The Economic Implications of an Electronic Monetary Transfer System

The Economic Implications of an Electronic Monetary Transfer System

Mark J. Flannery
Dwight M. Jaffee
Economics Department
Princeton University

Lexington Books
D.C. Heath and Company
Lexington, Massachusetts
Toronto   London

Library of Congress Cataloging in Publication Data

Flannery, Mark J
    The economic implications of an electronic monetary transfer
system.

    1. Money. 2. Electronic data processing—Banks and banking.
I. Jaffee, Dwight M., 1943– joint author. II. Title.
HG230.7.F56   332.7'6   73–1057
ISBN 0–669–84806–9

Printed simultaneously in Canada.

Printed in the United States of America.

International Standard Book Number: 0–669–84806–9

Library of Congress Catalog Card Number: 73–1057

To Our Parents

Contents

List of Tables

List of Figures

Preface

In recent years, and basically in the last five years, there has been awareness in the financial community and on the part of the public that the potential exists for a large-scale change in the current system of check use and monetary clearing. *Credit cards* have been interpreted by many as the first step toward a new system, and discussions and studies of the history, mechanics, and significance of credit card use have appeared. Looking into the future, *the checkless society* and *electronic money* have become passwords for the application of modern computer technology to the payments system. These have been discussed in the popular press and more complete studies are appearing even as we finish our work. In all the articles and studies we have seen, however, the analysis either has been very general, and therefore superficial, or it has been very narrowly directed. The key feature of our study, in contrast, is that it attempts to consider carefully and completely the full range of *economic implications* of an electronic transfer system. We must acknowledge, of course, that on this account we have been able to give only brief notice to the wide range of social concerns that might arise in this context. We hope, however, that we have succeeded in providing a complete, yet compact, discussion of the economic changes that may be anticipated upon the introduction of an electronic system.

We have faced a difficult problem in determining the appropriate level for the discussion. On the one hand, recent developments in the area of monetary economics have provided a set of tools, techniques, and analyses that can be applied with force and rigor to the questions at hand. Unfortunately, however, these methods require both patience and expertise on the part of the reader in moving through the complexities and mathematics. Thus, while we have made use of the results of these methods, we have generally not provided the details of rigorous proofs—even then, we feel we must apologize for the more difficult material in parts of Chapters 2, 6, and 7. On the other hand, we recognized from the start that the principles and basic foundations of economic analysis provide a necessary discipline if the study were not to become one of simple stargazing. We hope we have remained true to this framework even if it has meant a study that is more difficult in places than would have been preferred. The upshot, therefore, is that we have prepared a book that can be read easily, but we admit that some foundation in economics or experience in financial markets and matters will make the going easier. We think that the book will find direct applications in undergraduate and graduate courses on money, banking, and financial markets, and that it will prove useful to policy-makers in these areas for the decisions that they surely will have to make.

The study had its origins in Flannery's senior thesis submitted to the economics department at Princeton University in May, 1972. The thesis was then fully revised and expanded (including new material that appears as Chapters 2, 3, and 6) by both authors during the summer and fall of 1972. During the process of revision we have benefitted from many useful comments and suggestions. Professors Lester Chandler, Burton Malkiel, and Thomas Russell, and Mr. Barry Feldman, all of the Princeton economics department, read one version of the full manuscript. Professor Stephen Goldfeld of Princeton, Professors Henry Wallich and William Brainard of Yale University, and Dr. Robert Eisenmenger of the Federal Reserve Bank of Boston have also read at least parts of the manuscript and provided useful comments. To all of these individuals and to many others who helped us, we offer our sincere thanks.

Finally, in terms of other assistance, we have received logistic help from the Financial Research Center and economics department at Princeton University. Additionally, Flannery received summer support from the Savings Banks Association of New York State and Jaffee received summer support from the Monetary Subcommittee of the Social Science Research Council. None of these groups, or any of the individuals noted above, bear responsibility for the final results.

Mark J. Flannery   Princeton, New Jersey
Dwight M. Jaffee   December 1972

The Economic Implications of an Electronic Monetary Transfer System

1 Introduction

As is the case with many commonplace things, the U.S. payments system is a much-ignored phenomenon. Currency and checks have always been commonly used, they are felt to work well today, and most people believe that they will continue to be widely used in the future. However, even a cursory perusal of the banking literature since 1965 casts serious doubt on this last conclusion. One encounters numerous references to the "checkless society," the "cashless society," and the "payments system of the future." Clearly the banking industry, at least, is not content with the U.S. payments system as it currently exists.

The transition to the payments system of the future—or, as we shall refer to it in this book, the *electronic monetary transfer system* (EMTS)— has already begun; and there is good cause to believe that a complete revolution in the U.S. payments system is imminent. Financial institutions throughout the country are being swamped by the ever-mounting flow of paper that accompanies their activities. Perhaps the best known reactions to this problem are the plans of the New York Stock Exchanges to computerize their trading procedures, obviating the need for physically transporting and storing stock and bond certificates. But this "paper problem" is by no means confined to the stock exchange: the Federal Reserve system and commercial banks are being inundated with paper as the volume of checks rises seemingly without limit. The Federal Reserve has found the paper flows generated in its dealings with member banks to be, in the words of one writer, "increasingly frustrating and expensive." On June 17, 1971 the Board of Governors issued a "Statement of Policy on the Payments Mechanism" that stated the problem as follows:

> Increasing the speed and efficiency with which the rapidly mounting volume of checks is handled is becoming a matter of urgency. Until electronic facilities begin to replace check transfer in substantial volume, the present system is vulnerable to serious transportation delays and manpower shortages.

Clearly the Federal Reserve is prepared to take the initiative in responding to the situation at hand. As a first step, the Board of Governors, in February, 1972, issued a set of guidelines for the implementation of "regional (check) clearing centers . . . provided with automated clearing and telecommunications capabilities to serve as a basis for transition to widespread checkless—electronic—fund transfers."

1

As a result of the costs and inefficiencies of this current system for effecting payments, still other innovations have begun to occur. In 1966 the Federal Reserve Bank of New York commissioned a study by the Stanford Research Institute entitled *A Techno-Economic Study of Methods of Improving the Payments Mechanism*. This study demonstrated the cost savings that would accrue to the banking system if an electronic transfer system (like our EMTS) were to replace the current payments mechanism. In 1970 the Federal Reserve opened its new automated bankwire facility at Culpeper, Virginia, which is designed to effect electronically interbank funds transfers without the need for any paper exchanges. In the *Monthly Review* (May, 1970) of the Richmond Federal Reserve Bank (which operates this switching center at Culpeper on behalf of the entire Federal Reserve System) it is said that "there is little doubt that the Culpeper center represents one of the early steps leading invariably to an electronic payments system." More far-reaching still (because it involves nonbank sectors of the economy) are the SCOPE (Special Committee on Paperless Entries) programs that have been instituted in California and Georgia. A SCOPE program is an agreement between a firm and its bank, whereby the firm forwards financial information to a bank clearinghouse via computer tapes, and the clearinghouse instructs the firm's bank to transfer funds directly to the payees' banks, without the use of written payment orders. SCOPE programs also allow an individual to authorize his bank to pay certain recurring and/or fixed-sum bills from his account when they are presented directly to the bank. Each of these innovations represents a step away from the paper-and-check payments system of today and toward the EMTS.

Contrary to the stereotype of bankers as highly conservative businessmen, the history of commercial banking over the past 15 years contains a series of bold innovations. When confronted with rising costs, competition from other financial intermediaries, or the threat of deposit losses, banks have been quick to respond to the situation at hand. Certificates of deposit, the Eurodollar market, Magnetic Ink Character Recognition (MICR) coding on checks, the Federal funds market, bank credit cards, and other schemes have all evolved with the aid and encouragement of members of the banking community. In the area of electronic payment reforms as well, three separate EMTS pilot programs (each of which created a microcosmic EMTS for a sizeable community) have been sponsored and operated by commercial banks as an extension of their current credit card plans.

In sum, a conglomeration of factors seem to point toward the eventual emergence of an EMTS in the United States: the excessive cost of continuing to operate the current payments system; the technological feasibility of a totally automated system; a highly receptive attitude on the part of the Federal Reserve System; and the eagerness of most commercial bankers to stem the rising costs of their deposit and credit operations.

The replacement of the current payments system by an EMTS is bound to have far-reaching implications for the economy. A payments system is in many respects a social good, characterized by significant externalities and large fixed costs of operation. There is also an exceedingly high cost of transition when an economy changes from one payments system to another. Due to these facts, we would expect that the federal government will become involved to a significant extent in the transition to and operation of the EMTS—just as it has always regulated the payments system. Whether it owns the EMTS outright, merely regulates it, or some combination of the two, the state will have a hand in the payments mechanism of the future, and it is therefore a valid issue for public concern and discussion. Further, the mechanics of a nation's payments system can have serious effects on the daily workings of the economy and its individual economic units. The availability of credit, the level of welfare attainable by consumers, and the distribution of income can all be affected by the management of the monetary system. The replacement of cash by a less anonymous and less easily stolen medium of payment is also likely to have implications for the extent and success of criminal activities in the society. It is thus in the interest of economists, politicians, and private citizens to understand and control innovations in this area.

It has been frequently pointed out by writers on this subject that an EMTS will engender a myriad of political, legal, sociological, and ethical issues as well as those that are purely economic in scope. A study many times the size of this one could readily be filled with considerations of all these EMTS—related problems. However, the goal of this study has been narrowed to an examination of what we consider to be the purely *economic* ramifications of the emergence of an EMTS in the U.S. To this end, we will consider the economic conditions that have led to the need for a change in the current payments system, the technological developments that make that change feasible, and, most important, the implications of the new system for the operation of the economy.

In order to effect an analysis of this sort, one must first predict what the future EMTS will be like. Such a prognosis can be based only on data that are available at the present time, and consequently it will be subject to many potential inaccuracies. However, we have attempted to minimize the amount of analysis that requires accurate knowledge of the *details* of the EMTS; instead we base our analysis on what we consider to be valid and accurate assumptions concerning the *broad features* of the EMTS. For us, these economic and technical assumptions constitute the structure of the EMTS. We have tried to make the assumptions as general as possible; but should the system evolve in a significantly different fashion, then its implications may be different as well. This is not, however, a weak basis on which to proceed. First, as will be shown below, both the outline and most of the important features of the EMTS can be predicted with a reasonable degree of confidence even when the details themselves cannot be predicted. (For example, we assume that a large portion of consumer lending in the EMTS will occur in the form of prenegotiated lines of credit. We cannot, however, estimate *a priori* the quantitative extent of such credit lines.) Second, we feel that we have focused our attention on the relevant questions that must be considered, regardless of the particular details of the EMTS. In many cases, our analytic framework could be used equally well to determine the implications of a system that does not conform to all our assumptions.

We will be pursuing the method of comparative statics analysis—comparing the current monetary system with a fully operational EMTS. We will therefore ignore costs of transition between the two systems which, while they may be significant, are impossible to predict with any accuracy. The questions that we will consider in this work deal basically with the properties of the envisioned new transfer system and its effects on the U.S. economy: What are the efficiency implications of monetary transfer systems—and in particular of the EMTS? What effects will such drastic changes in the payments mechanism have on financial corporations? On manufacturing firms? On consumers and borrowers? What new financial services will be available under the EMTS and at what price? What will be the macroeconomic effects of these services?

1.1 An Electronic Monetary Transfer System

Before we begin our discussion of these and other economic issues, it will be helpful to sketch the major features of the future EMTS. This section is not intended to be an exhaustive description of the future payments system, but only to serve as a simplified example of how an EMTS will operate. Chapter 4 treats this subject at much greater length, and it is there that we present and defend our formal prognosis of the EMTS.

Our current payments system fulfills two distinct but very closely related needs of the society. First, it provides a means for settling debts. Money is the economy's most generic claim on real resources, and can therefore be used to settle the accounts that arise in the course of trade. The second function of the payments system is to control and measure debits and credits arising in the course of trade. On the wholesale or manufacturing level, this occurs primarily by means of trade credit (that is, the extension of short-term credits by one business firm to another). While at the retail level, this same function is effected through the use of credit cards. Our current system of payments can thus be generally characterized as the establishment of debits and credits followed by the use of money to effect final settlement; cash transactions are, of course, a special case in which settlement is immediate.

An EMTS must continue to fulfill the dual functions of credits and debits and of settlement. In contrast to the present system of several interfacing, but distinct payments methods, however, an EMTS is first and last an integrated real-time, electronic information system. It is a means of gathering financial information from literally millions of sources, processing it, and disbursing it back to the sources. Each economic unit in the society will have an account through which it can instantaneously effect funds transfers to any other member of the system. The EMTS will consist of a nationwide computer network which keeps track of individuals' credits and debits as trading occurs in the economy. Business firms and government offices will tie into the EMTS network using their own computers, while private individuals' means of access to the system will be a plastic identification card, quite similar to today's credit cards. Every retail establishment will have one or more on-line terminals which have the capacity to read identification cards and transmit sales and payment information to the local EMTS computer center. A careful examination of Table 1–1 will reveal some of the details that are involved in making payments through the EMTS. (Note that the discussion here is numbered so as to correspond to the numbering of the Table).

1.   A "point-of-sale transaction" is one in which an individual uses his ID card to pay a retail merchant for goods or services.
     (a) The ID card will have the buyer's account number, a nearly immutable photograph of the card's owner, and probably his signature as well. The latter two items should serve to discourage petty amateur thieves.
     (b) The terminal will be an input *and* output device for the computer system: the ID card will be read, and details of the transaction will be printed on the sales slip.
     (c) As he does today, the buyer may have more than one option concerning the timing of his payment. He may pay "cash" (i.e., instantaneous transfer of funds); draw on his bank line of credit (if he has one); or receive short-term credit directly from the merchant.
     (d) The fact that the customer's account is checked *prior to* the sale eliminates today's risk of a bad check or bad credit risk. The "magnetic code" referred to can be explained as follows. In order to protect an account holder from the fraudulent use of his account, each time a transaction is made the bank computer will generate a random number which it stores in its disk files and writes magnetically on the plastic card. Prior to the next transaction with this account, the computer compares these two random security codes to insure that a valid card is being used to activate the account. Other means, of course, are necessary to prevent the use of a valid, but stolen, card (see 5 below).
     (e) The sales slip serves as the buyer's record of expenditure (it is his "check stub").
     (f) If the customer has overdrawn his account, perhaps he can negotiate with the merchant for credit . . . or perhaps he will go home empty-handed.
2.   One's pushbutton home phone can be used to pay bills received in the mail or to transfer funds among financial institutions. This part of the table is

Table 1-1
EMTS System Procedures

Procedure	Consists of Following Steps
1. Point-of-sale Transaction.	1. (a) Seller inspects ID card. (b) Seller inserts card in terminal and sales slip in printer. (c) Seller keys in total amount and terms of sale (e.g. cash, bank credit line, seller credit.) (d) Appropriate local center checks validity of buyer's account number and magnetic code as well as balance in account. If valid, debits buyer's account and credits seller. (e) Terminal prints out buyer's account number, amount, terms of sale, and date. (f) Overdrawn account signals problem on terminal. (g) Invalid account or fake card causes card to be locked in terminal.
2. Home phone transaction (optional). Available during specified hours to cardholder on phone number he specifies as a "protected phone."	2. (a) Buyer dials special local number. (b) After receiving "go-ahead," buyer inserts card into dialer unit (or keys in his account number) and hangs up. (c) Local center computer dials "protected phone" number stored in disk and gives "go-ahead" signal. (d) Buyer keys in account number of payee and trade terms, and receives voice validation. (e) Buyer can find out status of his account by keying in appropriate code, if this option is desired.
3. Preauthorized transactions for repetitive payments.	3. (a) Buyer signs agreement with his bank indicating sellers, terms, maximum amounts. (b) Local center effects transactions during nonpeak hours.
4. Corporate or government-initiated transactions via computer.	4. (a) On-line: corporate or government computer dials up local center's computer. (b) Random security code is exchanged. (c) Transactions consisting of seller's account number, amount, terms of trade, etc. are transmitted. (d) Standard verification techniques used to detect transmission and computer errors. (e) Off-line: transmission of information possible via magnetic tape and courier or mail.

Table 1-1 (continued)

Procedure	Consists of Following Steps
5. Reporting lost or stolen card.	5. (a) Immediately go to nearest police station, give name, address, secondary identification. (b) Go to local bank next morning to get new card.

Table adopted from B. Cox, A.W. Dana, and H.M. Zeidler, *A Techno-Economic Study of Methods of Improving the Payments Mechanism*, Stanford Research Institute (Menlo Park, 1966), pp. 73–74.

self-explanatory. One might, however, note that the option discussed in 2 (e) would be most helpful to people who today have trouble keeping their checking accounts in order.

3. Preauthorized transactions constitute a specialized SCOPE program for individuals. An individual who is confronted with many fixed bills per month (e.g., auto, mortgage, and insurance payments) or small variable payments (e.g., utility bills), can authorize his bank to make payments for him directly to the issuers of the bills.

4. Since they would have their own computers, a corporation or government unit will not need an ID card as a means of access to the EMTS.
   (a) An on-line computer transmission would be used for highly important payments, where time is of the essence.
   (b) This security code is similar to that described in 1 (d) above.
   (c) The terms of trade for a firm, as for a consumer, could be cash, bank credit, or interfirm trade credit.
   (d) This sort of technique is commonly used in data processing operations today to detect machine error in the transmission and/or processing of data.
   (e) Routine payments, which are known in advance of the date they must be made, could be handled off-line. Examples of this would be stock dividend checks, accounts payable, or wages.

5. Because the status of the buyer's account is checked before each and every transaction, a lost card can be simply marked "cancelled" in the bank's computer storage, and no one will be able to use it. (See 1 (d) and 1 (g)). Therefore, if a lost or stolen card is reported promptly, there is no danger of loss to the owner or to the issuer of the card. In contrast, with today's bank credit cards an individual may be held responsible for up to $50 worth of goods charged on his lost card, and the issuing bank must pay the rest.

From this table and discussion it should be clear that an EMTS will continue to perform the basic functions of today's payments system. However, the means by which debt settlement occurs will be radically altered. The use of cash and currency will drop drastically; bad debt losses of the system will be reduced; and both the pecuniary *and* nonpecuniary transactions costs that must be borne by the society as a whole, and by its individual economic units, will be considerably lowered or eliminated altogether. It is the central thesis of this study that *quantitative* changes of this magnitude in the speed and ease of making financial transactions must necessarily precipitate *qualitative* changes in the structure and functioning of the financial system and all that is affected by that system.

1.2 Plan of the Book

This study assumes the existence of an EMTS similar to that described in Table 1-1. We are interested in economic analyses of the implications of this system for the United States. To that end, the study is organized in the following manner.

Chapter 2 reviews the economic properties and historic features of resource transfer systems. We develop both the logical and historic background leading up to the introduction of electronic transfer, and in this setting the economic gains and efficiency of an electronic transfer system become evident. The material requires some background in the microeconomics and money and banking literatures, and it can be omitted without a serious loss of continuity.

Chapter 3 discusses in detail the present system of payments. Here we describe the various types of instruments that serve as money in the U.S. economy, as well as some of the recent innovations that have emerged in the system in response to inefficiencies and high transaction costs. In particular we consider bank credit card plans as the starting point, albeit an inefficient and costly one, for the EMTS.

Chapter 4 considers some of the problems associated with the design of an EMTS. It is here that we present in detail the type of payments system that we envision; its economic characteristics will be our primary concern, but physical and technical characteristics are also discussed in considerable detail.

Chapter 5 discusses the changes that will occur in the economy's depository financial intermediary system. The low transactions costs and high information flows of the EMTS are shown to necessitate a drastic reorganization of this sector of the economy. Indeed, many specific proposals for reform in this area have been set forth in the past few years, and these will be evaluated in the light of the EMTS.

Chapter 6 presents a more detailed discussion of the implications of the EMTS for the portfolio and liability management of financial intermediaries. The specific topics that are covered include consumer loans and lines of credit, the interest yields on time deposits, and the various cost and yield factors relating to demand deposits. The material in this chapter requires some mathematical background, but it is hoped the argument can be followed even with difficult sections omitted.

Chapter 7 describes the effects that the EMTS can be expected to have on other sectors of the economy. Manufacturing corporations, retail establishments, and household units, in particular, are considered in detail. Section 7-3 of this chapter, like parts of Chapter 6, requires some mathematical background.

Chapter 8, following the microeconomic issues of Chapters 6 and 7, focuses attention on the macroeconomic effects of the EMTS. EMTS implications for the real sector, the monetary sector, and for monetary policy are considered separately and as they relate to one another. It is concluded that the most far-reaching effects of the EMTS are to be found at the microeconomic, not the macroeconomic, level of the economy.

Chapter 9 concludes the study with a summary of major points and important conclusions.

2

Systems of Economic Exchange

The major part of this study is concerned with a detailed analysis of the effects of an electronic monetary transfer system (EMTS) on the various sectors and economic units in the economy. Because of the many ramifications of an EMTS and because of the extensive scope of our study, it is possible to lose sight of the fact that a change to an EMTS is at the fundamental level a change to a new system of economic exchange and settlement. The purpose of this chapter, therefore, is to place the EMTS in its proper historical and economic perspective. We will review the available economic theory on exchange and settlement, set up a structural framework for analyzing alternative systems of exchange and settlement, and, finally, indicate on this basic level the major changes that are involved in the adoption of an EMTS.

2.1 The Literature on the Theory of Economic Exchange

The notion of the exchange of economic resources is perhaps among the most intuitive, and surely is among the most important, basic concepts in economic analysis. The economic analysis of an individual in isolation is relatively straightforward: given the individual's criterion or utility function over alternative sets of consumption, and given the technologically feasible set of production and storage activities open to him, the problem is to maximize the utility indicator subject to the technological constraints. The solution to this problem yields a variety of efficiency conditions that the individual should meet, but otherwise there is little more to be said. Expanding the analysis to include two or more economic units, with the possibility of economic exchange between them, on the other hand, opens many additional issues: How will production be arranged, and will there be specialization in resource use? How will the distribution of goods be determined? Will some, or all, individuals gain from economic exchange? How will trade be arranged, and how much of one good will exchange for another? These are the types of questions that have formed the basis of microeconomic general equilibrium analysis and they all depend, at least implicitly, on the assumption that economic exchange can occur.

It is, thus, striking that the available microeconomic theory pays relatively little attention to the mechanics and institutions of the transfer of economic resources. This lack of attention has been apparent in both the classical and neo-

11

classical traditions, and it has been generally true of modern mathematical analyses of general equilibrium systems as well.[1] In all of these approaches, the concept of economic exchange has been accepted as an axiom or primitive concept, much in the way that mathematicians accept the point or the line as a primitive assumption. The available theories and models therefore yield results that apply only to the most abstract and generalized systems of exchange and settlement, and consequently they are of little value in dealing with questions that directly concern the specific properties of alternative systems of exchange and settlement.

An important side effect of the lack of attention to exchange and settlement has been a relatively sterile theory of money. One of the major economic roles of money is associated with its medium of exchange function, and, lacking a rigorous analysis of exchange and settlement processes in the economy, it is not surprising to find that a rigorous theory of money is also absent. This has, in fact, shown up very clearly in the economic analysis of money. For the classical authors, money was a lubricant that oiled the wheels of industry; it was accepted that money was critical to the functioning of an industrial economy and that barter was inefficient.There was little attempt, however, to explain how money did these things. Consequently a theory that could explain how things would change if the monetary system changed in some way was never developed.[2] Similarly, the early neoclassical writers, although they were more aware of the problem and made some attempt to integrate money with utility theory, continued to deal with highly abstract models of the role of money in economic activity. Indeed, it is ironic that many of the abstractions used in the more highly developed neoclassical studies of exchange, such as Walras' for example, are operationally feasible only in the context of a computerized information system.[3]

More recently, the main focus in discussions of monetary theory can be viewed as a response to John Hicks' suggestion in 1935 that monetary theory be integrated with the established tenets of price and value theory.[4] The developed literatures that are now available on the term structure of interest rates, portfolio selection, the cost of capital, and related subjects are some of the major results. However, the outcome has not been a satisfactory theory of money or of exchange. In fact, instead of monetary theory taking its place alongside value theory as part of a consistent theory of economic behavior, it appears that value

---

1. For examples, see, respectively: John Stuart Mill, *Principles of Political Economy,* (New York; Augustus M. Kelley (Reprint), 1969); Léon Walras, *Elements of Pure Economics,* William Jaffe translator, (London: George Allen and Unwin Ltd., 1954); and Gerard Debreu, *Theory of Value,* (New York: John Wiley & Sons Inc., 1959).

2. See David Hume, "Of Money" in *Essays,* (London: Oxford University Press, 1963).

3. Walras, *op. cit.*

4. John Hicks, "A Suggestion for Simplifying the Theory of Money," *Economica,* (February 1935).

theory has to a significant degree simply taken over monetary theory. The consistency has been obtained, but so far only at the expense of an independent body of theory relating to monetary matters.

It is in this setting that a revival of interest in the specification of the role of money in systems of exchange and settlement has occurred. The challenge is clear; Paul Samuelson has stated it as follows: "Indeed, we still lack in 1972 a really adequate theoretical structure that encompasses the foundations of a monetary economy. On to the drawing boards!"[5] The responses to this challenge, at least so far, have been attempts to incorporate transactions costs, various constraints on trading possibilities, and restrictions on the existence of markets into existing models of general equilibrium. It is hoped that in this way a more complete specification of monetary influences and of the role of money in the economy can be provided. While the spirit of these recent studies is in many ways pertinent to our consideration of the EMTS as an exchange system for the U.S. economy, we shall not review them in detail here because their complex, mathematical results are unnecessary for our purposes.[6] Instead, we shall begin by presenting a more general framework for the analysis of systems of economic exchange that illustrates the basic principles involved.

2.2 The Structure of Economic Exchange Systems

Our starting point will be the notion of the *transfer of economic resources*. A transfer will be defined by three elements: the economic units involved in the transfer; the economic resource that is being transferred; and the quantity of that resource. More formally, this may be symbolized, as one example, by the notation $\overline{A\ x_i} \rangle B$, that is, economic unit A transfers x units of economic resource i to economic unit B. We will treat this concept of transfer as axiomatic. It should be pointed out, however, that in so doing we implicitly presuppose definitions for three still more basic concepts. These are the notions of: eco-

---

5. Paul Samuelson, "Samuelson on the Neoclassical Dichotomy: A Reply," *Canadian Journal of Economics*, (May 1972), p. 292.

6. Recently published studies in this area include Karl Brunner and Allan H. Meltzer, "The Use of Money: Money in the Theory of an Exchange Economy," *American Economic Review*, (December 1971); Robert Clower, "A Reconsideration of the Microfoundations of Monetary Theory," *Western Economic Journal*, Vol. 6, pp. 1–9; Frank Hahn, "Equilibrium with Transactions Costs," *Econometrica*, (May 1971); Jurg Niehans, "Money in a Static Theory of Optimal Payments Arrangements," *Journal of Money, Credit, and Banking*, (November 1969); Jurg Niehans, "Money and Barter in General Equilibrium with Transactions Costs," *American Economic Review*, (December 1971); Thomas Saving, "Transactions Costs and the Demand for Money," *American Economic Review*, (June 1971); Ross M. Starr, "Exchange in Barter and Monetary Economies," *Quarterly Journal of Economics*, (May 1972); and E.C.H. Veendorp, "General Equilibrium Theory for a Barter Economy," *Western Economic Journal*, (March 1970).

nomic *resources*, the goods and services that are exchanged; *property rights*, the legal or social recognition of ownership; and *economic units*, the entities that have property rights over economic resources.

Although the task of properly defining economic resources, property rights, and economic units will present serious problems for an institutional study of exchange systems in different societies, they need not detain us here. There is, however, still another dimension of economic transfer that is critical to a conceptual development of a complete system of economic exchange. Economic transfer, as it has been defined, is a unilateral movement of economic resources; that is, the goods move in only one direction, from one unit to another. It may be noted that "gifts" fall into this class. More generally, however, it is a basic assumption in economic analysis that economic transfers are reciprocated by a *quid pro quo*. That is, transfers are assumed to be at least bilateral, in that for any transfer from unit *A* to unit *B* a transfer of equal value is made from unit *B* to unit *A*.[7] It is thus useful to define an *exchange* of economic resources as the initial transfer of resources taken together with the reciprocating *quid pro quo*, and to define a *system* of economic exchange as the institutional structure through which exchanges are carried out.

An important objective of recent studies of general equilibrium models has been to integrate a particular system of exchange with the rest of the model. This has been attempted in most cases by postulating an "exchange technology" which defines the feasible set of exchanges that may occur and the costs associated with them.[8] Although the mathematical statements of these technologies are quite abstract and difficult, the underlying notions of transactions costs and trading constraints are largely intuitive and it is to these topics that we now turn.

2.2.1 Costs of a System of Economic Exchange

It was recognized even by the earliest classical writers that a critical characteristic of a system of exchange is the cost of operation associated with its use. Costs are important for two reasons. First, given that a society has a fixed endowment of factors, resources devoted to running the transfer system must necessarily reduce the output of other goods and services. The costs of operating various exchange mechanisms therefore are of major importance in determining

---

7. Multilateral transfers would occur if *A* transfers goods to *B*, *B* transfers goods of the same value to *C*, and *C* transfers goods of the same value to *A*. The multilateral transfer of goods should not be confused with medium of exchange systems as are discussed below. With a medium of exchange system, transfers are typically bilateral with *A* sending goods to *B*, and *B* returning the equal value of medium of exchange to *A*. Of course, as we develop below, a system with bilateral medium of exchange transfer may have many of the properties of a system with multilateral goods transfer.

8. See, for example, Hahn, *op. cit.*

which system will actually be chosen. Second, to the extent that a system of exchange does affect the set of commodity transfers (by means of constraints and costs imposed on traders), it will be an important determinant of the economy's final equilibrium trading pattern.

As we have noted, recent mathematical specifications of systems of exchange have treated transactions costs at a quite abstract level, while our main interest here is with the more specific and institutional forms that these costs may take. Given the potential complexity of systems of exchange, on the other hand, it is not our intent to compile a complete catalog of the full detail and variety of costs that may arise. Rather, we will here limit ourselves to distinguishing between the *direct* costs of economic transfer and the *indirect* costs. We shall argue that direct costs are common to almost all systems of exchange, whereas the indirect costs will vary between systems and will in many cases serve as the critical variable distinguishing the various possible systems from one another.

The direct costs of economic transfer are to be interpreted as the costs associated with arranging and carrying out what may be described as the "real" aspects of the commodity movement. More specifically, the direct costs may be separated into two categories—*search* costs and *delivery* costs. Search costs are the costs involved in finding a trading partner and arriving at mutually advantageous terms of exchange. In general, both parties to an exchange will have to face these search costs. The delivery costs include the large variety of expenses involved in effecting the physical and legal transfer of the goods. These would include, for example, transportation costs and insurance fees. In addition, it should be noted that there is a *risk* in exchange, which may be translated into the terms of a *direct* delivery cost, owing to the possibility that one or the other party may fail to meet the terms of the exchange agreement.

The direct costs of search and delivery are basic to any system of exchange, although, of course, they may vary depending on the specific properties of the goods to be transferred, the location of the trading units, and the amount of trade. It is possible, however, to reduce the direct costs by introducing additional institutions that expedite the exchanges. These additional institutions will generally have costs associated with them, and we refer to these as indirect costs. Three basic types of institutions have been introduced to reduce the direct costs of exchange: *markets, brokers,* and *mediums of exchange*. Markets may be interpreted here in the literal sense, for example, of a location set aside for trading. It is clear that markets will reduce the direct costs of search since all traders will then have at least a common trading area. On the other hand, markets have costs of their own—for example, the land that must be set aside for the market. In a similar way, brokers may be defined as economic units that specialize in arranging exchange. It is apparent that brokers will serve to reduce the direct costs of search while at the same time they introduce costs of their own. There is thus an obvious tradeoff available to the society, with optimality requiring that brokers and markets be expanded until the marginal reduction in direct costs just equals the marginal rise in indirect costs. In addition, the extent to which markets and brokers are used, and the specific forms that they take in an economy, will depend on the *pattern* of economic exchange to be carried out in the system.

The third type of device that may be introduced to reduce the direct costs of transfer—a medium of exchange—raises even more possibilities. A medium of exchange may be defined as an entity that is generally accepted as the *quid pro quo* for an economic transfer solely because the recipient anticipates that other traders will accept it as payment in future transactions. The introduction of a medium of exchange will generally be associated with a reduction in both the search and delivery direct exchange costs.

With respect to the reduction in delivery costs, two conditions must be met by the medium of exchange. First, the introduction of the medium of exchange must reduce the total number of transfers of other commodities. To see how this can occur, we must distinguish between the *gross flows* and *net flows* of a system of exchange.[9] The gross flows include all economic transfers that occur in the system. The net flows are the difference between individuals' initial endowments of commodities and their final consumption sets. Gross flows can never be less than net flows, and they will be greater whenever some trade is undertaken for purposes other than direct consumption. Thus, a medium of exchange can reduce the total number of goods transfers by reducing the gross flows that are not undertaken for direct consumption. The second condition that must be met by a medium of exchange is, of course, that it be relatively inexpensive (in terms of delivery costs) to transfer. This condition is important because, in general, the introduction of a medium of exchange will increase the absolute number of transactions that must occur; even though transfers of goods decrease, monetary transfers increase even more. The cost savings arise, therefore, in the substitution of the medium of exchange transfers for the gross flows of commodities that are more costly to effect.

The reduction in search costs upon the introduction of a medium of exchange arises basically because all exchanges now involve only one commodity, rather than two. In a probabilistic sense, this greatly increases the likelihood of finding a trading partner. Alternatively, this savings may take the form of reducing the number of markets and/or dealers that are used in the system. To take a specific example, in a system with n goods to be exchanged and no medium of exchange, it is possible that as many as $n(n-1)/2$ markets will operate; this would allow each good in the system to trade against each other good. In a medium of exchange system, on the other hand, there will be need for only n markets since each good will trade only against the generalized *quid pro quo*.[10]

As is the case for the introduction of markets and dealers, the advantages of

9. For further elaboration, see Niehans, "Money in a Static Theory of Optimal Payments Arrangements," *op. cit.,* pp. 706–710.

10. See Robert Clower, "Introduction," in *Monetary Theory, Selected Readings,* Penquin Books, Baltimore, 1970, pp. 11–14.

a medium of exchange must be weighed against the indirect costs that it introduces. We have already noted, for one thing, that the use of a medium of exchange may increase the total number of transactions that occur, and given that such transactions are not totally free, this cost will have to be considered. A second cost of a medium of exchange is the risk of theft. The medium of exchange is particularly vulnerable to theft for exactly the same reason it is useful in the economy: it is accepted in trade. A third cost results from the fact that whatever entity is used as the medium of exchange, it is not then available for direct consumption or investment. This last factor has led, of course, in the extreme case to the use of fiat mediums that are essentially costless to produce.[11] As a general rule it can be seen that for a medium of exchange to be introduced efficiently into an exchange system, it must be the case that the savings in direct costs outweigh the new indirect costs that are introduced.

There is one further form of innovation that can allow savings even on the transfer costs of a medium of exchange. This is to use a clearing system in which a transfer agent maintains the accounts of individuals in the system and credits or debits the accounts as directed.[12] There are several advantages to this system: there is less risk of theft; the medium of exchange need not be physically transferred; and the cost of maintaining a stock of the medium of exchange may be eliminated. Again, however, it is to be stressed that new costs are introduced. With a clearing system, for example, fraudulent transfer—a check with insufficient funds—becomes more likely, and the transfer agent must also be compensated for his services.

2.2.2 Trading Constraints

The concept of trading constraints that appears in the literature on systems of exchange is closely related to, but distinguishable from, transactions costs. Trading constraints occur in a system of exchange when specific classes of exchanges are not allowed to occur. In this form, trading constraints are similar to transactions costs, since both serve to limit the ability of an individual to transform his endowment of goods and wealth into a more desirable consumption package. Trading constraints are more restrictive, however, in that they directly reduce the feasible set of trades open to an individual. Two examples can perhaps clarify the concept most readily.

One instance of trading constraints occurs when certain markets in an economy do not exist. An interesting example, and one that has been important

---

11. See Harry Johnson, "Inside Money, Outside Money, Income, Wealth, and Welfare in Monetary Theory," *Journal of Money, Credit and Banking,* (February 1969), pp. 30–45, for a more formal discussion of the advantages of replacing a commodity money with a fiat money.

12. See Hicks, *op. cit.,* pp. 10–14.

in the theory of general equilibrium models, is when markets do not exist for trades in commodities for future delivery.[13] The case of missing markets is particularly interesting because it illustrates a situation in which an individual may be willing to pay the direct costs of trading in a market, but in which there are not a sufficient number of such traders to allow the indirect costs of running the market to be covered.

A second and perhaps more obvious restriction that must be enforced within a system of exchange is that individuals not be allowed to spend more on consumption purchases than the value of their initial endowment of goods and wealth. In the Walrasian general equilibrium model, this restriction is referred to as the *budget constraint*.[14] It is a relatively weak constraint and will automatically be met if all transfers involve an immediate *quid pro quo*. More restrictive forms for the budget constraint, however, are possible. Robert Clower has suggested that a basic requirement of a system with a medium of exchange should be that purchases can be made only with the medium of exchange *in hand*.[15] Thus, even if an individual has an endowment of goods with a value that exceeds his planned purchases, these goods will not be directly useful in affecting an exchange if Clower's constraint is operative. Relaxing the Walrasian form of the budget constraint allows for the possibility of borrowing against future income, thereby enabling individuals better to coordinate their consumption patterns and time preferences. The removal of Clower's constraint would allow more optimal allocations of an individual's wealth among the various assets available to him at any given time. In order to adjust or eliminate either of these constraints, lending must be able to occur in the economy, a possibility which we now consider.

2.2.3 Credit Institutions

Our discussion has so far focused primarily on cases in which the reciprocating *quid pro quo* of a resource transfer is rendered, in one form or another, immediately. There is another possibility, however, and the discussion of futures markets anticipates it: the settlement or *quid pro quo* payment may be deferred until some future date. To be more precise, consider the case of a resource transfer $\overline{A\ x_i} \, \backslash B$ in which unit B reciprocates by issuing a promise of *quid pro quo* at some future date. We shall refer to this promise as a credit for A, or symmetrically, a debit for B. There are two questions that should be considered; first, how does deferred settlement fit into a system of exchange; and second,

---

13. The role of futures markets in economic models is discussed in K.J. Arrow and F.H. Hahn, *General Competitive Analysis*, (San Francisco: Holden-Day, Inc., 1971).

14. See Walras, *op. cit.* pp. 153–163.

15. See Robert Clower, "A Reconsideration of the Microfoundations of Monetary Theory," *op. cit.*

what are the institutions that may be set up to handle such deferred settlements efficiently.

With respect to the first question, a particularly simple procedure is to treat the promise of future repayment, or in a legal context the loan contract, as if it were the *quid pro quo* itself. In other words, the complete economic exchange may, as one case, consist of the transfer of a resource from A to B and the reciprocal flow of a promise of future payment, that is a loan contract, from B to A. The loan contract is thus treated as any other commodity that can be used for immediate settlement.

An alternative procedure is to treat the promise of future repayment as a commodity flow. In this case there will be two complete exchanges involved in the full transaction. First, the initial real commodity flow will be exchanged for the standard medium of exchange; second, and simultaneously, the medium of exchange will be returned in exchange for the promise of future repayment. The net flows—the real commodity transfer and the promise of future payment—will thus be the same as the case in which the loan contract is accepted in settlement.

While these approaches have the advantage of fitting into our framework for systems of exchange, we must note immediately that they significantly change the interpretation of trading constraints. In particular, we have previously introduced the concept of a budget constraint as the restriction that individuals cannot purchase more than their endowment of commodities and wealth. If we are to assume, however, that individuals are free to issue debits as payment, then it is clear that the budget constraint will no longer be restrictive. Traders will be free to "create" a commodity endowment simply by promising to provide payment in the future, and thus they would be unconstrained in the purchases that they can make currently. Obviously, no real-life system possesses this characteristic. The problem, of course, is that when B gives A a credit, there remains the question of whether B can actually fulfill the promise at the specified future date.

This raises the basic question of how it can be certified that a promise of future payment, that is a credit, will be fulfilled. One possibility, in a system with a complete set of futures markets, is that the recipient of the credit A can verify that the borrower B has entered into futures contracts that do make allowance for the repayment of the loan. Once we shift to the realistic case in which relatively few futures markets exist, however, we are thrown back to the case that A can only depend on B's promise that he will undertake trades in the future such that repayment can be made. The upshot, then, is that accepting a credit as the *quid pro quo* will be risky for the lender, and that the risk will vary depending on the borrower.

Given the condition that loan contracts are intrinsically risky, we might consider how institutions can best be developed to deal with this risk. So far, our discussion has assumed that credits are granted by individual traders. This is certainly a possibility, but it means that the lender takes on the full risk of default.

An alternative possibility is that specialists in lending, we might call them lending agents, will come into existence. There are two fundamental advantages that lending specialists may have in bearing the risks of loan default. First, through expertise in the evaluation of loan contracts and through economies generated by evaluating a large number of loan contracts, loan specialists could obtain better appraisals of the risk inherent in each loan. This information could then be used in rejecting contracts where the risk is too great and in setting the appropriate risk premium (in addition to the interest rate) in cases where a loan is granted. Second, by granting a large number of loans, the loan specialist can achieve a lower overall risk than would have been obtained were the loans granted separately by individual traders. This reduction in aggregate risk is the direct result of the gains available from a diversified portfolio of a large number of relatively small individual contracts.

One other feature of loan contracts and credits concerns the form in which repayment is promised. Here it is traditional to distinguish the *standard of deferred payment* and the *medium of repayment.* The standard of deferred payment is the bookkeeping unit used for the denomination of the loan, and it has no direct implications for the operation of the exchange system. The medium of repayment, on the other hand, is the entity used for making the actual repayment, and thus it is of importance. In many cases the medium of exchange and the medium of repayment are the same, and this simplifies the system. Otherwise, the exchange ratio between the two mediums can create additional risk in the system if it should be expected to vary over time.

2.3 Classification and Examples of
Systems of Exchange

The previous section has outlined the basic structural features of systems of exchange. We have seen that an exchange technology, which consists of the means by which transfers are made and the reciprocating *quid pro quo* is returned, can be associated with the costs of its operations and the categories of trades that may occur. In addition, one must take into account the types of credit facilities and futures markets that exist. To make these concepts more concrete, and to set the basis for a comparison with an electronic monetary transfer system, in this section we consider some specific examples of how exchange systems may be organized. Then, in the following section, we will be ready to discuss the EMTS and its implications for the technology of exchange.

2.3.1 Direct Barter

Barter systems of economic exchange are characterized by the condition that goods exchange only for other goods. *Direct* barter systems, more specifically, are defined with the additional constraint that all goods entering into trade are desired only for the purpose of consumption (or investment) by the recipient. Direct barter thus rules out the possibility that some good or commodity may enter into trade because the recipient anticipates selling the commodity in some other market in the future.[16] Direct barter does not, on the other hand, rule out the possibility that credit or deferred settlement may occur, but the restriction does remain in this case that the repayment of the credit must be made only in goods desired for direct consumption.

Direct barter has long been considered an inefficient form of exchange. W.S. Jevons, in his classic study, *Money and the Mechanism of Exchange,* attributes the inefficiency of direct barter (or in his term *simple barter*) to the requirement that a "double coincidence of wants" must exist between traders before an exchange can occur.[17] That is, under direct barter, each transactor must have a direct demand for the other's commodity, and this has the effect of reducing the opportunities for trade, or, equivalently, of increasing the search costs of finding trading partners. It is apparent that this fits directly into our framework of transactions costs and trading constraints for evaluating systems of exchange.

It should be noted, however, that Jevons' view overstates the absolute inefficiency of direct barter. In particular, direct barter systems, at least in the forms that have occurred, frequently include some arrangements for deferred settlement.[18] The possibility of deferred settlement, even with the requirement that repayment must be in directly consumed goods, weakens the requirement of a double coincidence of wants. In addition, direct barter systems have generally occurred in small and compact primitive communities. Under these circumstances, it is clear that the traders will be well known to one another and that the variety of goods to be traded will be small. Consequently, the requirement of a double coincidence of wants becomes less restrictive.

Interpreted in the context of a large industrial economy, on the other hand, it is apparent that direct barter will be highly inefficient. Recent studies have shown, in particular, how Jevons' double coincidence of wants can be translated in a rigorous fashion into transactions costs and trading constraints.[19] With respect to transactions costs, it has been shown that if specific commodities have lower trading costs than others, then it is efficient to use these commodities as mediums of exchange. With respect to trading constraints, it has been shown that the requirement that individuals trade only for goods to be directly consumed has the effect that certain net flows of goods for consumption cannot be

---

16. This is developed more formally by Starr, *op. cit.*

17. W. Stanley Jevons, *Money and the Mechanism of Exchange,* Thirteenth Edition, (London: Kegan Paul, Trench, Trubner and Co., Ltd., 1902), p. 3.

18. The anthropological and economic characteristics of primitive exchange systems have been discussed in Paul Einzig, *Primitive Money*, (London: Eyre Spottiswoode, 1949).

19. See Starr, *op. cit.* and Veendorp, *op. cit.*

achieved by direct barter trading. Thus, as a rule, direct barter will be inefficient except in the context of a small, primitive system.

2.3.2 Indirect Barter

The natural extension of direct barter, is a system of *indirect* barter, in which specific commodities serve the specialized function of medium of exchange, such that they are accepted in trade in anticipation of their use in trades to be made at a later time in another market. Indirect barter shares with direct barter the requirement that goods exchange only against other goods. The distinguishing feature of indirect barter is, therefore, that one or more of the goods can take on a medium of exchange function, and it is for this reason that transactions costs and trading constraints may be changed.

The savings in transactions costs upon the introduction of a medium of exchange, as noted in Section 2.2.1, occur in the form of lowered delivery costs and search costs. For these savings to be realized, however, the medium of exchange must be efficiently chosen such that it has low handling costs. Indeed, long lists have been compiled enumerating the desirable properties for a medium of exchange.[20] These include such factors as portability, durability, and divisibility. Given the nature of these properties, it is not surprising that the precious metals have frequently been used as the circulating medium of exchange in indirect barter systems. The precious metals do have the drawback, however, that they withdraw from consumption or investment use a valuable commodity, and as we shall see in a moment, this has been one impetus for devising alternative systems that do not rely on a commodity medium of exchange.

With respect to trading constraints, the key advantage of an indirect barter system is that it allows a multilateral transfer of goods. In contrast, goods exchanged between two individuals in a direct barter system cannot again enter the trading system, and thus only bilateral goods transfers can be achieved. The advantages of multilateral transfer can, at least in principle, be quite important, since it is easy to show conditions under which a bilateral transfer system can achieve only a more restricted set of feasible trades than a multilateral transfer system.[21]

2.3.3 Warehouse Receipts

Further savings in transactions costs can be achieved in an indirect barter system when warehouse receipts are substituted for the commodity itself as the

---

20. See Jevons, *op. cit.,* pp. 30–66.
21. See Starr, *op. cit.* and Veendorp, *op. cit.*

medium of exchange. This system requires that some individual or enterprise provide a warehouse in which the commodity serving as the medium is stored. Traders "deposit" this commodity at the warehouse and receive receipts. The receipts then circulate as the actual medium of exchange.

The system may also be extended to allow drafts (bills of exchange) to be drawn against the warehouse in lieu of the physical transfer of the warehouse receipts. Individuals would then essentially be maintaining "accounts" at the warehouse, and the warehouse itself would be functioning as a transfer agent. If the system had more than a single transfer agent, then there must also exist a further institution through which transfers between warehouses can be affected. Otherwise, transactors with their accounts at different warehouses would not be able to trade with one another. One means by which this situation can be avoided is the establishment of a "clearinghouse" at which the various warehouse agents meet in order to settle their accounts.

The gains achieved in moving to a warehouse receipt system depend critically on the magnitude of the costs that can be eliminated when it is no longer necessary to transfer physically the commodity serving as the medium of exchange. Indeed, to the extent that the transfer of warehouse receipts is costless, this element of delivery costs would be totally eliminated. This, however, would be the only gain over indirect barter; in particular, the trading constraints are still identical to those of indirect barter.

The further emergence of a draft system with accounts at clearing agents would similarly depend on the cost reductions engendered by a system in which transfers could be made in any amount desired without splitting physical entities. The draft system entails, however, at least a slight change in the applicable trading constraints. Individuals may now take advantage of the lag between the time when the draft is written, and the time the draft is presented to the transfer agent, in order to make additional deposits with the trading agent. In other words, a draft system allows for the possibility of "float," and this affects the trading options open to an individual at any specific moment.[22]

2.3.4 Fractional Reserve Banking Systems

The warehouse receipt system with a transfer agent may be considered as a special case of banking systems in which banks maintain a one hundred percent reserve base against accounts in the form of the medium of exchange commodity. From this starting point, it is clear that the warehouse manager may find it profitable to combine his transfer agent function with a lending function. In particular, loans may be granted in the form of accounts with the transfer agent.

---

22. More precisely, float may be interpreted as an implicit short-term loan made by the seller of a commodity to the purchaser that exists during the time period in which the seller is presenting the transfer draft to the purchaser's agent.

Assuming for the moment that the loan funds are maintained as accounts with the transfer agent, or that they are transferred to other account holders who continue to hold them with the transfer agent, the total liabilities of the transfer-loan enterprise (and we should now really call it a bank) would consist of the original accounts plus the loan-induced accounts. Similarly, the assets would consist of the original reserve commodity and the newly issued loan contracts. This form of organization may be termed a *fractional reserve banking system,* since the total accounts outstanding exceed the amount of the reserve commodity held, the difference being the loan assets.

From the standpoint of the warehouse manager, the profitability of this new banking venture can be very great since no real resources are used, yet interest can be charged on the loans. There is, of course, the risk of default on the loan contracts. There is also the risk that account holders may wish to redeem their accounts for the reserve commodity, or to transfer their accounts to other transfer agents, in amounts greater than the actual commodity reserves held by the bank. Thus, for the venture to be profitable, the interest rate on loans must be set at least high enough to compensate for these risks. Given that the warehouse manager has not had to commit any resources of his own, however, it would appear that in general this condition could be met with interest rate levels sufficiently low to generate a significant loan demand.

While this development of fractional reserve banking systems appears straightforward, we should consider the reaction of the original account holders at the one hundred percent reserve bank to this change. In particular, these individuals would presumably be aware that the shift to a fractional reserve bank creates the risk for them that the bank may have insufficient commodity reserves to redeem their account. Given a choice between a fractional reserve bank and a one hundred percent reserve bank, they would choose the latter, everything else the same. Thus, for the warehouse manager to induce his transfer agent customers to maintain their accounts, he would either have to pay interest on accounts or reduce his transfer agent fees. For fractional reserve banks to exist, then, it must be the case that the interest income generated by the lending business is sufficient to compensate both the warehouse manager and the bank's account holders for the risks and costs implicit in such activities. Given the dominance that fractional reserve banking has achieved in modern transfer systems, this condition is presumably easily met. On an *a priori* basis, however, the success of fractional reserve banking appears quite remarkable.

2.3.5 Zero Reserve Banking and Fiat Issue Systems

As the logical extension of a fractional reserve banking system, it would appear possible that the commodity reserves of the system could become a progressively smaller proportion of the outstanding accounts, and that in the limit this proportion could approach zero. In fact, however, it is unlikely that a zero reserve banking system would be reached, or even approximated, in this manner. In order for the bank to expand its loans, which is the mechanism for lowering the reserve ratio, it would have to continue to lower the interest rate it charges. At some point, however, the risk on the loans that are being demanded at the margin (that is, the combined risks of default and insolvency) will exceed the interest rate that is being offered, and thus it would not be profitable for the banker to expand his loan portfolio any further.[23]

A zero reserve bank can be achieved, however, through an alternative strategy. This requires that account holders give up all rights to convertibility and that deposits at the bank become the medium of exchange in and of itself. If the condition of nonconvertibility is accepted, then the bank could disburse the reserve commodity as a dividend to the account holders and thus induce them to accept the change. From a social point of view, such a system of exchange has the added virtue of freeing the total reserve commodity for use in consumption or investment.

Zero reserve banking systems of this form are sometimes termed *pure inside money* systems, since the quantity of loans and deposits that are created are fully determined by the banking system itself. A prime difficulty of inside money systems with no convertibility is that there is no incentive for the managers of the institution to consider default risk on loans. Since the bank uses no scarce resources in creating loans, it loses nothing should default occur. Similarly, the bank's management could issue loans to itself in the form of accounts and spend the proceeds on real goods and services. In either of these cases, the total quantity of loans and deposits could be expanded without limit as long as the public continued to accept and use the accounts as the medium of exchange. Ultimately, of course, the value of bank accounts in terms of real goods would begin to decline toward zero and acceptance of the accounts as the medium of exchange would come to an end. Until this point is reached, however, the bank management would have the benefit of a true Widow's Cruse.[24]

The upshot of the argument, therefore, is that a zero reserve banking system tends to be unstable since bank management has an incentive to increase the

23. In addition, if the bank is a monopolist in the loan market, then it would have no inducement to lower the interest rate below the point that maximizes the revenue from the lending business. See James Tobin, "Commercial Banks as Creators of 'Money'," in Deane Carson, editor, *Banking and Monetary Studies,* (Homewood: Richard D. Irwin, 1963).

24. See Tobin, *op. cit.* This problem of instability does differ, however, between a system with one monopoly bank and a system with a large number of small and competing units. With a monopoly bank, it is possible that the owners of the bank would discount the expected future profits of running a stable system, and would find it profitable not to "break" the system by overissue. With a system of numerous banking units, each unit would want to maintain reserves against possible adverse inter-bank clearings, and this would also have a stabilizing influence on the system. Even taking these points into account, however, it is clear that banking systems do have significant tendencies toward this instability.

loans outstanding as fast as possible. In practice, of course, this stability problem has been well recognized in banking law. Banking institutions have long been required to maintain minimum reserve ratios that are typically greater than the ratio that would be freely chosen. In addition, bank law generally prohibits management from making loans to itself.

Having just noted that banking law generally precludes the operation of zero reserve systems, we shall now find, ironically, that the government is the one agent in the economy that can, in fact, run essentially a zero reserve system. In particular, we can define a *fiat issue system* as one in which the government issues nonconvertible notes as payment for resources that it purchases from the private sector. The evolution of a fiat system can be described much as we have done above, but with the government replacing the warehouse (and later the bank) as the agent responsible for the medium of exchange. As we have already noted for a zero reserve banking system, there is the obvious advantage that resources are not kept idle as backing for a medium of exchange. This, in fact, is the primary economic incentive to develop such a system.[25] Furthermore, the stability of a government fiat issue system depends on the same factors as were the case for a zero reserve banking system—namely that the owner, in this case the government, not abuse the privilege by overissue.

There are basically two reasons why a government-run fiat issue system may be stable whereas a private zero reserve banking system is not. First, unlike a private banking system that would be motivated by profit to overissue, a government run system, if it is properly managed, would maintain stability as one of its objectives. Monetary history, of course, is replete with examples where governments have succumbed to the temptation to overissue, with the result that the system broke up. But these are presumably exceptions, not the rule. Second, governments can create a demand for their fiat issue by requiring that it alone be acceptable in payment for taxes and duties owed to the government. While this is neither a necessary nor sufficient condition for the government's fiat issue to be generally acceptable in trade, it does provide one form in which a government can guarantee a market for its issue.

2.3.6 Integrated Fiat Issue-Fractional Reserve Systems

We have now reached the point at which we can describe the system that is most commonly used today—namely an integrated fiat issue-fractional reserve banking system of exchange. In this system the government issues a fiat currency in the form of notes as described in the previous section. There also exists a private banking system which operates in a fractional reserve fashion. The

---

25. See Harry Johnson, *op. cit.*

critical link between the two systems, and what integrates them, is that the banking system uses the government's fiat issue as its reserve commodity.

To describe the more specific properties of such a system, it is useful first to assume that the bank operates under a one hundred percent reserve rule. In this case, legally and fundamentally, the medium of exchange is the fiat issue of the government. The banking system serves only as a transfer agent, in accepting fiat issue accounts and transferring funds between accounts. It is also possible that, as a separate enterprise, there may be lending specialists who borrow and lend funds, making their profit on the margin between the borrowing and lending rates. For the moment, however, we assume that the lending agents are not integrated with the banking system.

Such a system possesses three important characteristics that make it an efficient institutional construct. First, there is no real commodity used as the medium of exchange or as the reserve backing. Second, the fiat issue, which stands in place of a commodity standard, is controlled by the government and is therefore likely to possess a degree of stability. Finally, the transfer function is organized in the private sector, presumably driven by the market to operate under efficient conditions.

Having set up the system in this way we can see, following our earlier discussion, that there would be incentive for both the bank and its account holders to shift to a fractional reserve system. Alternatively, this can be interpreted as a merger of the transfer agent and the lending agent, the important feature being that the combined institution can grant loans simply by creating account balances on its books. Compared with a fiat issue—one hundred percent reserve banking system, the important change here is that the economy's medium of exchange now includes not only the fiat issue and accounts with one hundred percent backing, but also the accounts created by the lending activities of the banks. This implies that the total stock of the medium of exchange is no longer controlled by the government alone, but rather will depend on the lending activities of the bank and the level of reserves of fiat issue that the banking system chooses to maintain. This raises questions concerning the *modus operandi* of monetary policy, questions to which we shall return later in the study.

2.4 An Electronic Monetary Transfer System

We can now turn to our main objective, the interpretation of the future EMTS as a system of economic exchange. In particular, we intend to discuss the EMTS within the framework of economic exchange systems that has been presented above. In the course of this section, we will be anticipating at a theoretical level a number of issues that will be considered in greater detail and in a more institutional context later in the study.

2.4.1 Specification of the EMTS
Exchange System

An EMTS will fundamentally be an automated transfer agent. Our previous discussion has indicated that transfer agents may be integrated into an exchange system in any of several ways. One possibility, for example, is that the EMTS could be set up as a one hundred percent reserve transfer agent with no loan functions. The reserves of the EMTS would presumably consist of the same fiat money base as the current banking system. For an individual to build an account balance with the system, he would either deposit fiat money balances or would be the recipient of a transfer from someone else in the system. The total volume of balances in the system would thus be totally dependent on the amount of fiat money deposited in it, while transfers between account holders would leave this total unchanged.

If such a one hundred percent reserve regime were adopted, and if this form of transfer were to dominate traditional check transfers in terms of costs, then banks would lose their fractional reserve banking status. Individuals would no longer maintain bank demand deposit accounts for the purpose of check transfers, and the banks would thereby be reduced to the status of lending agents who bid for funds (perhaps in the form of time deposits) and then make loans, much as savings and loan associations do at the present time. As we have indicated, however, the incentives for a profitable merger of the transfer agent and lending agent functions are substantial and one would therefore expect economic forces to precipitate a merger of the two. In fact, we will argue (in Chapter 4) that the EMTS is most likely to emerge in the U.S. as a consequence of the banking system's efforts to lower its costs of operation. That is, the banks will create the EMTS in the process of moving from the present paper system of funds transfer to an electronic system.

On the basis of these principles, therefore, we are able to conclude that the EMTS will not be operated *solely* as a means for transferring funds. This fact, taken together with institutional factors developed in later chapters, leads one to expect that the U.S. banking system is likely to be directly involved in the EMTS operations. Indeed, it is expected that some of the most important changes precipitated by the EMTS will be felt in the banking sector.

As one important example of this latter situation, the level of reserves maintained by the banking system could be directly affected by the EMTS. In the current system, currency and demand deposits are both used extensively for transactions purposes, and thus the banks must be prepared to meet significant currency drains on their reserve positions from time to time. Under an EMTS, however, the use of currency in the system could diminish significantly, and therefore the likelihood of currency drains would be reduced. This would allow the banking system, if it were not restricted, to operate with substantially lower reserve ratios, and it is possible that banks' desired reserve ratios could even approach zero if the public's demand for currency were to decline enough. If such a system were left unregulated, it would therefore suffer from the instabilities that we have discussed above with respect to a zero or near-zero reserve system. In fact, however, it would appear reasonable to expect the monetary authorities to continue to regulate the banking system in the ways that it already does. In particular we would expect that reserve requirements will continue to be enforced, since their function will be critical to the system's stability.

2.4.2 EMTS Effects on the Pattern of Trade

For the EMTS actually to be adopted in the economy, the most obvious and important condition will be that it allow a higher level of welfare than is possible with the current technology of exchange. Such an improvement in the level of welfare will occur for two reasons: transactions costs will be reduced; and individual trading constraints will be altered.

With respect to transactions costs, the adoption of the EMTS will result in a reduction in both the exchange system's direct and indirect costs. Lower indirect costs, accruing in particular to financial institutions, will in fact be the major force leading to the emergence of the EMTS. By eliminating the need for physically clearing paper through the bank system, the cost of transfer agent functions will be reduced. Furthermore, as we will discuss below, the EMTS will make certain classes of lending functions considerably less expensive to undertake.

With respect to the direct costs of economic exchange, the costs associated with delivering the monetary *quid pro quo* to sellers will be the area most affected by the EMTS. This will occur in several ways. First, for individual transactors, there should be explicit reductions in transfer fees, corresponding to the lowered indirect transactions costs outlined above. Second, individuals will receive nonpecuniary benefits in terms of the convenience and accessibility of an electronic system. Third, the risk of insufficient funds will be fully eliminated as a result of the instantaneous balance verification and transfer available under the EMTS. Under a check clearing system, in contrast, it is only by undertaking special and costly precautions, such as bank certified checks, that the seller can be assured that the draft he receives will be accepted by the purchaser's bank.

The actual magnitude of these savings will depend on the specific features of the system that are adopted and of the fee and pricing methods employed. Thus, we shall defer a discussion of these details of the system for Chapters 4 and 7. It may be noted immediately, however, that an interesting feature of a computer-based transfer system will be the combination of a large fixed cost of creating the system with a very low marginal cost per transaction; the true marginal cost could, indeed, approach zero. If the system were implemented optimally, with marginal cost pricing, the fees for transfers would also approach zero. This, of course, would provide strong incentive for individual traders to join the system. On the other hand, the large fixed costs of initiating the system may well mean that some form of government subsidy will be required if the implementation of an automated payments system is to occur.

The second major impact of the EMTS will result from changes in trading constraints. The EMTS will directly affect the form of individuals' budget constraints in several ways. On the most general level, the EMTS will be cheaper to operate than our current system. The emergence of an EMTS will, therefore, be analogous to the replacement of a commodity medium of exchange by a fiat issue, in that real resources will be freed for use outside of the transfer system. The economy's collective budget constraint, and thus individual constraints, will accordingly be shifted outward.

A second important effect impinging directly on individual's budget constraints, will derive from the EMTS capacity to store and process large amounts of data. We have already indicated how the existence and/or improvement of credit institutions allows individuals to expand their consumption possibilities. The information storage and processing capability of the EMTS will make it feasible for financial information on individuals to be available on a real-time basis, and thus the costs of administering consumer loans will be reduced at the same time the risks of default on such loans are lowered. There should thus be a greater availability of credit to consumers in the economy, and a corresponding increase in individuals' ability to control their budget constraints over time.

Still another change in effective constraints will accompany the elimination of float resulting from the system's instantaneous transfer of funds. In particular, individual traders will no longer be able to make use of funds that have already been marked for disbursement. On this level of the individual, therefore, it might appear that the elimination of float is actually a disadvantage. It must be noted, however, that there are always two parties to float, and that if one individual is the recipient of deferred payment, then the other party to the transaction receives late payment. Thus, for the individuals involved there are no net gains from the elimination of float.[26] On the social level, however, there are at least two reasons why the elimination of float is advantageous. First, in terms of monetary policy, the elimination of float will generally improve the accuracy of short-run forecasts by the monetary authority (see Chapter 8). Second, individuals expend resources in trying to take advantage of float; but this is not a socially productive activity (although it may be privately profitable) and thus the elimination of float will release the resources used in float endeavors to more productive purposes.

The instantaneous transfer of funds will also have a still more general effect in the economy. It will lead individuals to distinguish more sharply between

---

26. Of course, to the extent that the monetary authority is willing to provide the private financial system with float, then the elimination of this float would be a net loss to the private sector.

settlement on current transactions on the one hand, and lending and borrowing activities on the other. Under the current system these two activities are frequently integrated. For example, the present existence of check float, which we have just discussed, may be interpreted as an integration of settlement with lending for the period of the float. More generally, many retail establishments and credit card companies allow a grace period of over a month on bills due. During this period the purchaser is receiving an interest-free loan. The inefficiency of this arrangement arises because someone must, in fact, bear the cost of this free loan. Unfortunately, however, the price of the loan is typically built into the price of the good itself, and thus individuals who do not, or worse still who cannot, take advantage of the credit purchase plan end up subsidizing those individuals who do. Under the EMTS, in contrast, merchants' motivation to extend such "free credit" will be substantially eliminated; settlement, instead, will generally be instantaneous. Credit plans for financing certain purchases could still be organized, either by banks or by individual retailers, but the provision of credit would be distinct from the settlement. We can thus anticipate a more efficient system in which the cost of loans will be paid explicitly by those taking advantage of the service.

2.4.3 Conclusion

The basic purpose of this chapter has been to place the EMTS into perspective with respect to other economic exchange systems. We have seen that the main function of the EMTS will be its ability to expedite the transfer of funds, but that, in addition, by integrating an EMTS with the full exchange system a large number of other changes are likely to ensue. It is not possible on this theoretical and abstract level, however, to discuss in detail the specific changes that are likely to occur. Consequently, in the remaining parts of this study our attention will be focused on institutional factors pertinent to the U.S. economy. We begin in Chapter 3 with a detailed discussion of the features of the current U.S. monetary system that are related to the emergence of the EMTS.

3 The Present Monetary System

The discussion in Chapter 2 distinguished three main systems of economic resource transfer and settlement: barter, circulating medium of exchange, and book credit. The discussion indicated, furthermore, that it is possible for the different systems to coexist in an economy. Such is precisely the case in the United States. In this chapter we review the role of the various types of transfer which together make up the present U.S. monetary system. We will evaluate the economic and social strengths and weaknesses of each type of transfer in preparation for the argument, presented in the next chapter, that the economy as a whole will benefit from the emergence of an EMTS. Because our primary concern in this study is the EMTS, two subjects in this chapter will receive special consideration. First, Section 3.4 describes a giro payments system. While the giro has no part in the U.S. payments system today, it is quite common in Western Europe and its procedures provide an interesting comparison with the operation of our traditional demand deposit payment process. Second, bank credit cards are discussed in Section 3.7. Because bank cards represent a highly important stepping-stone to the EMTS, the details of their operation and their efficiency characteristics are presented here at length.

3.1 Nonmonetary transfer: Barter

Nonmonetary transfer occurs when goods or services are exchanged directly for other goods or services. In the U.S. this occurs essentially on two levels. At the noninstitutional level, there is the relatively primitive form of barter exchange. This is evident in newspaper want-ads offering to swap a car for a boat, violin for cello, etc. The economic motivation for such barter trades has a variety of sources. It is perhaps in part an attempt to eliminate, or at least to share, the risk of trading second-hand merchandise. (For example, you can't be sure that my car won't break down, and I don't know that your boat won't leak; but perhaps misery loves company.) It may also be an attempt to minimize the number of transactions required to achieve the desired exchange of resources. If I sell my car for cash, and then use that medium of exchange to buy a boat, two transactions have occurred. If I barter, I can eliminate one of these exchanges. A third possible explanation for barter occurs in the exchange of similar commodities. For example, the trading of a house in London for a similar house in New York is not uncommon. Barter may be a reasonable system of settlement in such cases

Table 3-1
Components of the U.S. Money Supply
($ billion, end of year)

Year	Currency	Demand Deposits Adjusted[a]	Total
1945	26.5	75.9	102.3
1950	24.5	90.0	114.6
1955	27.8	107.4	135.2
1958	28.6	112.6	141.1
1960	28.9	112.1	141.1
1962	30.6	117.1	147.6
1964	34.2	125.2	159.4
1966	27.6	132.8	170.4
1968	42.6	157.0	199.6
1970	47.8	161.6	209.4
1972	55.4	197.0	252.4

[a]Demand Deposits Adjusted—total demand deposits less government balances, interbank balances, and cash items in the process of collection.
Figures may not add to total due to rounding.
Source: *Federal Reserve Bulletin,* various issues.

because of the likely occurrence of a double coincidence of wants—an individual wishing to rent an expensive residence in London may also be likely to require one in New York. If such joint probabilities are sufficiently high, transactions costs may be lower through direct barter than with indirect monetary settlement.

The second form of barter in the U.S. occurs on an institutional level, in the form of fringe benefits provided by business firms to their employees. Many companies today provide insurance benefits, privileges at the company store, free meals, or some comparable kind of compensation which is offered in addition to employees' base pay. In 1969, such barter-type benefits provided by U.S. business represented 2.9 percent of the total payroll; that is, 14.8 billion dollars.[1] Such fringe benefits may be offered as an attempt to gain economies of scale (group insurance programs or free meals), to minimize transactions costs (a company store), or to reduce the income tax liability of employees, as well as for noneconomic motives.

It is unlikely that the volume of noninstitutional barter transactions is significant in comparison to the rest of the transactions in the economy. Furthermore, transactions are effected in this manner for reasons largely independent of any particular medium of exchange. Similarly, the bulk of fringe benefits supplied to employees have no direct relation with the payments mechanism, but are the pro-

1. Chamber of Commerce of the United States, "Employee Benefits 1969," (Washington, D.C., 1970), Table 6. Only payments in kind for which the employee's salary is not explicitly reduced are included in this gross figure; for example, the company's share of group insurance premiums, free or subsidized lunches, etc.

duct of other economic and social conditions. We would therefore expect the volume and characteristics of barter in the U.S. to be substantially unaffected by the EMTS.

3.2 Outside Money: Currency

Coin and currency, the fiat monies of the U.S. government, are, *in quantitative terms*, relatively unimportant parts of the monetary transfer system. For example, in Table 3-1, it can be seen that throughout the post-War period, currency has composed only 25 percent of the total (narrowly defined) money supply. In addition, it appears that the velocity, or rate of turnover, of currency is significantly less than the velocity of demand deposits. Table 3-2 presents figures on the velocity of demand deposit balances during the post-War period. In 1972, demand deposits adjusted in the U.S. supported over 14 *trillion* dollars worth of transactions; and the corresponding velocity of these funds was 91 turnovers per year! (Even if we remove the mammoth influence of New York City banks and those of six other money market centers, which are involved in a large number of purely financial transactions, demand deposit velocity is still 49.) While there are no comparable figures for the velocity of cash, it has been estimated that currency accounts for less than 10 percent of the dollar volume of transactions in the economy.[2]

Despite this predominance of demand deposits in the dollar volume of transactions, coin and currency remain highly important segments of the money supply for certain sectors of the economy. Nonfinancial firms tend to hold relatively little cash: intercorporate payments are virtually never made with currency, and retailers strive to minimize the amount that remains in their cash registers. The household sector, however, has a substantial transactions demand for currency,[3] which is the result of four broad factors.

First, currency is used for small purchases—for example, vending machines, lunch, and small retail purchases. For these relatively small transactions, the service charge and inconvenience involved in writing a check make cash the means of payment most often utilized. In addition, there are some instances in which coins are the sole possible means of payment. In Table 3-3 we can see how the relative amount of coins outstanding has increased sharply since World War II—reflecting, *inter alia*, an expansion in the use of coin-operated vending machines and the like.

---

2. Lawrence S. Ritter and Thomas R. Atkinson, "Monetary Theory and Policy in the Payments System of the Future," *Journal of Money Credit and Banking,* II (November 1970), pp. 493-503.

3. Philip Cagan, *Determinants and Effects of Changes in the Stock of Money* (Columbia University Press: New York, 1965), and George Garvy and Martin Blyn, *The Velocity of Money* (Federal Reserve Bank of New York, 1969).

Table 3-2
Bank Debits and Turnover Rates
(Debits in $ billion; turnover in times per annum)

Year	Debits				Turnovers			
	Total	New York City	Six Other Cities[a]	All Other Centers	Total	New York City	Six Other Cities	All Other Centers
1945	924	383	200	342	*	24.1	17.5	13.5
1950	1,380	509	299	572	*	31.1	22.6	17.2
1955	2,044	766	432	845	*	42.7	27.3	20.4
1958	2,440	959	487	994	*	53.6	30.0	22.9
1960	2,839	1,103	578	1,158	28.2	60.0	34.8	25.7
1962	3,436	1,415	702	1,319	31.3	77.8	41.2	27.7
1964	4,816	2,013	1,065	1,738	35.5	90.7	41.7	30.0
1966	6,406	2,844	1,405	2,157	56.9	121.8	53.2	34.2
1968	8,753	4,077	1,902	2,774	65.9	147.7	61.1	37.5
1970	10,896	5,016	2,480	3,400	77.0	170.6	76.7	42.6
1972	14,788	6,605	3,491	4,682	90.6	215.7	95.4	48.8

a"Six other cities" = San Francisco, Los Angeles, Chicago, Detroit, Boston, and Philadelphia.
*Not available.
Source: *Federal Reserve Bulletin.*

Table 3-3
Coin and Currency Outstanding
(as a percentage of total cash in circulation: December figures)

	Coin	Small Denomination Currency						Large Denomination Currency			
		$1	$2	$5	$10	$20	Total	$50	$100	$500 and over	Total
1945	4.4	3.6	0.2	8.1	23.7	32.2	67.8	8.1	14.7	4.4	27.4
1950	5.6	4.0	0.2	7.3	21.6	30.7	63.8	8.7	18.1	3.5	30.4
1955	6.3	4.2	0.2	6.9	21.2	31.9	64.4	8.7	18.1	2.4	29.3
1958	6.7	4.6	0.2	6.7	20.5	31.9	63.9	8.6	18.2	2.0	29.0
1960	7.3	4.6	0.2	6.8	20.3	32.0	63.9	8.5	18.1	1.7	28.4
1962	7.8	4.6	0.2	6.7	20.0	32.2	63.7	8.4	18.2	1.5	28.2
1964	8.5	4.5	0.2	6.3	19.0	32.0	62.0	8.5	19.1	1.4	29.0
1966	10.0	4.5	0.3	6.1	18.0	31.7	65.6	8.2	19.5	1.1	29.0
1968	11.1	4.0	0.2	5.8	17.2	32.3	59.5	8.2	19.7	1.0	29.0
1970	11.0	4.0	0.2	5.5	16.0	32.5	58.2	8.5	21.1	0.8	30.5
1972	11.0	3.8	0.2	5.2	14.8	32.9	57.8	8.8	22.7	0.3	32.2

Note: Figures may not add to 100 percent due to rounding.
Source: *Federal Reserve Bulletin.*

A second reason for using currency occurs when a credit card or check is not acceptable to the seller. When traveling or moving, for example, the individual and his home bank may be completely unknown, making it impossible to use a personal check. In such cases currency is often the only feasible means of payment.

Third, there is a demand for cash notes with which to undertake illegal activities since a check could provide evidence for police or the tax collector. The anonymity of currency motivates this type of use.

Finally, many people find the use of a checking account to be expensive and/or inconvenient. Some 25 percent of American households have no checking account.[4] They either find the bank service charges involved to be too great (particularly for small balances and a low level of expenditures); or their work precludes easy access to a bank office during the latter's business hours. In addition, individuals in low income brackets may find that their checks are not generally accepted. Whatever the case, there appear to be individuals, largely in lower income ranges, for whom cash represents a free and readily available means of paying bills and transacting business.

In spite of its current popularity, however, there are sizeable problems associated with the use of currency. The loss of notes through carelessness, fire, or some other mishap, is an ever-present danger. But even more important, at least in terms of the attention it receives, is the threat of loss as a result of robbery. The use of safes and cash registers in the society represents substantial capital investment;[5] and theft occurs despite such protective measures. The cost of robberies in the economy consists of both the dollar value of money and goods taken (which in 1970 amounted to over $82 million),[6] and the detrimental effect which an ever-present threat of robbery or mugging can have on the quality of life in the society. The dollar cost of the latter item is, of course, unassignable, but it seems obvious that the widespread use of currency, which often requires people to carry significant amounts of money with them, is a major cause for many of the robberies which do occur at the present time.

So far we have considered only the transactions function of currency. There are, however, two other aspects to the use of currency in the U.S. First, cash can be used as a means of storing wealth. In the 1930s public confidence in the banking industry was at a nadir, and many people did indeed hold part of their wealth as cash. But the existence of federally-insured bank and nonbank accounts today

---

4. "Bankers Debate Free Checking," *Banking,* LXV (July 1972), p. 27.

5. Carl Gambs, "Economics of an Automated Payments Mechanism," Ph.D. dissertation submitted to Yale University, 1972. Gambs estimates the total value of cash registers in the U.S. to be $2.5 billion.

6. J. Edgar Hoover, *Uniform Crime Reports for the United States,* U.S. Government Printing Office (Washington, D.C., 1971).

has made this use of cash obsolete. (Again referring to Table 3-3, we note the steadily declining relative amount of large ($500 and above) bills in the money supply. This may reflect a reduced demand for money as a store of wealth).

Currency is also part of the high-powered money stock supplied by the Federal Reserve System. To the extent that the public varies its holdings of cash and coin, the amount of demand deposits that can be supplied by the banking system varies inversely. We will discuss the ramifications of the EMTS for this aspect of currency use in Chapter 8.

3.3 Inside Money: Demand Deposits

As shown in Table 3-2, demand deposits account for the bulk of payments in the economy. This segment of the money stock, which is under control of private financial institutions, is the part destined to be most affected by the introduction of the EMTS.

As a preface to our discussion of demand deposits, it will be helpful to sketch in greater detail the nature of check-writing in the U.S. In 1970 there were over 22 billion checks written, with a total value of $13 trillion.[7] Underlying these aggregate data are the following features:[8]

1. Only 100 million checks (less than 0.5 percent) transferred amounts in excess of $10,000, yet these large checks accounted for almost half of all funds transferred.
2. The average check size was about $560, yet over 50 percent of all checks were written for amounts less than $25.
3. Individuals owned 36 percent of all domestic privately-owned demand balances, and they initiated 52 percent of all checks written.
4. Businesses held approximately 64 percent of domestically-owned balances, and wrote 43 percent of the checks.
5. Government, at all levels, wrote one check out of every twenty in the economy.

From these data we can draw two general inferences: First, that checks serve a number of diversified purposes for many different types of check-writers; and second, that a very small portion of all checks account for the majority of checks' dollar volume.

---

7. Ritter and Atkinson, *op. cit.* and George W. Mitchell, "Paying and Being Paid—The Convenience and Economics of Electronic Transfer of Funds," in *The Payments Mechanism . . . Another Look,* Federal Reserve Bank of Boston, 1971.

8. Mitchell, *op. cit.,* reports these statistics.

3.3.1 The Nature of Checks

At the start it is important to note that a check is neither legal tender nor a direct claim on real resources. It is a negotiable demand intrument—a bill of exchange—whose negotiability is described and guaranteed by the Uniform Negotiable Instruments Act. This fact can present difficulties when one wishes to use his personal check as payment, especially in an area where the bank is not well known. Fraud is relatively easy to perpetrate, and even an honest man's check can be returned to the payee marked "insufficient funds." Such occurences greatly increase the risk involved in accepting checks as payment. Since demand deposits are not legal tender, no individual is required to accept payment by check and due to their potential problems, many people (including many retailers) are reluctant to accept checks from strangers.

A demand deposit account does, however, provide several advantages over currency for its user. First, funds in a bank account cannot be stolen or lost. Second, one need not go to a bank to "get money," but can simply write a check for most expenditures and bills. In other words, checks reduce the nonpecuniary costs of making payments. Third, checks can serve nonfinancial purposes as well as being a means of paying debts. A cancelled check is legal proof that a payment has been made. (This is a form of security very much demanded by Americans. The idea of a truncated check flow system—where the physical check is stored at the bank where it is first deposited, and the payor receives only an itemized list of deductions from his account—is highly unpopular in this country, where the possession of cancelled checks is regarded as insurance against having to pay the same bill twice.) Cancelled checks are also used as proof of expenses for tax purposes. Finally, it is possible in some cases for a dissatisfied customer to stop payment on his check, thus forcing the seller to provide adequate goods or service before he will be paid. For the firm there are additional benefits attached to the use of checks. First, the maintenance of a sizeable demand deposit balance at a bank precipitates a good customer relationship, which is often essential in order to procure commercial loans. Second, a savvy corporate treasurer can stretch his firm's working capital by playing the float on the checks written by the firm. Finally, demand balances are frequently held as compensation to one's bank for financial services performed, thus reducing explicit charges for such services.

The process by which funds are transferred by check is complicated, primarily because the check is a bill of exchange. In order for individual A to effect payment to individual B, several financial institutions usually must become involved, as shown in Figure 3-1. To initiate payment, A conveys his check to B, either by hand or through the mail. B must then present the check to his bank, which will credit B's account and send the check along to its next stopping place. Depending on the location of, and relationship between, A's and B's banks, the check will be sent to a local bank-owned clearinghouse, to the local Federal Reserve Bank, or to the B bank's city correspondent. Each recipient of the check

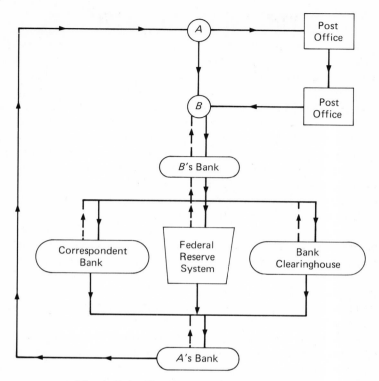

Figure 3–1. The Check Collection Process.

credits its previous holder for the amount of the instrument, and thereby becomes a "holder in due course." Finally the check will be presented to A's bank for payment. If payment is made, A's account will be debitted and he will eventually receive his cancelled check. However, if the check is rejected for any reason by A's bank, each holder in due course demands the return of its funds from the previous holder, thus reversing the flow of check and funds which had occurred.

3.3.2 The Cost of Demand Deposits

Most of the over 22 billion checks written in the U.S. in 1970 were processed in the fashion described above.[9] It has been estimated that each check is handled an average of ten times, and passes through 2 1/3 banks before being returned to its source. Moscowitz estimates that the annual cost in 1970 to the

---

9. Some of these checks are "on-us" when received at the bank of first deposit, which naturally simplifies the payments process a great deal.

private banking industry (before service charge income) for maintaining demand accounts was approximately 2.5 percent of demand deposit balances. This implies a total cost of roughly $4.5 billion, or an average of 20¢ per check.[10] The Federal Reserve System incurs still further expenses in its handling of checks.

By 1980 this volume of checks in the U.S. is likely to double.[11] The processing of paper poses two major challenges for the banks. The first, and more important, problem is that the cost of handling checks has been rising steadily, and seems destined to continue its upward trend. Despite the early and sizeable investment of commercial banks in electronic data processing equipment, the servicing of checks and checking accounts remains a labor-intensive operation. The 1972 Automation Survey of the American Bankers Association indicates that 80 percent of all demand deposits in the country are currently handled by machine. This leaves relatively few accounts, which probably originate an even smaller share of total checks, unautomated. But even the completely automated banks are confronted with a bottleneck under the current system: the technology of check clearing has already been mechanized to as great an extent as is practical.[12] Regardless of the preprinted MICR routing numbers, the amount of each check and its processing date must still be encoded on the check by hand. This means that, *ceteris paribus*, the labor input to demand deposits in the future will have to increase *roughly in proportion with check volume*. Given that the current upward trend in real wages will continue, the net result will be sharply rising costs for the maintenance of the check as it currently exists.

The second challenge inherent in this check-clearing process is float. In Figure 3-1, there are time lags involved with each movement of the check instrument, and consequently many institutions pay out funds before they themselves are credited by the next holder of the check. For the financial system as a whole, net float is zero—the Federal Reserve Banks alone are net extenders of float. However, individual banks devote considerable resources to "playing the float;" that is, a single bank can increase its reserves by garnering early payment of items due it and postponing the outflow of funds payable. Resources expended in this manner are a net loss to society.

The prohibition of interest payments on demand deposit accounts has, of

---

10. Warren Earnest Moscowitz, "The Cost and Profitability of Demand Deposits: A Review of the Literature," unpublished, 1971. There are many problems entailed in estimating the cost of demand deposits for a multiproduct commercial bank. In arriving at these figures, Moscowitz used the *Functional Cost Analysis, 1970 Average Banks.* These figures are basically accounting data and therefore assign portions of overhead, officers' salaries, etc. to the cost of demand deposit accounts. The marginal cost of demand accounts, of course, includes no such general overhead allocations. By eliminating certain of these costs, one can calculate the marginal cost of demand deposits (before service charges imposed) to be about 1.8 percent of total balances—or approximately 14¢ per check written in 1970.

11. Ritter and Atkinson, *op. cit.,* and Mitchell, *op. cit.*

12. Norman Strunk, "Electronic Funds Transfers: The Game Plan," *Savings and Loan News,* August 1971.

course, been a major reason why banks have been able to continue operating these accounts profitably. Net of interest payments, time and savings deposits are far more profitable than demand deposits because of the higher operating costs of the latter. However, when interest payments are deducted from gross income, demand deposits prove to be the more profitable items.[13] Rising market interest rates in the post-Accord period, along with the introduction of new, automated check handling techniques enabled banks to cope with their higher check clearing costs. However, the benefits of extended automation are substantially at an end, interest rates are not likely to continue on their upward trend, and it is projected that the volume of checks will continue to rise.

As a result of these cost pressures the banking industry has begun to seek new innovations in the area of making payments. SCOPE in California and the "Bill Check" plan originated by the Georgia Tech Research Institute for the Atlanta Federal Reserve District are two examples of the extent to which banks are willing to alter their traditional methods of operation in order to reduce costs. In both these programs, employers will be encouraged to transfer employee's "paychecks" directly into their bank accounts by supplying computer-readable payment orders to a local clearinghouse. Individuals can also pre-authorize the payment of certain recurring bills. "Bill Check" operates in the following manner: a customer simply signs the bill presented to him by a cooperating company and returns it to that company. The firm then forwards to the Atlanta Federal Reserve Bank a computer tape containing each customer's name, his bank, and the amount owed. The Federal Reserve Bank will sort the tape, and order each individual bank to pay the sum of its customers' accrued debts to the billing company.[14] SCOPE provides similar services to its members. Both SCOPE and Bill Check are designed to reduce the number of checks that must be handled physically by the banking industry.

The Federal Reserve as well has become increasingly concerned with the time, cost, and effort necessary to transfer funds by means of checks. In March, 1972, the Board of Governors announced plans to require simultaneously the overnight payment of all checks in the banking system (which would entail a change in Regulation D), and to lower reserve requirements against the demand deposits held in most banks. These actions will be taken in conjunction with one another so that the banking system will not lose free reserves when float is reduced by national overnight check clearing. The payment process will be speeded up by using the Federal Reserve's Culpeper wire service and more than fifty regional clearing centers to effect interbank settlements.[15] The larger customers

---

13. Richard E. Bond, "Deposit Composition and Commercial Bank Earnings," *Journal of Finance,* XXVI (March 1971), pp. 39–50. Also see Moscowitz, *op. cit.,* p. 20.

14. *Banking,* LXIV (April 1972), p. 22.

15. *Banking,* LXV (July 1972), p. 54. The change in Regulation J went into effect on September 21, 1972, and the Federal Reserve Board of Governors announced its intentions to make overnight check clearing a reality by the end of 1973.

of member banks are also being encouraged to make funds transfers in excess of $1000 by means of the Federal Reserve's wire. On August 12, 1971 the charge for using the Federal Reserve's wire facility to make these large third party payments was eliminated.

In addition to excessive and rising costs, today's check clearing system can be indicted on economic efficiency grounds. To begin with, a check costs the private banking system a marginal expense of about 14¢ to process (see footnote 10, this section). Yet the marginal charge for writing a check is usually 10¢ or less. This results in an inefficiently large volume of checks being written, since the price to the payor is less than the marginal cost to his bank.[16] This particular situation obtains as a result of the legislated prohibition of interest payments on demand deposits: placing price below marginal cost provides the depositor with an implicit interest payment for the use of his money. The solution provided in this manner is, however, far from optimal—depositors are not properly compensated (in an efficiency sense) for the use of their funds, and too many checks are written. Further, the pricing arrangement completely ignores any costs incurred by the Federal Reserve in check handling, thus separating still further the marginal private cost of writing a check from the marginal social cost.

It has also been shown by numerous writers that the prohibition of interest payments on demand deposits causes economic units to tie up real resources in making an excessive number of shifts between money and earning assets. The costs of making these shifts are an absolute loss to the society. Moreover, Harry Johnson contends that the banking system does not provide a sufficient amount of demand deposit balances: since the marginal cost of creating one dollar of bank money is practically zero, he argues, efficiency dictates that money should be created until the utility derived from holding an additional dollar is also zero.[17] This obviously does not obtain today—due both to the prohibition of interest payments on demand deposits *and* to the process by which banks grant loans. We will discuss this topic further in Section 4.4.

The role of demand deposits in financing the society has expanded rapidly in the postwar period, and the commercial banks have consequently found themselves confronted with continually rising costs of operation. The check can thus be said to have sown the seeds of its own destruction. The rising costs of check clearing and demand deposit accounting have caused the banks to seek new, less expensive devices for effecting payments in the economy—devices which will eventually make checks obsolete.

---

16. This point was brought out by Thomas Russell, "Economics of Bank Credit Cards," Ph.D. dissertation submitted to Cambridge University, 1972. Furthermore, there are costs to merchants associated with the receipt of checks—often explicit fees for an item deposited to his account. Such costs are external to the check-writer, so that, again, there is an overuse of checks in the economy.

17. Harry Johnson, "Inside Money, Outside Money, Income, Wealth, and Welfare in Monetary Theory," *Journal of Money Credit and Banking,* I (February 1969), pp. 30–45.

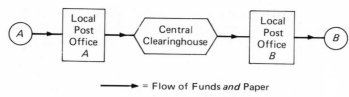

= Flow of Funds *and* Paper

Figure 3–2.   Transferring Funds with the Giro.

3.4 Giro Transfers

Indeed, forty-four countries around the world have already decided that checks, if not obsolete, at least can be improved upon for many purposes. These countries have instituted giro systems (pronounced "geero" or "jeero"—from the Greek word meaning "circle" or "ring") as adjuncts to bank checks and their currency. Although no U.S. giro exists, this type of system embodies important concepts which will be central to the EMTS. As one Federal Reserve official explained, "All of the point-of-sale 'electronic money' experiments I've heard of seek to duplicate the giro by permitting the customer to initiate, or at least participate in the initiating of, a direct payment out of his account to the creditor's, without a return flow of paper."[18]

Most giro systems currently in existence are operated by the national post office. For purposes of illustration we can consider the British system which began operations in 1968.[19] The British Post Office owns and operates the central giro clearinghouse as well as the local post offices where mail (and now money) is distributed.

In contrast to a check, a giro payment order instructs the post office to credit a payor directly with funds transferred out of the payee's account. Figure 3–2 illustrates the giro payment process. To initiate payment, individual *A* brings (or sends) a payment order form to his local post office. The office debits *A*'s account and sends the payment form to the National Giro Centre by special overnight post. The Centre debits post office *A*'s account, credits post office *B*'s account, and forwards the order form to post office *B*. Individual *B*'s account at his local post office is then credited, and *A*'s payment order is finally sent to *B* as notification of the payment which has already occurred. In this example both *A* and *B* are giroists (i.e., giro account holders); but it is possible to transfer funds in a similar fashion when nongiroists are involved.

Noteworthy characteristics of the giro are: (1) The flow of paper and information is far less complicated than for checks—compare Figures 3–1 and 3–2. Paper and information in a giro system flow in the *same* direction at all times.

---

18. James T. Timberlake, "Electronic Money—A Closer Look," in *The Payments Mechanism . . . Another Look,* Federal Reserve Bank of Boston, 1971.

19. Much of the information in this section is derived from F.P. Thomson, *Money in the Computer Age* (Pegamon Press: London, 1968).

(2) Since the national clearinghouse provides overnight processing, outstanding float is less than for a check system. (3) One can make payments, deposits, etc., at any post office in the country. This is *far more convenient* than banking, whose offices are not so commonly located and whose business hours are usually less extensive. Giroists deposit funds at their local post office, just as they would at a commercial bank. The account balances earn no interest, but the charge for transferring funds within the system is also zero. Operating costs are covered by earnings from loans made by the National Giro Center using the funds on deposit with it. (Sweden has used its giro as a source of low-interest loans for government favored long term investment projects.)

In his study of the national giro in Great Britain, F.P. Thomson presents estimates of the cost to nonfinancial parties of making payment by various means. It is on the basis of these cost estimates—which show that a giro will reduce tremendously the cost to nonfinancial economic units of making payments—[20] that Thomson argues for the adoption of the giro; at no time does he refer to cost pressures on British banks as indicative of a need for payment reforms. Regardless of the precise absolute costs of similar payments in the United States, the point to be emphasized here is this: the cost to nonbank members of society of making payments with checks can be considerable, and modification of our demand deposit system can yield substantial savings for nonfinancial economic units. These savings must be added to those of the commercial banks and the Federal Reserve in determining whether an innovation in our payments system is desirable for the society as a whole.

3.5 Trade Credit

It is common in the industrial sector of the U.S. economy for firms to extend short-term loans directly to one another in the course of carrying on trade. To the extent that such credit allows firms to receive goods without paying cash in return, it must be counted as part of the payments mechanism.[21] The

---

20. Thomson calculates that the total cost, exclusive of bank charges, of making a single payment by check is about $1.65. The cost of a similar payment made through the giro is $0.30—a reduction of over 80 percent. These calculations include the cost of postage, clerk's and typist's time, stationery, bookkeeping, etc., for a process in which the payor includes a cover letter with his check and the payee returns a receipt. The absolute accuracy of these estimates is not crucial, but only their relative magnitudes.

21. There is some question as to how industrial trade credit (or *any* credit, for that matter) should be reckoned in computing the total money stock. Robert Clower asserts that trade credit is an important component of the money supply; while Arthur Laffer more specifically claims *unextended* credit (i.e., funds in the industrial sector available for the financing of new trade credit) to be the relevant figure. See Robert W. Clower, "Theoretical Foundations of Monetary Policy," in G. Clayton, J.C. Gilbert, and R. Sedgwick, *Monetary Theory and Monetary Policy in the 1970s* (Oxford University Press: London, 1970). Also Arthur B. Laffer, "Trade Credit and the Money Market," *Journal of Political Economy*, LXXVII (March/April 1970), pp. 239–267.

importance of trade credit in the economy is shown by the fact that total gross trade credit outstanding in the U.S. at the end of 1971 stood in excess of $195 billion. This is over 85 percent of the narrowly (and conventionally) defined money stock.[22]

Trade credit is most often priced with a discount period and a net period; for example, 2/10, net/30. That is, 2 percent of the bill is discounted on payments received within ten days of delivery, while the full face value of the invoice is due within thirty days. By extending such credit, the seller is financing the inventory of his customer for the time until the balance is paid. The customer who regularly foregoes his 2 percent cash discount (and, we assume, pays only on the thirtieth day) is thus continuously postponing his payments by 20 days relative to customers who settle within 10 days. But the cost of this 20-day loan to the late payer is quite high: On a $100 account the annual interest cost of borrowing $98 for 20 days is

$$\frac{2}{100} \cdot \frac{360}{20} = 36\%.$$

Therefore, someone who regularly foregoes the cash discount must either be unaware of the true cost of this working capital, or unable to procure funds at a lower cost from any conventional source. Once the firm has obtained credit there is always the option that it can make payment later than the net period prescribed by the seller, with the result that extra liquidity is gained and the effective interest rate on the loan is lowered. (This is commonly called "stretching" accounts payable or "leaning on the trade.")

However, such a process cannot operate for the entire nonfinancial sector simultaneously. Suppose Company A buys material from Company B on credit whose terms are 2/10, net/30. If, at the end of the 30 day net period, A finds itself in need of funds, it can try not to pay B for, say, another 30 days. B has thereby been forced to extend a loan to A for one extra month, and consequently may find itself short of working capital. Company B can then lean on its trade with Company C, thus passing along the financial pressure. But eventually some firm (say it is C) will buy from the original company A on credit, and proceed to stretch its accounts payable. The funds which A retained by withholding payments from B are then transferred to C. The process has come full circle, and all firms in the sector are in the same cash position they would have been in without any account stretching. It follows that for very short-term periods, trade credit can allow interfirm activity to increase without any increase in the firms' cash reserves. However, since funds will quickly "leak" out of the industrial sector (such as to pay a wage bill to the household sector), trade credit cannot be used as a net source of capital during extended tight money periods.

It has been characteristic of the postwar economy that trade credit extended

---

22. Flow of Funds data, Federal Reserve *Bulletin*, July 1972.

varies in a highly procyclical fashion. In addition, the change in the distribution of trade credit during tight money periods is primarily that larger firms lend on extended terms to smaller firms. This is apparently the result of the fact that during such periods it is the smaller firms that find it difficult or impossible to procure commercial loans. Supply of commercial loans is rationed. Several writers [23] have asserted the existence of a certain class of (large) firms who, because of the long run value of their "customer relationship" to their bank, are virtually never denied a loan request. Moreover, larger corporations generally find it relatively easy to procure funds in the capital markets, regardless of monetary conditions. This combined easy access to bank loans and the capital markets, even during times of contractionary monetary policy, makes it possible for the larger nonfinancial firms to increase their net extensions of trade credit. Trade credit is often considered to be a necessary selling expense, and to the extent that a firm can aid a customer in financing his inventory, demand for that firm's output will be increased. Therefore, the firm that can procure funds from the financial sector and redeploy them in the form of trade credit will find itself at a significant advantage over a competing firm that cannot afford to increase its credit offerings.

It should be stressed that trade credit by itself is not a *source* of liquidity for the industrial sector, but only a device by which available liquidity can be redeployed. Even so, it has frequently been pointed out that, when trade credit is used in this fashion, it can ameliorate the effects of contractionary monetary policy on small firms in the economy.[24] The economic rationale for credit rationing by commercial banks, implications of the EMTS for corporate loans, and the role of trade credit in the future U.S. economy will be discussed further in Chapter 7.

3.6 Nonbank Credit Cards

Expansion in the use of consumer oriented credit cards in the U.S. over the past twenty years has been extensive. From a market that was virtually nonexistent before 1950, credit card programs have multiplied and grown to a point where, by 1970, over 89 percent of all American households owned at least one

---

23. Dwight M. Jaffee, *Credit Rationing and the Commercial Loan Market* (John Wiley and Sons, Inc.: New York, 1971). Edward J. Kane and Burton G. Malkiel, "Bank Portfolio Allocation, Deposit Variability, and the Availability Doctrine," *Quarterly Journal of Economics,* LXXIX (February 1965), pp. 113–134.

24. F.P.R. Brechling and R.G. Lipsey, "Trade Credit and Monetary Policy," *The Economic Journal,* LXXII (December 1963), pp. 618–641. Jaffee, *op. cit.* Allan H. Meltzer, "Mercantile Credit, Monetary Policy, and Size of Firms," *Review of Economics and Statistics,* XLII (November 1960), pp. 429–437. M.I. Nadiri, "The Determinants of Trade Credit in the U.S. Manufacturing Sector," *Econometrica,* XXXVII (July 1969), pp. 408–422.

kind of card.[25] Moreover, many people, particularly wealthier individuals, have several credit cards. The 1970 volume of credit generated on nonbank credit cards was over $54 billion, a figure which is projected to reach $94 billion by 1980. Credit cards can be used to effect nearly any kind of retail purchase. Indeed, one would find it a far easier and shorter task to compile a list of things which cannot be charged than of those which can. The majority of purchases made with the cards represent convenience credit with payment due within thirty days; however, a growing number of card issuers are introducing "easy payment" plans for their goods, thereby entering the consumer installment credit field.

Today there are three general types of charge cards available: the so-called travel and entertainment (T&E) cards, oil company cards, and the cards or charge plates of private retailers. We will consider each type of plan separately. [26]

3.6.1 Travel and Entertainment Cards

The first nonoil company to issue charge cards in large numbers in the U.S. was Diners' Club, which commenced its credit operations in 1950. After a difficult startup period the company began to earn a profit, and in 1958 two competitors were attracted into the (then adolescent) industry—American Express, and shortly afterward, the Hilton Credit Corporation. In the ensuing years the three rivals continued to expand quickly, until, by 1970, 14.6 percent of all households possessed either a Diners' Club, American Express, or Carte Blanche (Hilton's brand name) card.

The operations of these card plans are all similar and relatively simple. The issuing firm accepts applications from individuals for membership in the program. Those who are accepted pay an annual membership fee and receive a plastic identification card that is honored by all of the plan's member merchants. In order to make a payment, the cardholder simply signs a receipt that has been imprinted with his card. The merchant forwards these receipts to the card company, which pays cash (less a discount of up to 10 percent) for them, and assumes responsibility for collection of the debt from the customer.[27] The card-

25. All data in this section, unless specifically noted, were obtained from research reports of Arthur S. Kranzley and Company, Inc. of Cherry Hill, New Jersey—a business consulting firm specializing in bank charge card plans. These reports are dated May and June, 1971.

26. For a more complete discussion of the development and operation of contemporary credit card plans, See Dennis W. Richardson, *Electric Money* (The MIT Press: Cambridge, 1970), Chapter 5.

27. The merchant must pay an annual membership fee to the card company, in addition to these receipt discounts.

holder is billed each month for all his expenditures with the card, and is generally expected to remit his balance due within 30 days.

Originally the T&E cards were used primarily at restaurants, hotels, and nightclubs. Over the years, however, many new types of institutions have come to use T&E cards extensively. Car rental firms, airlines, and even gas stations now accept T&E cards as payment for their products. The benefits of these card plans for individuals are obvious: by using his card a traveller need carry far less cash and write fewer checks. He can also postpone paying for his expenditures for at least 30 days. (These two features are especially convenient for a firm that procures cards for use on expense accounts.) Moreover, the T&E cards are sufficiently scarce so that there is some degree of status attached to owning one. The merchant, for his part, can offer a charge plan (which encourages spending, particularly for tips and less necessary items) without the need for an expensive collection and credit program of his own. He, too, gains some measure of prestige by being associated with a well-known, exclusive T&E plan.

3.6.2 Oil Company Cards

As early as the 1930s, paper charge cards were being issued by the larger American oil companies. Volume remained quite small, however, until the 1950s, when auto sales, oil company sales, and the demand for convenience credit at gas stations all experienced an era of rapid growth. Today there are more than 100 million oil company cards outstanding in the economy. In 1970 they had penetrated 69 percent of American families, and generated over $6.5 billion in sales. As is true of the T&E card, the realm of oil company credit cards has expanded immensely. In addition to gasoline, the cards' original purpose, repairs, tires and parts for automobiles are chargeable, as well as a myriad of other goods and services—from auto rentals to hotel rooms.

While the T&E companies were set up solely as profit-making ventures, oil company credit operations are considered ancillary to the sale of goods and services. Convenience credit is a form of nonprice competition which is designed to build customer loyalty to a particular oil company. Purchasing a loyal customer in this manner is not cheap: the cost to the company of opening a new account is estimated to be between one and two dollars, after which operating costs claim between 2.5 percent and 7 percent of credit sales, depending on the efficiency of a given operation.[28] "Credit cards cost a fortune, but you have to have them," said one oil company official.[29]

Customers would be foolish not to take advantage of the free credit cards being offered by the gas companies. They provide a more convenient form of

---

28. Richardson, *op. cit.*, p. 65.
29. *Ibid.*

payment for routine (and necessary) purchases, and the companies increasingly are offering revolving charge plans with which to finance one's larger expenditures (at 1 1/2 percent per month on the unpaid balance).

The oil companies, however, have generally not derived profits directly from their credit operations; rather, they consider such credit to be the key to their market shares, and thus a necessary cost of conducting business. Several attempts have been made in the past to unify the billing operations of all major credit cards. All have met major opposition from oil companies who are jealously and tenaciously guarding the loyalty of "their" segment of the market.

3.6.3 *Retail Cards and Charge Plans*

A similar quest for customer allegiance is to be found at the root of most retailer-operated charge plans. These retail plans have achieved an even greater degree of penetration in the society than those of the oil companies. In 1970, 78.5 percent of U.S. households held one or more retail cards, and they charged a total volume of $43 billion in retail sales. The bulk of these credit plans are small—with far fewer accounts than the average oil company plan. They therefore suffer from many diseconomies of small scale—high fixed costs per account, poor collection facilities, high cost of working capital, excessive bad debt losses, etc. Yet retailers are driven by competition to maintain these expensive programs. Account holders are viewed as comprising a specially selected mailing list for advertising and they are considered to be a body of loyal and desirable customers.

The smallest retailers, who find it too expensive or too complicated to offer their customers a charge plan, feel handicapped in their ability to compete with larger stores. This is one of the reasons why bank charge card plans have become so widespread in recent years. Convenience credit is a much-demanded commodity in the economy, and both merchants and customers are willing to pay highly for it.

3.7 Bank Credit Cards: Forerunner of Electronic Transfer

Growth in the area of bank credit cards since 1965 has been staggering. Between 1965 and 1970, for example, the number of commercial banks involved in credit card plans increased from 79 to 8900. In 1965, 4.8 million bank cardholders made purchases totalling 330 million dollars; whereas the 1970 figures reveal that sales of 6.5 *billion* dollars were financed by the bank cards of approximately 30 million Americans. Such card plans have frequently been called "the link to the cashless checkless society of the future," and we shall see that this is at least partially true. Like giro payments systems, bank credit card plans of today are providing an important precedent and preparation for the EMTS. In this section we will first sketch the operating process of today's national bank card plans, and then we will discuss the *raisons d'être* of bank cards and their economic characteristics.

3.7.1 *The Mechanics of Present Bank Card Systems*

Early experience in the field demonstrated that there are two necessary preconditions for operating a profitable card plan. The bank must induce a sufficiently large number of people to hold its card, and it must also provide cardholders with a large and varied merchant membership in the market area. Only then will sales revenues provide enough commissions for the bank to cover its costs. A contrast can readily be drawn between the BankAmericard plan which developed successfully in the mid-sixties, and Chase Manhattan's abortive effort which was terminated in 1963 due to chronic losses. Both banks started card plans early, but the restrictive branch banking laws of New York State severely limited Chase's market region. Chase was simply unable to generate enough purchases, because physical restrictions on its office locations made it impossible to induce a sufficient number of people to hold the Chase card. In contrast, California banks are allowed to branch anywhere in the state. The size of California combined with the prevalence of Bank of America throughout the state easily lead to sales revenues sufficient to cover the fixed costs of operating the Bank-Americard system.

Learning from the example of Chase and others, later entrants to the field formed regional associations. Banks wishing to issue charge cards simply agree to honor one another's cards, and form a nonprofit association to handle interbank paper and funds transfers. In May 1970 there were nearly twenty such nonprofit bank charge card associations in the operation in the U.S. The system operates as follows.

Each member bank in an association issues its own cards and signs up its own merchants. (The details concerning billing procedures, merchant discounts, etc. vary by bank.) A cardholder will make a purchase by selecting his goods and presenting his bank card to the retailer. If the purchase value is above some specified ceiling (usually about $50) the merchant must call the card's issuing bank in order to check on the credit status of its holder. Upon receiving authorization for the sale, a receipt for the purchase is imprinted with the customer's card and the merchant forwards the receipt to his bank. He receives immediate credit for some fixed percentage of the face value of the receipt (typically the bank will discount receipts at 3 to 6 percent) and the consumer will be billed by his bank at monthly intervals. See Figure 3–3. He will have perhaps 25 days after the billing date in which to pay the balance due, after which the amount outstanding becomes a loan at 1 to 1½ percent per month.

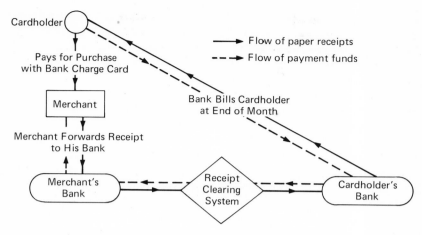

Figure 3–3. Bank Card Billing Procedure.

What we have omitted in the above scenario is the means by which the card-holder's bank pays the merchant's bank. This is where the associations are vital; and the clearing process is also an important precedent for the operation of an electronic network in the future. There are three situations which could arise in the clearing process, and we will consider them in their increasing order of complexity.

In the case where the merchant and the cardholder bank at the same institution, the transfer of credit is effected quickly and generally no other institution becomes involved. The bank pays the merchant's account immediately and collects from the cardholder at some later date. The transaction is similar to an "on-us" check, except that this charge transaction generates float that the bank must absorb in the form of an interest-free loan to the customer for an average period of 40 days (that is, an average of 15 days before the monthly billing date, and 25 grace days before the outstanding balance becomes an interest loan).

When the merchant and customer have different banks which belong to the same regional association we have a somewhat more complex situation. In this instance, all member banks figure on a daily basis the amount due to and receivable from each other association member, and net payments are made by transferring funds on the books of one of the association's primary banks. The time value of money is given greater recognition than in the previous case, since the consumer's bank pays less than the par value of the receipt to the merchant's bank. This discount is generally 1 percent, so the "float" generated by purchases is really a loan at the rate of 1 percent per 40 days—the interest being paid out of the merchant's discounts. As soon as more than one bank becomes involved, the imprinted receipts trade among banks at somewhat below par, essentially like acceptances.

The third possible situation would involve a customer and merchant whose banks belong to different credit card associations. For example, suppose an individual holding the card of a New York City bank travels to San Francisco and makes a purchase there. The merchant's bank in San Francisco will sell the imprinted receipt (at a discount) to the Western States Bank Association (WSBA), which in turn sells it to the Eastern States Bank Association (ESBA) and receives funds (again less than the par value). The ESBA then debits the account of the cardholder's bank (by an amount less than the face value of the receipt) and the cardholder is eventually billed by his own bank for his San Francisco purchase.

This receipt clearing system operates essentially like the Federal Reserve's check clearing process, and presents no conceptual difficulties. However, the fact that the Federal Reserve is unwilling to process imprinted receipts means that credit card banks must maintain two distinct clearing operations. Furthermore, for all card transactions except "own-bank" transfers, the amount of paper flowing through the banking system is no lower than the paper volume which would be generated by similar check payments: there is still one receipt per transaction.

Banks must also incur considerable extra expense by keeping separate accounting procedures for their credit card accounts. It has been suggested[30] that the end results of bank credit cards (that is, a negotiable credit instrument for the consumer and an easy means through which to generate consumer loans) could be achieved at lower cost by means of a plan similar to the "Eurocheque" plan currently popular in Europe. In this scheme, the bank charge card is replaced by a bank check guarantee card, augmented by an overdraft allowance for the cardholder. In this way, the bank would not have to arrange the clearing of its card receipts separately, but instead, cardholder's checks could be cleared through more normal (and cheaper) channels. In addition, the accounting could be incorporated into the bank's standard demand deposit procedures. While this plan may indeed hold promise in that it reduces the costs to a bank of operating a credit card-type plan, it in no way ameliorates the basic paper problem confronting the banking system. The adoption of such a plan would therefore do little to slow the emergence of an EMTS.

A sizeable problem connected with the operation of today's national credit card plans is the following. A San Francisco merchant, when faced with a potential $150 purchase, must contact the issuing bank in order to secure authorization for the sale (since the amount is over the card's ceiling limit). Now, the merchant must call his bank, which contacts the WSBA, who calls the ESBA, who receives approval from the customer's bank. Obviously all this requires more than an instant, and the time lag has at times proved very bothersome to customers and merchants alike. By January 1972 both national charge card plans (Mastercharge and BankAmericard) had, therefore, announced plans for national

30. George D. Edwards, "A Quick Fix for the Bank Card," *The Bankers Magazine,* CLV (Spring 1972), pp. 81–85.

computer networks that will automatically do the message switching involved. In the above example, the WSBA computer can obtain authorization directly from the New York bank's computer and relay the results to the merchant in San Francisco. Any member merchant will be able to dial a single telephone number and receive authorization within seconds, regardless of the location of the customer's bank. Such a national computer system with message switching capabilities will be the heart of a functioning EMTS.

Thus, to summarize, the pertinent features of today's bank card system are four.

1. It does nothing to decrease the paper burden on the banks: in 1971, 400 million sales receipts flowed through the banking system. Indeed, the banks' paper flows and operating expenses are *increased* by bank cards.
2. Customers are able to procure free 40-day loans for their purchases. Therefore, a rational consumer will generally choose his charge card over cash in making a purchase.
3. Merchants' charge card receipts are discounted by the bank, but no corresponding discount is offered by the merchants to their cash customers. Since the merchants often tend to raise prices in order to cover costs associated with the charge plans, these cash customers are subsidizing the operation of the plans.
4. The capacity to interchange information and funds between virtually any two points in the nation exists and is so organized as to be readily adaptable to computerization.

3.7.2 Economic Features of Bank Card Plans

Significant economic gains accrue to users of the bank card system. As with any charge card, the bank cardholder must hold less (noninterest-bearing) money to support his transactions and therefore is able to increase the income from his wealth; he writes fewer checks; he has a ready source of short-term credit; and he receives interest-free loans on the amount of his purchases for an average of 40 days. But the particular advantage of a *bank* card over nonbank charge arrangements lies in its general usability and convenience. There is a single card that must be carried, and but a single check to write at the month's end for all one's purchases. Merchants also derive considerable benefits from the system. Customers can buy on credit without the need for every small store's extending its own credit. The absolute cost of a given amount of credit in the society is thus reduced due to economies of scale and specialization; and the merchant can operate with less working capital since he receives immediate credit even for his charge sales.

These features all constitute gains for the society. But the existence of such gains does not necessarily imply that bank credit cards are an efficient payment medium. In fact, such cards are a step *away* from an optimal system in several respects.

1. They increase the amount of paper being exchanged among the country's banks. Credit card banks must maintain dual facilities for handling paper— checks and charge card receipts flow by distinctly different routes.
2. The marginal cost of using one's credit card to make a purchase is zero (actually it is negative, in the sense that payment is postponed by the use of the card.) Since the marginal cost to the banks of a card transaction is positive, cardholders will "overuse" their cards, just as they overuse checks.
3. Merchants provide no cash discount for noncharge customers, yet the seller receives the full value of such purchases—instead of, say, 95 percent of the price with a bank card purchase. For the cash buyer there exists a gap between the price to him and the marginal cost to the merchant of the good sold. This gap can only exist as a result of imperfections in the market; in this case, free access to bank cards does not exist.

The gains which accrue to society as a result of bank cards must be balanced against these inefficiencies. On net, however, the charge card plans would seem to yield significant advantages, since they are being widely used and have been earning profits for the banking industry.

The rapid move to credit card plans of late has been prompted primarily by this opportunity to gain a substantial profit. Consumers and merchants have shown themselves willing to support the costs of the new services through merchant discounts and interest payments on overdrafts. The banks, for their part, have been eager to provide new services for their smaller depositors. Since World War II, the banking industry . . .

> has moved away from wholesaling services for big, exclusive clients to retailing them for the public. The banks' courtship of consumers has been encouraged by continual pressure on the "spread" between what the banks pay for money and what they charge to lend it. The pressures come from the increasingly competitive capital markets, and from the growing savvy of corporate money managers who hate to leave funds sitting in interest-free demand deposits. For their profits, the banks have had to move deeper into consumer loans, where rates ran up to 18% a year.[31]

The data in Table 3–4 support the above conclusions in these regards. It is clear that commercial bank dealing with consumers have risen rapidly over the past quarter century. In particular, note that loans to individuals increased (as a per-

---

31. "Money Goes Electronic in the 70's," in *Business Week's* "Special Reports on Major Business Problems," 1970.

Table 3–4

Commercial Bank Loans

(as a percentage of total assets)

Year	Loans to Individuals	Commercial and Industrial Loans	Real Estate Loans	Total Loans
1946	2.7	9.5	4.8	20.9
1948	4.4	12.3	7.0	27.9
1950	6.0	13.1	8.0	31.4
1952	6.8	14.9	8.4	34.7
1954	7.3	13.4	9.1	35.6
1956	8.7	17.9	10.4	42.4
1958	8.7	17.0	10.6	42.1
1960	10.3	16.8	11.2	46.8
1962	10.3	16.4	11.6	48.2
1964	11.5	17.7	12.7	50.6
1966	11.9	20.0	13.4	54.7
1968	11.7	19.6	13.1	52.4
1970	11.4	19.5	12.6	51.7

Source: *Report* of President's Commission on Financial Structure and Regulation.

centage of total bank assets) over 400 percent after the war, while commercial loans doubled and real estate loans have increased about two and one-half times.

These very profitable consumer loans are easier to issue and maintain outstanding with a large card plan. That is, the bank can expect a certain volume of loans to be generated *for it* by the sales of its member merchants. Bank customers are able to finance a myriad of goods and services with bank loans—many of which would be too small to finance individually. Charge plans thus perform two lending functions for the banks: they increase the demand for consumer loans, and enable the banks to reduce the cost of issuing such loans, thereby lowering their breakeven point. (The Functional Cost Analysis of 1970 Average Banks shows that a two year consumer installment loan with a 6 percent add-on interest rate (11.08 percent true annual interest) had a breakeven size between $755 and $1137, depending on the lending bank's size.[32] This very high figure is due to the fixed costs of issuing any loan.)

But in addition to this profit motive, banks view credit cards as a means of holding consumer and merchant favor during times when other financial intermediaries (and rising rates on market securities) threaten to erode their share of the savings market. Many banks were lead to introduce credit card plans in order to gain a competitive advantage over other regional bank and/or nonbank competitors (or to counter a competitor's card plan). As we will see in Chapter 5,

---

32. More precisely the breakeven points are: a bank with less than $50 million in deposits—$755; between $50 and $200 million—$888; and over $200 million—$1137. The Analysis makes no reference to these apparent scale diseconomies.

the competition for savings funds became intense in the mid-1960s, and banking
institutions sought new means by which to differentiate themselves from rivals.
In addition, latecomers to the bank card field have viewed charge card plans
as an essential prerequisite for successful competition in the checkless society of
the future.[33]

3.8 Summary

This chapter has provided an overview of the current system of credit and
settlement in the U.S. The main features may be listed:

1. Nonmonetary transfer exists and will continue to exist on a small scale for
    specialized transactions.
2. Coin and small-denomination currency transfers play a somewhat more
    significant role in the economy, although almost solely in the household
    sector. Their use can be expected to continue in certain kinds of trans-
    actions, although in diminishing importance. (We will discuss this issue fur-
    ther in Chapter 7.) Large denomination currency transfers are minor at the
    present time and will become even more so.
3. Demand deposit transfers are the center of the current U.S. payments sys-
    tem. Unless other changes occur, the volume of check transfer will continue
    to grow rapidly, as will the cost (and even the feasibility) of maintaining the
    system. It is here that the impetus for an EMTS is seen most clearly.
4. Giro transfer systems, although not used in the U.S., have been extensively
    implemented in Western Europe and elsewhere. An important attribute of
    giro transfer is the small amount of paperwork involved, and for this reason
    giro principles should tend to become ever more important.
5. Trade credit transfer is second only to check transfer in importance in the
    current U.S. payments system. It would appear amenable to computeriza-
    tion and thus should continue its critical function for the business sector,
    albeit with some changes.
6. Bank and nonbank credit card networks have proven feasible and have
    grown quickly in the last ten years. In many ways they point to the future
    role of an EMTS, but with the important *caveat* that credit cards are still
    essentially a paper transfer system, while the EMTS has characteristics that
    are unique to a fully electronic system.

---

33. Donald M.T. Gibson, *The Strategic and Operational Significance of the Credit Card
for Commercial Banks,* Research Report No. 42 to the Federal Reserve Bank of Boston,
August 1968.

4

The Structure of an Electronic Monetary Transfer System

We are now prepared to move the discussion from what *is* to what *will be*. In this chapter we undertake to describe the electronic monetary transfer system (EMTS) as it is likely to emerge in the U.S. in the course of the next 10 to 15 years. We will begin where any economic analysis of a proposed investment project must begin—with a discussion of the costs and benefits associated with the EMTS. To predict the *exact* costs of the system at this time is technically impossible. But we believe that the evidence that *is* available tends to support the commonly-held (among bankers) belief that an EMTS will offer substantial cost savings for the society as a whole. The second section of this chapter is devoted to a consideration of the technical requirements that the EMTS must fulfill, and the types of hardware and software that will be employed toward those ends. The section is somewhat lengthy and considers exclusively noneconomic aspects of the system. We have, however, felt it necessary to clarify a number of issues. Too many articles and speeches on "our future payments mechanism" either ignore the technical problems involved in the EMTS or attempt to burden the system with "problems" which are in fact not nearly so serious as is alleged. It is hoped that this section of the chapter will shed some light on the physical EMTS, without an undue reliance on technical jargon. Section 3 then describes the economically relevant features of the EMTS; it considers the EMTS' general effects on financial activities in the economy. Finally the last section demonstrates how an EMTS will fulfill several important criteria for an efficient payments mechanism.

4.1 Economic Feasibility — EMTS
Costs and Benefits

Any attempt to estimate the cost of the future electronic payments system must be plagued by a series of unavoidable problems. What performance per dollar cost can be expected from fourth (and fifth) generation computers? How can message flows among regions of the country be estimated most accurately? How many computer centers, merchant terminals, etc., will be demanded? What type of communication links should be used—wires? microwave? satellite? Will these links be owned or leased by the operators of the EMTS, and at what price? In view of obstacles such as these, the cost estimates that have been produced to date must be viewed as approximations at best. We will therefore confine ourselves to indicating the order of magnitude of probable cost savings engendered by the EMTS. In particular we will demonstrate the plausibility of the view that the EMTS will, on net, reduce the society's cost of operating the payments mechanism by a substantial margin. Toward this end we can draw on the conclusions of three feasibility studies that have been performed during the past few years.

The first of these reports is not concerned with a complete EMTS, but deals only with the process of interbank payment communications. It was sponsored by the Bank Administration Institute (BAI),[1] and published in 1969. The system proposed by BAI would link together all commercial banks in the country for the purpose of quickly effecting interbank payments of cash items. Based on its data from 1967, the research committee concluded that an electronic interbank system would reduce bank operating costs attributable to demand deposits by $500,000 a day (from about $3 million to $2.5 million). Their plan mechanizes only the communications aspect of payments; in other words, much of the in-bank processing of payment information would still be done by hand. This fact necessitates a continued dependence on labor inputs to the payment process. While the BAI scheme somewhat reduces the banks' demand for clerical labor, a sizeable demand would still remain. A more revolutionary plan was not evaluated because of a desire to

> impose a minimum of change on bank customers. Consequently the model does not illustrate the full cost reduction potential of electronic systems. Preliminary investigations indicate that mechanization of the receiving operations and elimination of encoding, filing, check return and statement make-up operations might reduce per-unit payment processing costs substantially.[2]

The BAI cost data indicate that the elimination of these labor-intensive steps would reduce the banks' daily costs $1.6 million further—a total reduction of about 65 percent from the original $3 million daily cost.

A Stanford Research Institute (SRI) study [3] concerns itself with a system which extends to the entire economy, and eliminates much of the labor input to funds transfer. In a completely paperless financial system there will rarely be any need for physical input to the computers. Instead, a bank's deposit data will originate electronically—from a merchant's terminal, another bank's direct data transmission, or as a computer tape prepared by a nonfinancial firm. Once the necessity of a paper-to-machine transfer of information is eliminated, the cost of labor input to the payments process drops dramatically.

SRI's "Direct Funds Transfer" system is similar to our EMTS; however,

1. Robert H. Long and Linda M. Fenner. *An Electronic Network for Interbank Payment Communications: A Design Study,* Bank Administration Institute, Park Ridge, Ill. 1969.

2. *Ibid.,* p. 27.

3. B. Cox, A.W. Dana, and H.M. Zeidler, *A Techno-Economic Study of Methods of Improving the Payments Mechanism,* Stanford Research Institute, (Menlo Park, 1966).

their discussion places much greater emphasis on the point-of-sale (i.e., retail) aspects of the system, to the exclusion of intercorporate and interpersonal operations. The Stanford group estimated that 65–70 percent of bank demand deposit expenses are displaceable by an automated system—an estimate close to that derived above from BAI's data. The presentation of the SRI data is imprecise at some points; the size of the national EMTS system (and therefore its total cost) is expressed only as a range (e.g., "200 to 1000 local switching centers"); average costs are presented on the basis of an arbitrarily assumed number of transactions per month; and displaceable costs are computed *only* for the banking industry, thereby ignoring advantages and savings which will accrue to nonbank institutions. But despite all these problems, three conclusions can be drawn on the basis of SRI's data and analyses.

1. The EMTS *is* an economically profitable investment. For the 1966 volume of checks, the banks' cost of operating the payment mechanism would have been $800 million lower had an EMTS been in existence. (If the EMTS had handled all retail 30-day charge and installment credit transactions as well, net savings in 1966 for the economy would have been $3 billion.)

2. The average total cost of a retail transaction with an EMTS varies between 3¢ and 12¢, depending on the number of purchases effected with the terminal unit. Fully 91 percent of this average cost is attributed to the cost of operating a merchant's terminal and his communication tie with the local computer center. In other words, once information has entered the system, the average cost of *transmitting* it between two points is very small—between 0.27¢ and 1.08¢ per message.[4] A giro payment order would therefore be far cheaper to effect than a retail sale. In any case, all the transaction costs projected by SRI are well below the bank costs of 13¢ per check which they estimate will be displaced by the EMTS.

3. The *marginal* cost, as inferred from SRI's data, is virtually zero for any kind of transaction in the system. All the EMTS costs projected in the report are fixed, with no relation to the number of messages actually processed by the system. Such an assumption obviously understates the marginal costs to some extent, but it may still be a reasonable approximation.

The third research report is more recent, but also less specific on the issue of a full-scale EMTS. The Georgia Tech Research Institute study,[5] commissioned by the Federal Reserve Bank of Atlanta, suggested the immediate introduction of their "Bill Check" and paperless payroll crediting plans (see Chapter 3), and proposed a further study to examine the costs of implementing a point-of-sale electronic system as well. The report found preliminary evidence on the work-

---

4. The average cost per message in BAI's projected system is 0.2¢. Due to the high fixed costs of operating such systems we would expect the *marginal* cost to be still smaller than the estimates of either BAI or SRI.

5. Georgia Tech Research Institute, *Research on Improvements of the Payments Mechanism* (Atlanta, July 1971), as reported in *Banking,* April 1972.

ability and profitability of such a retail operation to be "promising." It is thought that a full electrified payments process will produce substantial cost savings for both the commercial banks and the Atlanta Federal Reserve Bank. In particular, it was estimated that a Bill Check payment will cost the banking system 25 percent less than a similar check transaction, and a paperless payroll deposit will save the banks over 60 percent of a check's cost. Furthermore, the preliminary evidence suggested that, as a result of new services which can be provided to merchants and individuals via an electronic point-of-sale transactions system, the banks could earn 22 percent on their invested capital from such a system.

A further indication of the cost advantages associated with automated banking techniques is to be found in recent experiments with robot tellers. "In its most highly developed form, the robot, or automatic, teller can dispense cash, accept payments, process deposits or transfer funds between accounts."[6] There are indications that overall operating costs can be lowered through the use of robot equipment in the performance of the more routine tasks connected with banking. For example, the Huntington National Bank of Columbus, Ohio has installed a completely automated branch office. It is capable of performing 80 percent of the services offered by a manned branch, but at one-tenth the cost.[7] (To date, however, most installed machines of this sort have suffered from a severe lack of use—largely because people are unfamiliar with them and therefore hesitate to deposit their funds with a robot.)

Overall, then, there is every reason to believe that the EMTS will cost less than the private banking industry's current demand deposit operation. However it is important to point out that this is *not* a necessary prerequisite for the EMTS to be considered a socially desirable innovation. Banking-oriented studies have concentrated on automation's effect on private operating costs, and the fact that the EMTS looks to be a profitable innovation is responsible for the progress and research that has occurred to date in the area of electronic payments. However, there is also the Federal Reserve System, which expends a sizeable sum yearly in support of the checking system. These costs will be largely displaced by EMTS procedures. Nonbank intermediaries and nonfinancial economic units will receive substantial benefits as well: a lower crime rate, reduced bad debt losses, foregone postage expense, lower transaction charges, reduced nonpecuniary transactions costs, etc.[8] Further still, the EMTS will engender a series of new services that are likely to be strongly demanded, among them preauthorized payments and bank lines of credit.

The introduction of an EMTS will thus have far-reaching effects for the entire society; it is by no means a project limited in scope to the commercial

6. *Savings and Loan News,* June 1972, p. 54.

7. *Ibid.*

8. These and other features of the EMTS will be discussed further later in the chapter.

banking industry as was, for instance, the introduction of MICR encoded checks. The conclusion to be inferred from the above discussion and the data presented in this section is this: when the society goes over from its present payments system to the EMTS, substantial pecuniary and nonpecuniary benefits will accrue in many sectors of the economy. With this foundation given, let us now turn to a detailed description of the transfer system itself.

4.2 Physical Structure of the EMTS

The concept of an electrified money system dates at least to 1954, when two M.I.T. professors suggested that the best means of handling the then-pressing problem of increasing paper flows in the banking system was simply to computerize the whole process and eliminate paper altogether.[9] From the present technological vantage point the details of an EMTS are quite different from those envisioned in 1954, but the concept remains substantially unchanged. Units of the economy will transfer money and credit among themselves without the use of paper. All accounts, records, and transactions will be controlled by a nationwide network of interconnected computers. We have shown in the preceding section that the EMTS is by no means a financial SST—that is, it is not a project which will be carried out simply because it is technologically *possible*. The evolution of an EMTS in the United States would be an economically and socially desirable occurrence. This section is devoted to a consideration of the technical problems associated with the construction of the EMTS. We intend to demonstrate that, while many of the details of design, security, etc., are in fact quite complex and uncertain at this time, the state of the art in computer science is such that the EMTS can readily be constructed on the basis of knowledge, equipment, and techniques that are available today.

4.2.1 The National Computer Network

It is doubtful that a national EMTS could have been constructed in the U.S. in 1954, and it is even more doubtful that any 1954 system would have been able to operate cheaply and efficiently enough to induce large numbers of people to use it. However, recent computer developments, in hardware *and* in software have made the EMTS both feasible and highly profitable. The extremely quick processing times of third generation machines and their storage devices have made it possible for a computer to store and process huge amounts of information in a brief span of time. Telecommunication principles developed in the

---

9. Robert H. Gregory and Henry Jacobs, "A Study of the Transfer of Credit in Relation to the Banking System," M.I.T. Dynamic Analysis and Control Laboratory Report No. 87 (Cambridge, 1954).

past few years enable computers to communicate with one another—to share data banks and divide their common workload. Equally important has been the innovation of computer supervisor programs that enable a single machine to handle many programming tasks virtually simultaneously.[10] In short, the hardware and software needed for the successful economic operation of a national EMTS already exists and is in use throughout the U.S.

Functions of the System. The EMTS, as an electronic information system, will be required to effect two principal tasks. First, it must provide every member of the system with a means to pay (and receive payment from) every other member. This is the system's *information switching* capacity, and it will be similar in concept to the various computerized reservations services in operation today. Through an airline office in New York City, for example, one can reserve a seat on a Los Angeles to San Francisco flight due to take off the following week. Or, through a motor inn chain, one may procure a hotel room for the next night in another city. In all these cases (airline reservation, hotel room, and the EMTS) the capacity exists to communicate a certain kind of information directly from one member of a computerized system to another. Further, the transmitted information is used to control the allocation of a scarce resource—airplane seats, rooms, or money. This analogy should not be overworked. There are significant differences among these systems, but it is apparent that the functional concepts of an EMTS are not without precedent.

In addition, the EMTS will be required to manage the account of every member in the system. This is the system's *information processing* capacity. To-

---

10. There are two means by which a computer can service more than one task "simultaneously."

A machine operating in a *multiprogramming* environment can have several programs in its main storage at the same time (for example, the IBM 360/65 can simultaneously contain up to 15). The Central Processing Unit (CPU) proceeds to work on Program A until it encounters a situation where it must wait. The most common occurrence of a "wait" could be when Program A needs to read (or write) data from (to) a storage device. It is characteristic of computer systems that, no matter how fast a data device *appears* to be operating, a CPU finds it painfully slow. Therefore, the CPU will give an order to read, say, a punchcard, and then must wait to get the data into storage. Instead of sitting idle during this wait period, a multiprogrammed CPU will begin work on Program B, which is also in main storage. Upon encountering a "wait" in B, the CPU turns to work on C, and so forth. In this fashion a computer can appear to be doing many tasks simultaneously, while in reality it is merely allocating CPU time very efficiently.

A *timeshare* system is one where the computer has only one program at a time in its main storage. But when Program A produces a wait period, the CPU stores Program A on a disk file and quickly reads Program B into storage from another disk. B is then executed until it produces a wait state, etc. Timeshare programs are usually entered and controlled through teletype units that are connected to the computer by means of telephone lines. (These remote units may be up to several hundred miles away from the CPU.) In a multiprogram system, an individual program can command only a fraction of the machine's resources (storage and input/output devices); whereas a timeshare user gets the impression (although false) that he is the sole user of the entire computer.

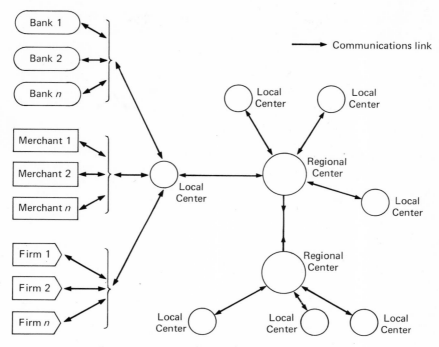

Figure 4–1. Information Flows in the EMTS.

day, in large and medium-sized banks and thrift institutions throughout the country, "on-line" banking and computerized accounting procedures are routine and largely error-free. There is no reason why these techniques will not be carried over into the real-time environment of the EMTS.

According to the SRI study [11] the carrier of all this information will be a network of 20 to 30 regional computer centers, 800 local centers, and communication lines among the centers. Figure 4–1 illustrates how these computer centers will provide the information switching capacity required by an EMTS. The optimal number and location of these centers can be calculated once cost data and message-flow estimates for various sections of the country have been obtained. The BAI study to determine the profitability of computerizing all interbank payments points out the tradeoff that must be optimized:

> The number and location of message switching centers are important in estimating network operating costs. If there are too few centers or if they are not placed so as to minimize circuit costs between centers and banks, then communication costs will be high. If there are too many centers, costs

---

11. Cox, Dana, and Zeidler, *op. cit.*

for circuits between centers and banks will be lower, but center-to-center circuit costs and switching center costs will be higher than necessary.[12]

Presently, detailed data on national financial flows exist only for the twelve Federal Reserve Banks and their 24 branches; but it will be necessary to accumulate data on financial flows within and among every region of the country, not just for these 36 Federal Reserve Cities. Therefore, a considerable research effort will be required before an optimal (that is, least-cost) computer network can be designed.

The type of communication lines between any two centers will vary according to the message loads expected. Today the Federal Reserve's Culpeper system and the privately-owned Bank Wire (an alternate means of interbank funds transfer) employ narrow-band teletype lines for communications. However, the BAI study cited above concluded that interbank traffic alone among the Federal Reserve cities was in most cases heavy enough to require voicegrade lines—and the EMTS will have to carry far more than just interbank payments. It is therefore probable that voicegrade lines will be the norm of the system, with microwave links (or other wideband facilities) established in the corridors of heaviest traffic. For every communication linkage in the system, the traffic load will influence both the type of data line employed and the equipment required by the computer centers. These details are closely connected with the geographic placement of centers, as discussed in the previous paragraph.

For a computer network of this sort, there are two types of communications that could be established. The system could either be of a (batched) message switching or circuit switching character. The BAI study concluded that, for its purposes, a *message switching system* was the proper choice. Interbank payments do not have to be effected instantaneously, but can be delayed for short periods of time. The BAI system would therefore work as follows: a bank in, say, New York, would wire a message containing payment instructions to its local computer center. If the payee bank is nearby, the local center can notify it directly that payment has been made to its account. However if the payee is in Chicago, the local center routes the message to New York's regional computer center, where the message is held until a sufficient number of other Chicago-bound messages are collected. Then the New York regional center sends its messages to Chicago in a batch. (The Chicago regional center then transmits the individual messages to the proper local centers, which in turn communicate with individual banking units.) The advantage of this batching process is that the number of distinct data transmissions is reduced, and redundant address information on each individual message can be eliminated.

However, such a message-switching system would be completely unsuitable for an EMTS, where constant direct access to one's account is an important

12. Long and Fenner, *op. cit.*, p. 12.

aspect of the system's security.Only if the payor's demand account is inspected prior to every transaction can the payee be certain that sufficient funds are available. It is for this reason that the EMTS must, like our telephone system, *switch circuits*. Only in this manner can the payee communicate directly with the payor's bank.

Efficient Use of Hardware. The issue of efficiency in the usage of equipment must inevitably arise in designing a system such as this one. There will, of course, be peak demand periods for the system's services, and hardware must be adequate to handle such peaks. What is to be done, then, with this idle computing capacity during off-peak times? It is here that multiprogramming and timeshare (see footnote 10) can make a major contribution. By utilizing general-purpose, multiprogrammable computers in regional and local switching centers, the owners of the EMTS can become large-scale sellers of their off-peak computer time. Non-EMTS tasks could be run in the "background"—that is, whenever an EMTS and a non-EMTS task are competing for the same computer facility, the EMTS task is given priority. Such schemes are common in large computer installations today. Users of such off-peak computer time would be numerous, including (among many others): small banks and other financial institutions who want computerized accounting procedures; research and business firms whose own computers are overloaded; nonfinancial firms who have their accounting done externally (see Chapter 7 for a full discussion of this implication of the EMTS); and government at all levels. The recent proliferation of computer leasing firms bears adequate testimony to the potential market that will exist for EMTS computers' free time.

It would also be possible (and desirable) to design the EMTS in such a manner that as much demand for the system's services as possible is shifted from peak to off-peak hours. For example, vending machines, transit systems, and other sectors that have a large number of relatively small transactions in the course of their business day could have off-line arrangements. Specifically, when the customer wishes to make a purchase, he enters his card into the vending machine, which would read the account number of the purchaser and store the amount of the charge and the account number on a small magnetic tape. At the end of the day, the tape would be forwarded to the local computer center for reading and processing. This process would be ideal for sellers who are unconcerned with verifying their customers' accounts prior to sales. Retail firms may well have two distinct methods of being paid—an on-line terminal for high-security transactions involving expensive items; and an off-line magnetic tape process for less valuable exchanges. In this way, many small transactions could be cheaply effected through the EMTS at off-peak times. Such a process bypasses the EMTS security measures, but for smaller transactions this will probably not be a serious problem.

4.2.2 Access to the System

Given the existence of this national computer network we must specify the means by which individual economic units will connect into the communication system. As was the case with the characteristics of individual communication lines, means of access to the system will vary according to the demands placed on the EMTS by each type of economic unit. We will consider here four specific kinds of institutions: banks, corporate and governmental offices, private individuals, and retail establishments.

Banks [13] will be the only institutions in the economy that must be on-line with the EMTS computer network at all times. A customer may at any hour wish to make a purchase through the EMTS, and his bank's computer must stand ready to effect payment any time it is demanded. As with the regional and local EMTS switching computers, banks' machines must be designed to accommodate peak message loads with little or no delay. There will thus be considerable off-peak excess capacity on these bank-owned computers, and we can anticipate that banks will do their computerized accounting, billing, loan evaluation work, etc., in the background on their multiprogrammable machines. It will be in their interest to price their payments services in such a manner that demand is transferred to off-peak times to as great an extent as is possible.

Financial and nonfinancial corporations and government offices as well, will have two means of access to the EMTS. First, they can use their in-house computer to order their bank to make payments to a third party. (See Table 1-1, part 4 (a).) Such on-line access will require a direct telecommunication link with the local computer center or with the firm's bank, and could be used to make very high-priority payments and/or to receive frequent notification of changes in the firm's account balances. Most writers on the EMTS seem to assume automatically that all transactions in the economy will be more efficiently made through on-line EMTS operations. However, efficiency and cost considerations combined indicate that there will be many kinds of transactions that will best be made off-line. Lower priority corporate transactions is one example; the smaller transactions mentioned in Section 4.2.1 is another. Even if a firm wishes to make some of its payments on-line there is no need to maintain a constantly open communication link. Rather, a "dial-up" telephone connection could be employed. In this fashion the firm would have to pay for the line only when it is actually in use. It seems unlikely that such important payments will be significant in number, and we can therefore anticipate that corporate on-line operations will not be very large.

A second means of access would be through computer tapes, punchcards,

---

13. It will be shown in Chapter 5 that the EMTS will cause a significant blurring of the distinctions among the various types of financial intermediaries. Therefore, "bank" as used in this chapter, will denote whatever assortment of institutions actually supply third party payments in the EMTS.

or other machine-readable input, which a firm would deliver to its bank. As with current SCOPE programs, the bank would then effect payments as directed by the tape, debitting the firm's account. A smaller firm, which is not completely automated, could keypunch its payment orders and forward the cards to its bank (or the bank may handle all the data processing as a service to its customers[14]). For routine payments, this off-line method would seem to be most suitable. One exception might be where a firm's bank is far away from the corporate offices. In such a case, a high volume of messages between the firm and its bank could make it profitable for data to be transmitted electronically (through the EMTS) rather than physically. The firm could either go on-line itself, or deliver the tapes to its local computer center for subsequent transmission to the bank during off-peak periods. Assuming that local EMTS centers can provide a reasonable level of service, the number of firms that will choose to acquire on-line capabilities for this reason will probably be quite small.

Private individuals will be the most numerous elements of the EMTS, and can be expected to effect a large number of comparatively small transactions. Their means of access must therefore be portable, cheap, fraud-resistant, and easy to use. Most writers agree that a modification of today's bank credit card fulfills these requirements and will become widely used in the EMTS. An individual's plastic ID card will have an indelible picture of the cardholder, his signature, and his account number. In addition there will be a magnetizable strip on the card, upon which the random security number described in Section 1.1 can be electronically written.

In the pilot studies of the EMTS that have been conducted thus far, an ID card of this sort (lacking, however, the magnetic security code) has proved to be highly satisfactory. In order to complete a sale, the customer's card is inserted into the merchant's terminal device (which was connected to the sponsoring bank's computer) and the amount of the sale is entered. The program in Upper Arlington, Ohio used IBM's Model 2730 credit card recognition device; the Hempstead, Long Island bank's program utilized a terminal manufactured by Electrospace Corporation of Westbury, New York; and the study conducted by the Bank of Delaware made use of special pushbutton telephones supplied by A.T.&T. In all these studies, customer acceptance of the card as an input device was quite good, and the equipment functioned well. With the addition of a magnetic security code to the ID card, this type of card-terminal input arrangement should prove to be totally acceptable for effecting retail sales.

Merchants, like banks, must stand ready to handle payments at any time; but, unlike the banks, this does not necessarily imply that merchant terminals must be on-line with the EMTS computer network at all times. It was pointed out near the end of Section 4.2.1 that merchants will be able to provide two

---

14. Chapter 7 considers changes that may occur in the bank-customer relationship as a result of the EMTS.

types of terminals through which to effect transactions. The high-security device would access the customer's bank in order to verify his account balance and to order the immediate transfer of funds. This type of device would have to be tied directly into the EMTS. As with corporate offices, however, this does not require the merchant to be permanently on line; a "dial-up" telephone connection would be sufficient. For less important (lower security) purchases the merchant terminal could simply record the details of the transaction on a magnetic tape. The contents of the tape could then be transmitted periodically to the retailer's bank, which would attend to the actual transfer of funds. Transmission of the purchase information could either be off-line (carrying the tape to the bank's office) or over telephone lines (perhaps using a high-security terminal as a transmission device).

It would also be highly convenient (for individuals) to provide a means for effecting payments from one's home. Pushbutton telephones provide a ready solution to this problem: The hardware exists today (and is in wide use) to convert the various tones of a pushbutton phone into a digital format processable by computer. (The Delaware pilot program is but one of many current examples.) The home user could dial his bank's computer telephone number, enter his account number, and begin issuing instructions concerning his finances. In this fashion, one could pay for mail-order items, be informed of his account balance, alter his savings accounts, etc. Nonpecuniary costs associated with handling one's finances will become nearly nonexistent.

4.2.3 Security in the System

There has been a great concern in the literature for the means by which EMTS account holders and their banks will be protected from fraud and theft. This concern is most likely rooted in the early experience of many bank credit card schemes, where bad debt losses and losses due to fraud and stolen cards frequently approach 2 percent of total sales during the startup period. As we have seen, the instantaneous inspection of a customer's bank balance will eliminate the possibility of an overdrawn check; and we will also argue in the next section that bad debt losses are likely to be reduced in the EMTS from their present levels. But there still remains the issue of fraudulent and/or stolen access to the EMTS, as well as the system's technical reliability.

Protection from Fraud. At the corporate and government level, fraud or theft would seem to be, at least potentially, a sizeable threat to the efficiency of the EMTS. In this regime, where money will be transmitted largely by wire, what is to prevent organized crime, or some errant but brilliant technocrat from falsifying payments out of other bank accounts and into his own? A person with a thorough knowledge of EMTS software, access to a computer, and physical access to the national computer network (possibly through wiretapping) could amass funds at the expense of other EMTS account holders in the absence of adequate protective measures. What is to prevent such illicit wiretap operations?

The cheapest defense available will be regular exchange of random security codes prior to any transfer of funds. Every corporate account would possess a randomly-generated number which is recorded by the corporation's computer and also by the bank's. Since this code will be changed after each exchange of messages in the system, a thief's task will be considerably complicated, for he must somehow acquire knowledge of the most recent security number. Even if this is achieved, the thief's use of a firm's account will change the security code that is stored in the bank's computer, so the next time the firm tries to access its account, it will be rejected, and the firm will know that it has been victimized. The more frequently this code is altered, the harder it is for a thief to procure the proper security code, and the sooner will any successful theft be discovered. While this last feature may seem of questionable value, in fact it is not: the firm's bank could be alerted, its records checked, and the payee of the false transaction discovered within minutes—all before the funds could be withdrawn from the system. If this protection is insufficient, it is also possible to install electronic "scramblers" at either end of a communication line, thereby making it necessary for any criminal to procure a similar scrambler in order to tap the EMTS. (We would expect security measures similar to those described above to accompany transmissions among regional and local EMTS centers, as well as for corporate transmissions.)

A firm's off-line transactions will entail a less complicated security problem, or at least one that is more traditional. It must merely insure that its computer input tapes, punchards, etc., are not stolen or tampered with while being transported. If a messenger were to be intercepted, the firm could immediately call its bank and freeze access to its account, thereby making the stolen input unuseable.

For an individual, the magnetic code on his ID card will provide protection; and it may also be feasible to equip merchants' terminals with scramblers. But for consumers there are two other protective schemes that are both simple and effective. First, an individual could be given the option of specifying some ceiling amount for purchases that can be made on his account without special prior authorization. A thief would be likely to exceed this limit in his desire to acquire goods quickly before the stolen card is missed and the account frozen. Second, the customer could be required to key a two or three-digit code into the terminal that would correspond to a permanent code stored only in the bank's computer. Without knowledge of this number, the ID card would be unuseable. (This scheme was actually used in the Hempstead EMTS pilot study.)[15]

---

15. Methods for providing positive identification of an EMTS cardholder have been multitudinous and varied. Two schemes which received the detailed consideration of the Personal Identification Project Committee of the American Bankers Association were voice-

Whatever the eventual details of the security measures built into the EMTS, we believe that theft and fraud represent at most minor obstacles to the operation of an EMTS. As the preceding paragraphs demonstrate, the system can be made complicated and protected enough so that it will be both expensive and technically difficult to use the EMTS illictly. Moreover, it is important to note that the present payments system is by no means totally secure and safe from theft. All the facts available to us now indicate that the EMTS will be *at worst* as secure as our present system; and at best the EMTS could provide users with far superior protection. The excessive concern for security that has been manifested in the literature is largely predicated on a false analogy between EMTS transactions and today's credit cards.

Proof of Payment.   Another question that has haunted the EMTS literature concerns the proof of payment that will be available in an electronic system. For payors in the system, payment proof could be provided by either a copy of the sales receipt printed by a merchant's terminal, or a descriptive bank statement that lists each payee as well as the amounts debited to the individual's account. A corporation will also receive descriptive bank statements—in the form of a computer listing of payees and amounts that have been charged against its account. (This is the way SCOPE programs operate today.) However, these receipts will only indicate that one's bank in fact initiated a transfer of funds. Further measures will be required in order to confirm that the payee received credit for the funds. Bank computers will have to keep track of both the amount and the source of each credit item received. The record of the payee's bank that he was the recipient of certain funds will then constitute further proof of payment for the payor.[16] In short, it seems that there are no *insurmountable* legal problems attached to the operation of an EMTS in the U.S.

Equipment Failure.   The problem of a power failure or computer "down time" is one with which the authors have frequently been confronted in discussions concerning the EMTS. It is certainly a serious issue, because banks' computers and EMTS switching centers must always be serviceable in order for the system to function smoothly. The problem is really comprised of two parts. The failure of a switching center in the communications network would be similar to

prints and fingerprints. In either case, a facsimile of the customer's print would be transmitted to his bank's computer for comparison with "prints" stored in the computer's memory. While these schemes would provide virtually 100 percent identification, it seems that the cost of implementing either plan would be prohibitive. The security afforded account holders by a frequently-changing random magnetic code number and the hand-entered code described in the text should be quite adequate, and nearly costless.

16. It is the payor's bank that has a problem if for some reason the payee's bank does not receive the funds which were transmitted. But this situation is no different from that which exists in the Federal Reserve wire system today. Similarly, California's SCOPE program lawyers anticipate no serious problems of this sort.

a local equipment breakdown in the telephone system. The national computer network could easily be designed so that a faulty center is bypassed, and neighboring centers temporarily control its message flows.

The failure of a bank computer would be more serious. However, neighboring banks (or perhaps local switching centers) could be designed to cover for one another in the event of a malfunction. A periodic transfer of the bank's deposit records (every several hours, at off-peak times) to its backup computer center would provide a reasonably recent set of records for the backup to work with. Both the failing bank's and the backup's customers would perhaps experience delays in making payments during the crisis, but hopefully computer failures will be small in number once the EMTS is fully functioning.[17] A further advantage of this type of backup arrangement would be that preventive maintenance could easily be performed on computers during off-peak hours. The bank's storage of account and transactions data will also have to be designed so that lost or damaged records can be reconstructed easily and quickly. Such a capability may best be combined with a backup arrangement of this sort.

4.2.4 Ownership of the System

The implications of an electronic payments system for our society will be immense and pervasive. Nonbank financial intermediaries will be unable to compete with banks unless extensive alterations are made in the regulations governing these financial institutions. Computer manufacturers, hardware and software leasing companies, and communications firms will all be greatly affected by the contracts awarded to build a communications system of this magnitude. The very existence of consumer finance companies and credit bureaus will be threatened. Therefore, the ownership of the EMTS will be of central importance for the determination of its design, cost, efficiency of operation, and accessibility to the public and to institutions in the economy.

The development of the EMTS in the U.S. will be an evolutionary phenomenon. Elements of the present payments mechanism will continue to coexist with the emerging future system for some time to come. It therefore seems most unlikely that any single entity will "own" the entire EMTS. Indeed, ownership of the current system is divided into many segments: the Federal Reserve System, the commercial banking system (with their clearing houses, credit cards, demand deposits, etc.), the Treasury, oil companies and the travel and entertainment card companies; etc. In a similar fashion, there is no logical reason for all the hardware of the EMTS to be centrally owned. Corporations, banks, and gov-

---

17. In computer systems today, software bugs (that is, undetected programming errors) account for the majority of machine down time. If all EMTS banks use similar or identical computer routines to manage the payment of accounts, one would expect software bugs to be quickly discovered and corrected.

ernment offices will own or lease their computer facilities; local communication lines may belong to some independent firm(s) that leases them to EMTS users; merchants will rent or purchase their terminals.

Ownership of the national switching network is not such a straightforward issue. It seems evident that the EMTS will be much like a public utility in the sense that two (or more) competing systems would not necessarily be socially desirable. If these competing systems were closed and separate, an individual or firm would have to maintain accounts in *all* existing electronic systems in order to be assured the ability to transact business through the EMTS.[18] The government will hopefully take steps to prevent such inefficiently competing systems from evolving, but what can we really expect in this area? On the one hand, we currently have the regulated, "natural" monopolies granted to telephone, electric, gas, and water companies. But on the other hand, we see two competitive national bank card plans in operation.

Whatever the eventual ownership, it would seem that some central planning and organization will be desirable in the design of the national switching system. As indicated in Section 4.2.1, the location and capacity of switching centers and communication lines will have a dominant effect on the overall efficiency of the EMTS. The Federal Reserve System, with its specialized knowledge of the nation's payments mechanism, may be in the best position to design (or regulate the design of) this segment of the EMTS. Furthermore, given the high fixed costs and externalities involved in such a communications network, the Federal government may be the only entity willing to undertake the design and construction of such a national system.

Whoever owns the system's hardware, the sole overriding requirement for the EMTS will be that the hardware and software used by all parties must be mutually compatible.[19] While this will necessitate a good deal of cooperation in the design and construction of the system, it no more requires central ownership of the physical capital than did the introduction of MICR coding in the early 1960s.

4.2.5 Summary

The more salient aspects of EMTS design as described in this section can be summarized as follows.

1. There are two separate functions performed by the EMTS, and responsibility for these functions will be sharply divided. The national network of com-

---

18. If an account holder can make payments to a member of any other system, then there is no problem. The inefficiency would arise *only* if each EMTS network were self-enclosed.

19. Mutual compatibility by no means requires the use of a single computer manufacturer's equipment throughout the system, but only that the hardware of the various suppliers be designed to be interfaceable.

puter centers and communication links will handle only the information *switching* capacity of the EMTS. The capacity to *process* the information and to effect payments will be lodged primarily in the (separately-owned) computers of the banking industry.

2. The EMTS will be a circuit switching communications system with its centers and communication lines designed to minimize the cost of building and operating a computer network capable of handling the nation's financial information flows.

3. Not all transactions in the future economy need be *real-time* EMTS transfers. There will exist a large number of opportunities for transferring demand for EMTS services to off-peak times, and taking advantage of such opportunities will reduce the amount of capital equipment needed to support the system.

4. Ownership of the system cannot be predicted at this time. Central ownership of the entire EMTS is in no way necessary for the proper (efficient) functioning of the system. Federal control over the design of the national switching network, however, may be desirable in order to insure the implementation of an efficient network.

5. The fraudulent use of accounts will be extremely difficult, if not impossible, due to security precautions that can be built into the system.

4.3 Economic Characteristics of the EMTS

Conceptually, the electronic system most likely to emerge in the future will be a synthesis of a modified bank charge card plan, a giro payments system, a SCOPE program, and a procedure for preauthorizing the automatic payment of selected liabilities. Innovation of this magnitude in the U.S. payments mechanism will have a myriad of ramifications, whose effects will be felt throughout the economy. This section enumerates the particular economic features of the EMTS that will be responsible for its widespread impact on the economy.

4.3.1 The Elimination of Paper

The first and most obvious aspect of this mechanized system is the nearly complete elimination of the paper flows that have come to cause such expense and inconvenience for many economic units. Banks' transaction records will produce itemized monthly statements[20] for account holders that can function as

---

20. With the complete automation of banking operations the cost of bank statements will probably decline somewhat. Concomitantly, the elimination of checks (which have heretofore served as both proof of payment (when cancelled) and as a notification that a debtor has initiated a transfer of funds into one's account) will make frequent bank statements a valuable customer service. We can therefore anticipate a trend toward more frequent statements to account holders.

receipts and proof of payment. With the exception of these monthly statements, the payments system will have almost no need of paper documents. Mailing, microfilming, storing, and transport costs will be nearly nonexistent.

It is highly improbable on the other hand, that cash will ever disappear completely—there will always be newspaper boys on the corner, illicit activities, and children's allowances. The banks will have to retain some means of providing their customers with cash, and perhaps we will see the widespread use of vending-type machines which dispense coins and bills on the insertion of an ID card.[21] Similarly, the check will continue to be used for certain kinds of payments.[22] However, noting that over 90 percent of the money value of all transactions carried on in the economy is currently paid by check, and that per-transaction costs will be considerably lower with the EMTS than with a check, then it is apparent that paperless payments will account for the great bulk (by value) of all transfers in the future economy.

4.3.2 Lowered Transaction Costs

Another characteristic of an electrified money system is a vast diminution in nonpecuniary transaction costs. Convenient and easy access to one's financial assets are bywords of the EMTS—from the home telephone, through the terminal units in any retail establishment, or by means of the preauthorized deduction of saving and investment funds from one's paycheck. This convenience will have great effects on the competition for savings funds in the economy, as discussed in Chapter 5.

A particular result of this decrease in financial transaction costs will be the disappearance of zero-interest demand deposits. More precisely, it will be argued in Chapter 6 that a logical result of the introduction of an EMTS will be that the accounts upon which one draws in order to make payments will bear interest. It should be noted here that there is a recent precedent for this type of account: In the second half of 1970 the Federal Home Loan Bank Board granted savings and loan associations the right to make third party payments for their customers. Prior to the rescinding of this right four months later, at least two savings and loan associations inaugurated *de facto* demand deposit accounts bearing interest at the regular passbook rate. The industry's newsletter, *The Savings and Loan News*, heralded such accounts as a "Foot in the Door" for electronic funds transfers. If savings and loans can find such payments arrangements profitable, then competition will surely force banks also to offer interest on their accounts.

The widespread operation of payments arrangements such as these will pre-

---

21. Such machines are already manufactured by several firms and are in limited operation. See the June 1972 *Savings and Loan News*, p. 54.

22. For example, an endorsed welfare or social security check helps insure that the proper recipient is still alive and residing at his alleged address.

cipitate a new kind of relationship between the demand deposit and time deposit accounts that have traditionally been available at commercial banks. An electronic order to transfer funds out of a cardholder's account will be similar to the transfer of funds from a savings account to his demand account, and the issuing of a check against the latter. An EMTS will allow an individual to gain the interest income of such a process without requiring the time and effort necessary today to effect such a transfer of funds. Whether large firms will be accorded this same type of transaction account is more questionable. The answer is intricately bound up in the question of compensatory balances versus specific bank fees for services rendered to firms. This issue will be considered in Chapter 7.

4.3.3 Consumer Lines of Credit

In addition to a unique identification number and an account at his bank, many EMTS account holders will also have a line of credit (or overdraft allowance) that can be drawn on at some predetermined rate of interest. Thus, suppose an individual has a $500 account balance and a $1000 overdraft privilege. In making a $1000 purchase he has two potential means of payment. He could transfer funds immediately to the merchant, using the overdraft allowance to create a $500 loan in the process, or he could authorize the transfer of funds to the seller for some time in the future, meanwhile transferring sufficient funds into his demand deposit account. In the latter case he incurs no immediate bank financing charges, but instead has received a loan from the merchant. Price competition among sellers will probably lead merchants to charge customers for the credit they receive. Thus, in recognition of the time value of money, the price paid for goods purchased with immediate payment will be discounted relative to the price inclusive of credit costs.[23] By choosing the second payment option mentioned above, the customer will have to forego this ("cash") discount.

A small credit line may be supplied to virtually every account holder. It has been suggested that many people will be reluctant to preauthorize payments from their account (especially in variable amounts, such as utility bills) for fear of accidentally overdrawing their balance. Individuals who cannot qualify for a sizeable credit line may therefore receive an automatic "convenience" overdraft allowance that must be repaid in full at the month's end. This insurance against an accidental overdraft should serve to encourage the preauthorization of routine payments. An alternate solution that has been suggested for this utility bill problem entails a modification of billing procedures. Instead of being billed for

---

23. Dwight M. Jaffee and Thomas Russell, "Are Credit Cards Inflationary?" unpublished, 1971. In this paper, the authors argue that, when a sufficiently large number of customers have the option of paying for goods with either cash or a credit card, the merchants will be lead by profit maximization and competition to offer cash discounts. A full discussion of the retail price effects of the EMTS is contained in Chapter 7.

actual electricity (gas, water, etc.) consumption during a given month, the individual would pay for some preestimated average consumption. Every year his payments would be compared to his actual consumption, and any differential applied to the *next* year's monthly estimate. In this way the customer would always know the exact amount of his preauthorized payment.

4.3.4 Increased Information Flows

Each transaction effected under the EMTS would be monitored by the cardholder's bank, thus providing an immensely important source of financial information. At the macro level, aggregation of these data can be used to provide monetary and fiscal authorities with detailed, precise, and real-time information about the economy. This situation should substantially reduce the recognition lag in monetary and fiscal operations. Internal Revenue Service access to the system would tend to discourage tax evasion and fraud. Funds for illicit operations (especially gambling) would also be far more difficult, if not impossible, to conceal from the authorities.

The ability of a bank to monitor constantly the financial condition of its depositors and debtors will enable it to evaluate loan applications more accurately. Moreover, the fact that the bank will be cognizant of *every* credit purchase made with its card (as opposed to the present bank card system where only the larger purchases are approved *ex ante*) gives banks far better control over the amount of credit issued to any one individual. The risk that a cardholder will default on credit items due will thus be considerably reduced by an EMTS.

Some of the economically relevant features of the EMTS may now be summarized:

1. The time value of money is everywhere recognized in the EMTS. Unlike bank credit card programs of today, credit will be extended only when it is paid for, and merchant prices will vary according to the time when payment is effected. Similarly, increased information flows and decreased transactions costs should serve to increase substantially the interest-sensitivity of the household and retail sectors.

2. Nonpecuniary costs in the financial system are reduced significantly. In particular, consumer loans are prenegotiated and can be drawn on at any time and in any amount up to the set limit. The physical location of savings institutions is irrelevant, and competition will center on interest rate levels and the quality of services provided by various institutions. In short, the EMTS will reduce imperfections in both the consumer loan market and in the saving sector of the economy.

3. The risk of default on consumer loans will be much lower than it is to-

day, since the bank will know the extent of all customers' accumulated debts—including preauthorized payments for the future.

4. The replacement of noninterest-paying demand deposits with interest bearing accounts at banks, combined with widespread access for individuals to lines of credit and a new relationship between time deposits and demand deposits, will require a new empirical definition of "money" and extensive research into the means by which financial activities in the society can be best controlled.

5. Changes in the financial environment will be greatest in scope for private individuals in the society. In contrast, firms, particularly the larger ones, frequently have access today to credit lines, the national banking market, and SCOPE-type arrangements with their bankers; and the so-called "revolution" of corporate treasurers over the past fifteen years refers to the very high interest sensitivity manifested by corporate depositors at commercial banks.

4.4 The EMTS as an Efficient Payments Mechanism

In Chapter 2 we presented an extensive discussion of transfer systems. In the course of that chapter we demonstrated that the entire evolution of transfer systems—from barter to full-bodied and commodity monies, to fiat and credit money—can be viewed as a progression to ever more-efficient means of exchange. The EMTS, as described in this chapter, has features which make it an extension of this evolutionary progression of transfer systems.

There are significant economic gains which accrue to a society that efficiently modifies its money system. Harry Johnson[24] writes about the gain in income that results in a society upon its conversion from commodity money to credit (or fiat) money. His argument is summarized here. Let there be an economy with an infinitely durable capital stock, in which all marginal efficiency conditions prevail; in particular we must be sure that there is but a single return to capital, r_0. Suppose that the total capital stock (including human capital) is $\overline{OW}_2$ in Figure 4–2; then income will be $r_0 \cdot (\overline{OW}_2)$. But if some of this capital is used as commodity money then it is "sterilized" in the sense that it produces no real income. Instead it yields utility to its holders. Capital as money will be demanded up to the point where the marginal utility of money is equal to the marginal (opportunity) cost of using capital as money; that is, at P on the demand for money curve DD'. The society will be foregoing real income in the amount of $r_0 \cdot (\overline{OM}_1)$ in order to derive monetary utility from the capital. If the government decides to issue fiat money, and replaces $\overline{OM}_1$ of real capital by a similar value amount of paper money (whose economic cost, let us assume, is

---

24. Johnson, *op. cit.*

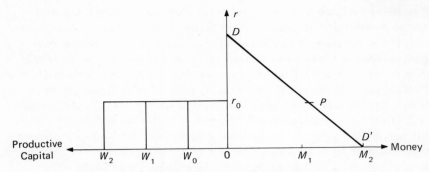

Figure 4-2. The Payment of Interest on Money.

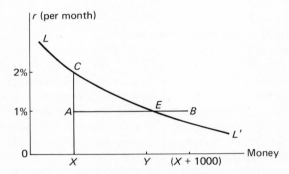

Figure 4-3. The Line of Credit as a Source of Liquidity.

zero), then the economy again has real income of $r_0 \cdot (\overline{OW_2})$; but it also receives an amount of monetary utility equal to DPM_1O.

In this situation depicted in Figure 4-2 there is an opportunity cost associated with an individual's holding money instead of productive capital, as reflected in the downward slope of the demand for money curve DD'. By paying no interest on its money, the state is foregoing a potential surplus for the society of PM_1M_2. Pareto optimality indicates that money should be produced (issued) up to the point where the marginal utility of holding money equals the marginal cost of producing money balances. The state or banking system should therefore issue $\overline{OM_2}$ of fiat money, and induce people to hold it by paying interest r_0 on it. In this manner the opportunity cost of money is zero, and the income of society is maximized at $r_0 \cdot (\overline{OW_2}) + DOM_2$.[25]

25. Edgar L. Feige and Michael Parkin, "The Optimal Quantity of Money, Bonds, Commodity Inventories, and Capital," *American Economic Review* LXI (June 1971), pp. 335-349. See section 6.3.1 for further discussion.

The presence of a guaranteed and divisible line of credit deserves further mention as well, because it makes it possible for an account holder to adjust his money holdings over a far greater range than is possible today. For example, suppose an account holder in the EMTS has a liquidity preference schedule LL' in Figure 4-3. The terms of his account are such that he can obtain an automatic loan of up to $1000 at a (marginal) cost of 1 percent per month. If he currently has X, then the supply of money curve confronting him is $OXAB$, and he can achieve an optimal point at E where he derives a consumer surplus CAE.

Now remove the bank card with its prenegotiated line of credit and reconsider the situation. In order to expand his money holdings beyond X the individual must first spend time and money for the fixed costs of obtaining a bank loan.[26] Call the sum of these fixed costs F. Then, even if the *marginal* cost of his borrowed funds is 1 percent (as in the EMTS case), there will be some "breakeven point" of loan size below which F outweighs CAE. For sufficiently small $(Y - X)$ the fixed costs involved in finding a suitable loan will prevent the individual from achieving optimality. No such constraint exists for an EMTS cardholder. So long as his optimal point lies between zero and $(X + 1000)$ on LL' it can be reached.

The EMTS described in the previous section of this chapter fulfills nearly all of the requirements for a more efficient monetary system: First, interest will be paid on demand deposit balances, meeting an important condition for an optimal system. Second, transactions between financial assets will occur at lower cost—both pecuniary and nonpecuniary. Together with increased competition in the financial sector, this should precipitate more optimal positions in financial portfolios and quicker reactions to changes in market conditions. Third, transactions from demand accounts for the purchase of real goods and services will be achieved at lower cost. In addition to direct cost savings by consumers, there is the less obvious saving that accrues in the form of more optimal goods inventories being held by individuals.[27] Finally, new flexibility in capital markets, particularly in the form of bank overdraft facilities, will allow the consumer to determine his consumption stream with a flexibility not heretofore available.

The low cost to users, opportunities for greater interest income from one's wealth, increased services, and the sizeable profit potential available to financial institutions will combine to insure the actual emergence of an electronic monetary transfer system in the United States. And the economic features embodied in that system will result in a highly efficient payments system for the economy.

---

26. The non-pecuniary costs are likely to be the dominant factors here—especially in times of tight money when the banks are far less willing to extend consumer loans on the consumer's terms.

27. Feige and Parkin, *op. cit.* Dwight M. Jaffee, "Transactions Costs and the Optimal Supply of Money," unpublished, August 1971.

5 Implications of the EMTS for the Depository Financial Intermediary Sector

Depository financial intermediaries in the United States—that is, the commercial banks (CB), savings and loan associations (SLA), and mutual savings banks (MSB)—currently are the repository of more than half of all the household sector's financial assets except corporate stock holdings.[1] As a group, these financial institutions serve the economy in a myriad of ways: they improve the allocation of capital in the economy and lower the cost of borrowing; the effects of monetary policy are transmitted to the real sector through the commercial banking system; the thrift institutions (SLA and MSB) are major sources of mortgage funds for homebuilding; and millions of individuals have entrusted their savings to one or more of the financial intermediaries (FI). For these and similar reasons, the future of FI in the U.S. must be anticipated and in some way controlled.

The EMTS obviously presents the potential for dramatic ramifications in the present savings system. The types of accounts offered by the various FI have reached the point where there is little or no real difference among them (at least in the eyes of the general public) and consequently the competition for savings has been centered on interest rates (that is, price competition) and convenience factors ("one-stop banking," etc.). The emergence of an EMTS will completely eliminate the latter element. Since everyone will be able to control his finances from his home, the physical location of an institution will be of little importance. The EMTS thereby threatens to alter drastically the market shares of the individual FI.

This chapter will sketch the pattern of inter-FI competition for savings deposits that has prevailed over the past quarter century. We will be especially interested in noting the economic forces that have shaped the activities of different FI; and the economic effects that different asset and liability structures have had on institutions. We will then superimpose the EMTS, as described in Chapter 4, over these historic trends and attempt to predict the future shape of the financial intermediary system and the competitive environment in which it will operate.

In the course of this discussion we will ignore the actions and effects of nondepository financial intermediaries in the economy. Instead, we reserve consideration of these institutions—life insurance companies, mutual funds, consumer finance companies, credit unions, etc.—for the last section of this chapter.

---

1. Samuel B. Chase, Jr., "Financial Structure and Regulation: Some Knotty Problems," *Journal of Finance* XXVI (May 1971), pp. 585–598.

The reason for this course of action is a straightforward one: the implications of the EMTS for these nondepository intermediaries are relatively minor (as will be discussed in Section 5.6), whereas the operations of commercial banks, mutual savings banks, and the savings and loan associations stand to be profoundly affected upon the introduction of an EMTS.

Before we begin, however, it is necessary to make one additional assumption about the operation of the EMTS. Simply put, it is this: regardless of who owns and/or controls the various components of the transfer system, all depository FI must have equal access to it. In other words, no single FI will be able to gain a price advantage over the others as a result of transactions costs in the system. Otherwise, if the banking system, for example, were to gain control of the EMTS (say as a result of its current credit card operations), it would surely be eager to exclude its competitors from the system. Such discriminatory action would lead to severe competitive disadvantages for the thrift institutions (as will be demonstrated below), and therefore, it is to be doubted that the government would allow such exclusion.[2] As will become clear in the discussion below, the accuracy of this additional assumption is vital to the prosperous future of nonbank intermediaries (NBI); moreover, the assumption seems to be economically logical and politically inescapable.

5.1 Competition Among Depository Intermediaries Since World War II

5.1.1 The Period 1945 to 1965

The two decades following the Second World War witnessed the rapid growth of the savings institutions relative to the CB. Encouraged by a large demand for residential mortgage funds, a generally upward sloping term structure curve in the money market, and certain institutional factors, NBI expanded until they controlled 33 percent of all FI assets. Correspondingly the CB share of all depository FI assets dropped from 86 to 67 percent in the course of twenty years.[3] Aggressive competition on the part of the NBI (and particularly the savings and loan associations) for the favor of the small saver left the banks far behind.

But in truth the CB were satisfied with their share of savings funds until the late 1950s, and their poor growth record prior to that time seems to reflect this

---

2. Paul S. Nadler says in this regard, "One can conclude, then, that either the banks will offer the checkless society to their competitors willingly, or they will be forced to do so by governmental intervention." (Nadler was speaking before an American Bankers Association convention in 1966.) This quote is taken from Carl Gambs, "Economics of an Automated Payments Mechanism," Ph.D. submitted to Yale University, 1972.

3. These figures are contained in the *Report of the President's Commission on Financial Structure and Regulation.* Reed O. Hunt, chairman (Washington, D.C.: Government Printing Office, 1971).

fact. The massive government debt issues of the war period left the banking system satiated with liquid reserves, and there seems to have been little pressure on the banks during the fifties to relinquish the safety and security of such portfolios. In addition, the relatively low yield on government bonds made them a desirable source of funds for any commercial loan expansion the banks did wish to undertake. However something happened around 1958–1962 to change this. The effects of this change can be seen in Tables 5-1 and 5-2. Note particularly the jump in loans to individuals and real estate loans that occurred between 1957 and 1959, financed largely by a reduction in the portfolio of government securities. By 1970 we see that the proportion of commercial loans as well had risen from its 1957 level. The banking system began to shift resources out of low-risk, government security portfolios and into riskier assets, and at the same time they entered into a period of intense competition for savings funds.

What was the cause of this change? While it is difficult to assign the change to any single source, two factors do appear to be substantially responsible. One factor was a *ceteris paribus* rise in the demand for loans. According to the staff of the Federal Home Loan Bank Board (FHLBB), CBs began to seek new time and savings deposits at this time largely because the "demand for bank funds pressed on supply, and the potential earnings from available investment outlets became more attractive."[4] In other words, an exogenous shift in the demand for loans resulted in relatively higher commercial loan rates. In a perfectly competitive market, the rate on risk-free government securities will be separated from the rate on risky private loans by some fixed amount representing the real costs and risks associated with holding either type of asset. When loan rates rose relative to government securities in the late fifties, funds flowed out of government securities and into loans as an adjustment to the unusual rate differential. The net result, for the banks, was a higher overall return on their portfolios.

Second, it is probable that there were costs involved with a CB entering the competition for savings. In general bankers had traditionally depended on demand deposits for their loanable funds, while savings had been left in the background. Banks realized that if rates on their time deposits were to rise sufficiently, many of their larger customers would shift out of demand deposits and thereby raise the average cost of deposit funds to the bank. Throughout the decade, SLA had been vigorously competing for savings funds, with the effect that CB time and savings deposits were growing comparatively slowly.[5] Further-

---

4. Federal Home Loan Bank Board, "Cycles in Mortgage Credit Availability and the 1966 Experience," in *A Study of Mortgage Credit,* Subcommittee on Housing and Urban Affairs, Committee on Banking and Currency, United States Senate, May 22, 1967, (Washington, D.C.: Government Printing Office), pp. 19–40.

5. In the period 1947–1959, bank time and savings deposits grew at an annual rate of about 5.1 percent. In contrast, the NBI expanded their deposits at a rate of 10.3 percent per annum; for SLA alone the rate was 15.6 percent. Clearly there was a substantial market for small savings accounts, one which the banks were unable or, more probably, unwilling to enter prior to 1959.

Table 5-1
Selected Loans and Investments of Commercial Banks
(all insured banks, $ billion)

Date	12/31/47	12/31/57	12/31/59	12/31/70
Total Deposits[a]	135,981	200,485	219,012	479,174
Demand Deposits[a]	106,935	142,827	151,538	246,168
Time and Savings Accounts[a]	34,954	57,658	67,473	233,006
Total Loans and Investments	114,274	168,595	188,790	458,919
Total U.S. Treasury Securities	67,941	57,580	58,348	61,438
Real Estate Loans	9,266	23,003	27,948	72,302
Commercial and Industrial Loans	18,012	40,380	40,022	111,540
Loans to Individuals	5,654	20,122	24,032	65,556
Prime Rate Charged by Banks	1.75%	4.50%	5.00%	6.75%
Rate on 3–5 Year Governments	1.54%	3.04%	4.95%	5.86%
Rate on 4–6 Month Commercial Paper	1.19%	3.81%	4.88%	5.98%
Rate on Treasury Bills (90 days)	0.95%	3.04%	4.49%	4.87%

[a]These figures were obtained from the Report of the Presidents Commission on Financial Structure and Regulation.

Source: *Federal Reserve Bulletin*, various issues.

Table 5-2

Selected Loans and Investments of Commercial Banks

(as a percentage of total deposits)

Date	12/31/47	12/31/57	12/31/59	12/31/70
Total Deposits	100%	100%	100%	100%
Demand Deposits	78%	71%	69%	51.5%
Time and Savings Accounts	22%	29%	31%	48.5%
Total Loans and Investments	84%	84%	86%	96%
Total U.S. Treasury Securities	50%	29%	26.5%	12.8%
Real Estate Loans	6.8%	11.5%	12.8%	15.0%
Commercial and Industrial Loans	13.2%	19.7%	18.2%	23.3%
Loans to Individuals	4.2%	9.6%	10.8%	13.6%

Note: All figures derived from data presented in Table 5-1.

more, in the postwar period the banks experienced a historically slow rate of demand deposit growth; from 1947 to 1959, CB demand deposit balances grew at a rate of only 2.5 percent per year, compared with a 7.9 percent annual increase in time and savings deposits at all depository FI. During this time the velocity of money rose quickly as firms and individuals came to economize on their holdings of demand deposit balances. (Table 3-2 reflects this rise in velocity.) It was becoming evident that "the real choice was not between demand deposit growth and time deposit growth, but between time deposit growth and no growth."[6] By 1959 or 1960 the commercial banks had reached a threshold, where the extra costs (in terms of interest expense and lost demand balances) of actively competing for savings funds were finally exceeded by the costs to the banks of insufficient loanable funds and slow growth. Only when this threshold had been reached did the banks as a group enter into serious competition with the NBI.[7]

Whatever the real cause of this shift in bank behavior, until the early sixties the competition for savings funds (such as it was) can be characterized by the permanent and significant interest rate differential that separated the accounts of banks and nonbanks.

The Growth of Nonbank Intermediaries.   It is, however, unrepresentative to treat the savings institutions as a unit. During the postwar period it was the SLA that accounted for most of the growth of the savings industry. From 1945 to 1965 the SLA share of FI deposits rose from 5 to 23 percent; while during the same time the MSBs did little more than retain their 9-10 percent of the market (see Table 5-3). Alan Teck[8] has undertaken a study of this phenomenon, and he presents three major reasons for SLA predominance in the savings field.

First is the interest rate advantage enjoyed by SLA over MSB. The magnitude of the consistent rate differentials that have existed can be seen in Table 5-4. The MSB, restricted by their location in older urban centers and unable to be chartered in most states,[9] were excluded from the areas of rising demand for mortgage loans that developed in the suburbs and the population-growth areas of the West. SLA, on the other hand, freely followed the migrating population

---

6. Herman E. Kroos and Martin Blyn, *A History of Financial Intermediaries* (New York: Random House, Inc., 1971), p. 225.

7. Concomitantly there came into existence a market for the negotiable certificates of deposit which New York banks began to issue in substantial volumes in 1961. The effect of such certificates on the banking industry's ability to attract deposit funds is discussed at length below.

8. Alan Teck, *Mutual Savings Banks and Savings and Loan Associations: Aspects of Growth* (New York: Columbia University Press, 1969).

9. MSB are chartered in only 18 states, most of which are in the northeast. One would suspect that the national figures presented here are biased against the MSB due to the very rapid postwar growth of SLA in California, where mutuals are not chartered. However, Teck also presents data separately for the geographic areas where both forms of FI operate, and similar trends are evident.

Table 5-3
Total Deposits of Depository Financial Intermediaries, 1945-1970
(in millions of dollars)

Year	Commercial Bank Time & Savings Deposits[a]	Savings and Loan Association[b]	Mutual Savings Banks[b]
1945	$ 29,964	7,365	15,334
1946	33,613	8,548	16,813
1947	34,954	9,753	17,759
1948	35,528	10,964	18,400
1949	36,049	12,471	19,287
1950	36,491	13,992	20,025
1951	38,292	16,107	20,900
1952	41,365	19,195	22,610
1953	44,794	22,846	24,388
1954	48,256	27,252	26,351
1955	49,951	32,142	38,182
1956	52,122	37,148	30,026
1957	57,658	41,912	31,684
1958	65,681	47,926	34,031
1959	67,473	54,583	34,977
1960	73,284	62,142	36,343
1961	82,812	70,885	38,277
1962	98,227	80,236	41,336
1963	111,694	91,308	44,605
1964	127,539	101,887	48,849
1965	147,676	110,385	52,443
1966	161,103	113,969	55,006
1967	184,339	124,531	60,121
1968	205,926	131,618	64,507
1969	196,859	135,670	67,086
1970	233,006	146,744	71,580

[a]Insured commercial banks only.

[b]Deposit figures for savings and loan associations and mutual savings banks are "Savings capital" and "Deposits" (including checking accounts), respectively.

Note: Data are as of yearend. For earlier years, they may not be strictly comparable with later data.

Source: The *Report* of the President's Commission on Financial Structure and Regulation.

Table 5-4
Interest Rates Paid on Savings Deposits
by Financial Intermediaries 1945-1970[a]
(average annual rates, in percent)

Year	Commercial Banks[b]	Savings and Loan Associations[c]	Mutual Savings Banks
1945	0.87	2.46	1.7
1946	0.84	2.36	1.7
1947	0.87	2.38	1.62
1948	0.90	2.43	1.66
1949	0.91	2.51	1.82
1950	0.94	2.52	1.90
1951	1.03	2.58	1.96
1952	1.15	2.69	2.31
1953	1.24	2.81	2.40
1954	1.32	2.87	2.50
1955	1.38	2.94	2.64
1956	1.58	3.03	2.77
1957	2.08	3.26	2.94
1958	2.21	3.38	3.07
1959	2.36	3.53	3.19
1960	2.56	3.86	3.47
1961	2.71	3.90	3.55
1962	3.18	4.08	3.85
1963	3.31	4.17	3.96
1964	3.42	4.18	4.06
1965	3.96	4.25[a]	4.11
1966	4.04	4.48	4.45
1967	4.24	4.68	4.74
1968	4.48	4.71	4.76
1969	4.87	4.81	4.89
1970	4.95	5.14	5.01

[a]Data for years prior to 1965 may not be strictly comparable with those of later years.

[b]Insured commercial banks only.

[c]Member associations of the Federal Home Loan Bank System only.

Source: The *Report* of the President's Commission on Financial Structure and Regulation.

and took advantage of the high mortgage rates engendered by the postwar housing boom. It is also important to note that special SLA tax treatment helped them retain their interest advantage. The special exemptions from taxation of new SLA in the process of building up loss reserves have been *highly* significant in affecting the profits and dividends of young associations.

Moreover, by virtue of their concentration in major financial centers (55 percent of MSB assets in 1964 were located in New York City, Boston, and Philadelphia), MSB faced considerable competition from the country's most aggressive CBs and the primary securities markets. Teck's examination of the savings institution-bond market situation leads him to conclude that the "data all support the thesis that sensitivity to bond yields is stronger in the major financial centers than in outlying areas."[10] The mutuals were therefore more liable than SLA to suffer deposit outflows in times of rising interest rates, due to their general propinquity to securities markets.

The last advantage for the SLA is the less restrictive branching laws under which they have operated. This gave them an advantage over MSB in the states where both types of institutions operated; the SLA were able to offer more offices, in more convenient locations, than the mutuals.

As will be shown below, these facets of competitive activity are equally applicable to the operation of all FI. Lacking significant product differentiation, the intermediaries strive to distinguish themselves by price competition (interest rates and free gifts) and convenience factors (nonpecuniary "price" competition). Each individual institution must likewise be prepared to protect itself from deposit outflows to other FI and/or to the capital markets.

Competition From Commercial Banks—CDs. By the early sixties, commercial bank lending had expanded to the point where the banks were eager to compete for more savings deposits.[11] The slow growth of demand deposits, combined with the successful competition of NBI, had served to limit the amount of funds available to the banking sector. Concomitantly, interest rates in general were experiencing an upward trend; and in particular an increased demand for commercial loans had caused their rates to rise relative to the rates on mortgages.[12] So, at the same time that banks began to seek more savings, they also found themselves in a better position to compete.

Once the banks entered the savings area they competed with a vengeance. A strong pressure for acquiring reserves was accompanied by the development of new techniques for more intensely utilizing available reserves—for instance the Federal funds market. More germane for the purposes of our discussion here, however, are the means by which banks attempted to attract funds from domestic nonfinancial sources. In this case the single greatest weapon available to the CB was the ability to offer deposit accounts of varying maturity and interest rates, the introduction of negotiable certificates of deposit being by far the most dramatic example.

---

10. Teck, *op. cit.,* p. 115.

11. The loan/deposit ratio of CB almost tripled in the period 1945–1959, going from 17 percent to 46.4 percent.

12. For comments on postwar interest trends, see Jack R. Vernon, "Competition for Savings Deposits: The Recent Experience," *National Banking Review,* IV (December 1966), pp. 183–192.

Certificate of deposit (CD) is a generic term that generally refers to any fixed-maturity time deposit at a commercial bank. The larger denomination CDs are frequently negotiable, being traded in a secondary market that is normally quite active. These negotiable certificates (of $100,000 or more) are issued in various maturities, primarily to corporations, financial institutions, or state and local governments as short-term investments competitive with Treasury bills, banker's acceptances, and finance company paper. But CDs are also issued in much smaller denominations to private individuals and other noninstitutional savers (these are often called "savings certificates"). In these cases, the CD is a nonnegotiable time deposit, whose rate of return varies with maturity. For the banks the most desirable characteristic of CDs of any size is that it enables them to take advantage of the fact that different people and institutions have varying interest rate sensitivities. In other words, opportunity costs of money vary considerably among savers. With CDs, the banks succeeded in creating a segmented market for deposits with several different products and prices, and as a result they did not have to offer higher rates on all their outstanding deposits in order to attract new funds.

CDs had been issued by various commercial banks in relatively insignificant amounts since 1900.[13] But it was not until 1961 that the certificates became a widespread and major source of reserves. In February of that year the First National City Bank of New York began to issue negotiable CDs, and at the same time several government securities dealers announced that they would make a secondary market for the instruments. Many CB—especially the prime New York City banks—had been losing funds to the capital markets, and negotiable certificates of deposit provided them with a means of competing for interest-sensitive, market-oriented funds. From 1961 to mid-1966, the regulatory atmosphere was quite favorable to such competition. The Federal Reserve raised its Regulation Q ceiling on such deposits no less than four times between April 1961 and December 1965. These ceiling increases allowed CDs to remain competitive with other short-term open market instruments, thus providing issuing banks with a constant source of relatively stable funds.

One can appreciate the banks' success in this competition for funds by considering the following figures, presented in a Federal Reserve System study. After their introduction in 1961, CB negotiable certificates of deposit comprised 10.1 percent of the total deposits of all issuing banks by mid-1966. The largest New York banks became even more dependent on CDs: in May 1966 CDs comprised 17.9 percent of the total deposits of the large New York banks issuing such certificates. Overall, bank time deposits grew at an annual rate of 15 percent between 1960 and 1965.

---

13. Parker B. Willis, "The Secondary Market for Negotiable Certificates of Deposit," prepared for the Steering Committee for the Fundamental Reappraisal of the Discount Mechanism, March 1967.

The smaller, nonnegotiable CD also proved to be a successful competitive device. Regulation Q ceilings were initially the same for all time deposits of the same maturity, regardless of denomination. Therefore, the banks could bid aggressively, unencumbered by Regularion Q, for the funds of smaller savers who were responsive to interest differentials. In contrast, NBI offered only passbook accounts and were unable to differentiate among their depositors. Passbook rates at NBI still remained significantly higher than bank passbook rates, but the interest-sensitive depositor was offered a maturity-interest income tradeoff by the banks that was simply unavailable at the more restricted thrift institutions.

As a result of the popularization of multimaturity time deposits at CB (and somewhat later at NBI), the meaning that can be assigned to the "average" rates paid on savings by various FI (such as those presented in Table 5-4) is difficult to specify. Since the market for small savings is segmented in order to take advantage of varying interest sensitivities, the response to an institution's savings rate is a function of both the level of these rates *and* the particular rate structure offered on deposits of various sizes and maturities. As we have noted above, at no time did the CB passbook rate exceed that of NBI. However, the fact that many savers have procured higher yielding time accounts results in an average yield for CB deposits higher than that for NBI in 1969 (see Table 5-4).

Elements of Competition. As described by Vernon,[14] the major forces of competition between banks and NBI were two: the CB were able to offer "full-service," "one-stop" banking with demand deposits, consumer loans, and other services; whereas the NBI had only a rate advantage on which to base their competition for the small saver's passbook account. Vernon maintains that the presence of a 1/2 –1 percent rate differential was essential for the nonbanks to retain their market share. Grebler concurs, asserting that without a rate advantage for the NBI . . .

> Commercial banks, with their superior market penetration, offering broader services and greater convenience, will capture the savings market to the detriment of the thrift institutions.[15]

It seems that we have encountered here the same facets of competition noted in Teck's study of savings institutions: interest income and convenience. These two, combined with the imminent threat of disintermediation shared by all FI in times of rising interest rates, are three factors that are of *central import in assessing probable effects of the EMTS on the financial intermediary sector.* It is to a consideration of the possibility of disintermediation that we now turn. Our example will be the experience of the thrift institutions during 1966.

---

14. Vernon, *op. cit.*

15. Leo Grebler, *The Future of Thrift Institutions,* (Joint Savings and Loan and Mutual Savings Bank Exchange Groups, June 1969), p. 84.

5.1.2 The 1966 Credit Crunch

The thrift institutions, particularly SLA, are unusual among financial inter-mediaries in the manner in which they invest the funds that are deposited with them. The savings institutions concentrate their asset holdings almost exclusively in the longest and most illiquid market instruments—mortgages. These portfolios tend to turn over in the course of seven or eight years, while NBI liabilities are payable essentially on demand. Since the period from the mid-1930s to 1965 was dominated by an upward sloping term structure curve, the peculiar asset/liability structure of the savings institutions proved most advantageous. In the postwar period they competed successfully with the banks and were generally able to provide enough funds to finance the housing boom of the fifties.

However, late in 1965 there began a series of developments that eventually had drastic effects for the NBI. By this time, the economy had been expanding steadily for more than four years, following the 1961 recession. In the latter part of 1965 demand for credit of all kinds increased sharply, driving up interest rates. As is common in such cases, short-term rates rose more rapidly than long-term rates, and in order to help banks maintain their volume of CDs outstanding, the Federal Reserve raised its Regulation Q ceiling for certificates maturing in more than 90 days by a full percentage point—from 4.5 to 5.5 percent—on December 6, 1965. At this time, the FHLBB was trying to restrain SLA dividend rates by refusing expansion advances to SLA which offered dividends higher than 4.5 per-cent.[16] In response to the Federal Reserve's action, this latter rate was raised to 4.75 percent—above the CB's 4 percent passbook rate, but still below the 5.5 percent ceiling on savings certificates and negotiable CDs.

Expansionary pressures in the economy continued, and credit markets grew ever tighter. By the second quarter of 1966 the FHLBB had allowed further rate increases for SLA across the country. But institutions in the Southwest (particu-larly California and Nevada) were still losing ground to CB, and they therefore proceeded to offer passbook rates of up to 5.25 percent, despite the FHLBB advance policy. By June the demand for Federal Home Loan Bank advances had reached extraordinary proportions, as SLA drew on FHLB funds to cover deposit withdrawals. The availability of funds for expansion advances was thus consider-ably diminished, and they were severely rationed. This necessity reduced the efficacy of the FHLBB policy of tying expansion advances to dividend rates, and as a result this policy was suspended on July 1.

Throughout the country the NBI were under great pressure to meet the high interest rates being offered by the banks and in the capital markets. But they were in a quandary. First they were locked into portfolios with low rates of return compared to present interest levels. The savings and loan associations in

---

16. Prior to September, 1966 the FHLBB had no legal power to regulate dividend rates. It therefore was forced to use its power to withhold expansion advances in order to prevent excessive dividend levels at System member associations.

particular were almost completely illiquid at the height of the crisis, having nowhere to sell their mortgage assets. Second, and more ominous, the term structure curve was tilted *downward* in reaction to money market conditions. This eliminated (reversed) the favorable spread that had previously prevailed between the short rates paid on deposits and the long rates earned on assets. The result was a drastically lowered profit margin and reduced additions to bad debt reserves for NBI.

The year 1966 turned out to be dismal for the savings institutions. Deposit inflows dropped sharply throughout the year and in the third quarter the flow of savings to SLA nearly stopped. The relatively small cash flow generated by their long-term, nonmarketable portfolios proved insufficient in many cases to cover the liquidity needs of the SLA, and they were forced to draw heavily on Federal Home Loan Bank advances.

There were two principal reasons for these difficulties. First, and more significant, was the increased competitive edge enjoyed by the commercial banks. For many savers, the interest differential between NBI and CB had diminished to the point where the convenience (that is, lower nonpecuniary transactions costs) of a bank savings account outweighed the extra interest income of a nonbank account. For many others, who were not interested in the liquidity of a passbook account, the CB offered an appreciable rate advantage over NBI. As a result, the CB share of new over-the-counter savings in 1966 was 66 percent, compared with 59 percent in 1965 and 49 percent in 1964.

In a word, the savings institutions as a group felt strongly the effects of the new, higher rates offered on competing securities. They were forced to reduce the inflow of mortgage funds, and many institutions were faced with severe liquidity shortages as a result of the reduced inflow of deposits. The San Francisco FHLB District suffered most severely of all during 1966. In the course of the previous years, SLA in this area had bid aggressively for out-of-state, interest sensitive funds by offering rates above those paid in the rest of the country, and they had been quite successful. However, when interest rates began to exceed SLA dividend rates by a significant margin in 1966, these interest sensitive blocks of money fled the state in favor of more attractive investments.

The second major competitor for NBI savings was the capital market. The loss of funds by intermediaries directly to the market was a completely new phenomenon, one which caused the word "disintermediation" to be coined. For NBI, this was a relatively minor source of trouble in 1966; however the CB found it first difficult, and then impossible, to maintain outstanding their record level of CDs. By August, comparable market rates had surpassed the Regulation Q ceiling on CDs and there ensued a large runoff. Between August and November of 1966 outstanding negotiable certificates of deposit dropped from an all-time peak of $18.7 to $15.5 billion. Corporations were simply placing their investable funds directly in the capital markets. Similarly, in 1966 the household sector invested 24.3 percent of its new savings directly in primary securities. For 1965 the comparable figure was 5.4 percent, and for 1967 it was nearly zero.[17] "This year-to-year rapid shifting of resources between deposits and the direct market [has become] one of the more important facets of modern economic life, particularly since 1965."[18]

The crisis subsided only after the Federal Reserve lowered its Regulation Q ceilings in September. More important, Regulation Q was modified to allow for separate ceilings on time deposits in denominations above and below $100,000. In this manner the banks' ability to compete with the capital markets could be preserved, while maximum rates on smaller savings certificates could be set so as to produce a balanced competitive relationship between the banks and the NBI. In addition, the FHLBB was given legal power in September to set binding interest ceilings for member SLA. The Board immediately exercised this power, in conjunction with the Federal Reserve's new ceilings, in order to halt what many considered to be the excessively rapid rise in savings rates that had occurred during 1966.

In the wake of the 1966 debacle came predictions of recurring future crises for the savings industry. It was now realized that a consistently upward sloping term structure curve could not be assured. Due to severe balance of payments problems and historically high levels of interest rates, some thought that the yield curve would tend to be more nearly horizontal—perhaps varying in slope over the business cycle.[19] If such predictions were true, NBI would again face periodic liquidity crises on the scale of 1966. It was also pointed out that during the postwar period savers as a group had become more interest sensitive in a ratchet fashion. In other words, the sensitivity of depositors to competing interest rates was not likely to decrease in the future; if anything, it would increase further. The continued competition of market interest rates, and the recent decreasing savings rate differential between banks and nonbanks could well be indicative of continued difficult times for savings institutions in the U.S.

5.1.3 The Post-1966 Experience

It did not take long for the post-1966 prophesies of recurring disaster to be fulfilled. Credit conditions eased near the end of 1966, and 1967 proved to be an excellent year for NBI as they recovered a large portion of the funds that had been transferred to the capital markets during the previous year. But continued expansionary pressures in the economy, reinforced this time by an accelerating inflation, produced another tight credit market in 1969. This time the term structure curve had an even more pronounced downward slope than in 1966. The

17. U.S. Savings and Loan League, *Savings and Loan Fact Book 1971*, p. 11.
18. *Ibid.*
19. Irwin Friend, "Summary and Recommendations," in the Friend *Study*, Vol. I, pp. 1–66, 1969.

process of disintermediation and reduced liquidity positions repeated itself again: there was a reversal of savings flows to the NBI, large CD runoffs in response to high short-term market rates, and a high percentage of household assets were channelled directly into primary securities.

This time, however, the SLA weathered the storm considerably better than they had three years earlier. In the first place (and *extremely* important in the minds of FHLBB authorities), competition from the CB was not as intense due to relatively lower levels for the Federal Reserve's interest rate ceilings. Second, the SLA were more willing and able to offer higher dividend rates, largely as a result of the high-interest mortgages they had been able to place since 1966. Third, and of crucial importance for their long run stability was the fact that the thrift institutions were offering far more fixed-maturity deposits than ever before. In July, 1966 only 27 percent of all savings and loan associations offered time accounts that paid above the regular passbook dividend rate. Two years later it was 76 percent.[20] It seems that SLA had learned well from the earlier successes of commercial banks.

In spite of their success relative to 1966 there was still a net outflow of savings funds from the NBI in 1969.[21] And again, as in the previous credit crunch, the San Francisco district SLA were hardest hit. During 1969 their deposit balances dropped 1.4 percent, highlighting once more the effects of the two-edged sword of interest competition for deposit funds.

Responses to the Crisis. The runoff to CDs from commercial banks was considerably more severe than that experienced in 1966: bank CDs declined from a peak of $24 billion to just over $12 billion in the course of the year. The banks reacted to this disintermediation with rapid and bold innovation. Faced with a Regulation Q ceiling that prevented them from obtaining funds domestically, many large banks borrowed heavily in the Eurodollar market through their foreign subsidiaries. This market had been growing steadily since the late fifties, and had been used as a source of reserves during the 1966 period of tight money. But it was not until CD rates hit their ceilings in late 1968 and 1969 that U.S. banks perfected and expanded their access to European dollar markets "in an effort to meet both rising credit demands from their customers and a run-off of maturing CDs."[22] There were no reserve requirements placed on these funds (which were loans from the banks' foreign branches), and no interest ceilings either. The banks could procure any volume of reserves for which they were willing to pay. And pay they did—during June 1969 interest rates on Eurodollar loans averaged about 11 percent.

---

20. Federal Home Loan Bank Board *Report,* 1968, p. 16.

21. The record shows an increase of $6.5 billion in SLA and MSB deposits for the year. However, interest and dividends on the 1968 balance of savings exceeded this amount, so there was actually a net withdrawal of deposit funds. (See the FHLBB *Report* for 1969.)

22. "Eurodollars: A Changing Market," Federal Reserve *Bulletin,* October 1969.

Another innovation that took place in 1969 was direct borrowing in U.S. capital markets by banks who issued subordinated debentures. Had these instruments been issued directly by the banks, the Federal Reserve's reserve requirements would have been applicable to them. Therefore, many banks borrowed from their holding companies, which had previously issued commercial paper or debentures in order to procure funds.

In short, CB strove to avoid the limits imposed by the regulatory ceilings by competing for reserves directly in the capital markets instead of relying on deposit flows for loanable funds. Similar events were occurring among NBI and in the mortgage market.

In spite of the reduced share of the thrift institutions in household savings during the period 1969–1970, mortgage lending nearly maintained its 1968 level. First, and most important for the SLA, was the aggressive and helpful activity of the Federal Home Loan Banks. During 1966 the Federal Home Loan Banks had been fearful that large-scale borrowing in the capital markets was impossible for them, given the current credit conditions. Consequently, expansion advances nearly stopped as the Federal Home Loan Banks limited themselves largely to withdrawal advances in the amount of $938 million. The effect of this policy on housing starts in 1966 was catastrophic. In 1969–70, however, the Banks were more confident of their ability to place security issues; they had also accumulated a considerable amount of medium-term money during the easier credit periods of 1967 and 1968. Expansion advances were issued virtually automatically during 1969 to any association that had not already borrowed heavily. Net advances to the savings and loan industry exceeded $4 billion—about 20 percent or all new mortgage lending for 1969, and nearly 50 percent of new lending by SLA. Another impetus to SLA mortgage extensions was the reduced level of liquidity reserves that were required by the FHLBB. This action freed about $1.3 billion of SLA funds for investment in home mortgages.

The Federal National Mortgage Association (FNMA, or "Fannie Mae") also displayed new and substantial initiative in its support of FHA and VA mortgages. It floated large debt issues during 1969 in order to finance the purchase of $3.8 billion worth of government guaranteed mortgages. The Government National Mortgage Association (GNMA, or "Ginnie Mae"), a subsidiary agency of the Department of Housing and Urban Development (HUD) channeled $800 million into HUD-sponsored conventional mortgages. As a result of these two "Mae" programs and Federal Home Loan Bank advances, almost one half of 1969's $20.4 billion in net residential lending was financed directly by (or with the aid of) market securities.[23]

The basic cause for intermediaries' heightened activities in the money markets can be stated simply. Low levels for Regulation Q ceilings were needed to protect the NBI from severe savings outflows such as those experienced in 1966.

---

23. Figures in the preceding two paragraphs are taken from the 1969 FHLBB *Report.*

The cause of this situation was that . . .

> Commercial bank earnings, supported by the responsiveness of bank port-
> folios to rising market interest rates, would have supported a level of inter-
> est payments on time deposits in excess of the rate that could be paid by
> thrift institutions whose earnings are restrained by low returns on long-term
> mortgage loans acquired during periods of lower interest rates.[24]

The peculiarly specialized asset structure of the NBI was therefore the indirect
cause of bank market activities in 1969 and the direct cause of that year's unusual reliance on open market funds for financing residential construction.

5.2 Efficiency Aspects of the Current Regulatory Structure

Thus, based on the experiences of 1966 and 1969–70, we are able to indict
the depository financial intermediary system as presently constructed for its
potential instability and consequent threat to economic growth. But the various
constraints and ceilings that are today integral to the system are also the root of
some rather serious inefficiencies in the allocation of capital within the society.

The constraints encumbering depository FI today are of five general types.

1. *Regulations governing assets.* These include prohibitions and restrictions
   on the purchase of particular types of assets by FI. For example, SLA have
   only limited powers to hold nonmortgage loans, and there are limits on the
   geographical area within which mortgages can be extended.
2. *Regulations governing liabilities.* Restrictions on the types of liabilities that
   can be issued by FI are more pervasive than is commonly realized. NBI are
   proscribed from issuing demand deposit accounts or subordinated debentures; reserve requirements applying to similar deposits at different institutions often vary considerably; and some types of deposits carry special
   restrictions—for example the funds of state and local governments frequently must be invested in securities issued by the depositor.
3. *Regulations controlling deposit rate levels.* The complex set of rate ceilings
   that govern the time deposits of NBI and CB have been discussed in detail
   above. The prohibition of interest payments on demand deposits falls into
   this class as well.
4. *Regulations concerning services.* Written into the charters of each kind of
   FI in the economy are prohibitions against, or specific permission for, some
   or all of the following: the sale of life insurance, issuing or selling travellers'

---

24. Federal Home Loan Bank Board *Report,* 1968, p. 14.

checks, the operation of mutual funds, pension funds and trust departments, the sale of bookkeeping and data processing services to other institutions, etc.

5. *Regulations governing structure.* Finally, there are a series of complex regulations that control the chartering, branching, deposit insurance, holding company activities, and audit and supervision of each type of intermediary.

We will consider in this section three general kinds of inefficiencies that result from the current regulatory environment: the inefficient allocation of capital among industries, the effect of deposit rate ceilings on an FI's ability to intermediate, and the inefficient flow of capital among geographic regions. The common effect of these regulations is that FIs are unable to act properly at the margin when confronted with changes in capital market conditions. Furthermore, the introduction of an EMTS into the United States economy will greatly increase the importance of these weaknesses in intermediary structure.

5.2.1 Efficiency Across Industries

The various legal restrictions governing the portfolios of today's FI constitute a major impediment to optimal capital flows among sectors of the economy. Fand[25] describes the situation in the following stylized manner. Suppose there are two types of FI, such that one specializes in financing industry A and the other in industry B. If there is a sharp increase in the demand for loans by industry B, the rate of return on industry B's debt would rise. FI_B therefore experiences a rise in the return on its portfolio in direct proportion to the percentage of its assets that are invested at the new rate. If the portfolio of FI_B turns over in N years, then only $1/N$ of its assets earn the new rate of return each year, and so the intermediary's deposit rate will rise less than in proportion to the changed yield on the debt of B. Therefore FI_B will not be able to attract enough capital out of FI_A and the marginal return to capital across industries will not be equalized as quickly as it should be.

However had there been no restrictions on asset selections for the two FI, both FI_A and FI_B would have diverted funds from other investments into the higher-yielding B and efficiency would obtain more rapidly as the rate on B's debt rises relative to A's. Note also that in this second case the depositors as a group would receive higher interest income sooner and there would be no need for them to incur costs by transferring funds from FI_A to FI_B.

Thus absolute restrictions on an intermediary's asset choices lead to at least an inefficient short-run utilization of capital in the society. Moreover, to the extent that these restrictions confine an FI to a longer-term portfolio (that is,

25. David I. Fand, "Financial Regulation and the Allocative Efficiency of Our Capital Markets," *National Banking Review,* III (September 1965), pp. 55–65.

a higher N), there is a threat to the liquidity of some FI. (For example, let FI_A above be confined to making mortgage loans and the year be 1966.) Such regulations also make it impossible to adapt to marginal changes in the term structure of interest rates.

A recent example of the effects of this type of portfolio restriction can be found in mortgage lending during 1969. As interest rates rose, diversified mortgage lenders (primarily CB and life insurance companies) invested increasingly in multifamily dwellings. In so doing these institutions were attracted by higher yields and the common practice of acquiring an equity participation in the building in addition to interest on the loan. NBI are currently proscribed from participating in such equity agreements, and therefore were confined in 1969 to lower yielding, conventional or government backed mortgages. The result of this regulated market segmentation is, of course, higher than necessary yields on multifamily mortgages, and lower earnings for thrift institutions.

Still another example of regulated inefficiency is the consumer loan market. By all accounts, consumer credit is among the least perfectly supplied capital in the economy;[26] yet NBI, potentially among the most efficient lenders in this market, have but scant authority to issue consumer loans.

5.2.2 Efficiency of Deposit Rate Ceilings

In the Fand example above, if there were some means by which FI_B could separate new deposits from old ones, the full benefits of new investments in B could be passed along only to the new depositors. This would aid the marginal efficiency of capital allocation. In other words, as far as a marginally efficient allocation of capital is concerned, flexibility for FIs in the *issue of deposit liabilities* can substitute, at least to some extent, for flexibility in their *purchase of assets.* To the extent that there exists a truly segmented savings market, and to the extent that FI raise rates on some types of accounts and not on others in order to attract new funds, then they are tending toward efficiency in the allocation of their new capital. At present NBI have some powers to issue nonpassbook accounts, and CB are better off still. However, all depository FI are regulated as to the maximum interest rates that can be offered on their deposits, and these ceilings can sharply curtail the institutions' ability to attract new capital in this fashion. The devices used by banks, thrift institutions, and government agencies to procure funds directly in the capital markets for the purpose of replacing deposit funds lost during 1966 and 1969 is ample evidence of the efficacy of Regulation Q type restrictions. Let us examine some of the economic effects of these restrictions on the market.

---

26. See, for example, David Fand, "Savings Intermediaries and the Consumer Credit Markets," in the Friend *Study,* Vol. IV, pp. 1437–78, 1969; or George J. Benston, "Savings Banking and the Public Interest," *Journal of Money Credit and Banking,* IV (February 1972), pp. 133–226.

The imposition of interest ceilings was originally designed to reduce the threat of bank insolvency which was alleged to have resulted in the early 1930s from the "excessive" interest rates previously paid by banks for deposit funds. One can only wonder, however, how a regulation that forces banks to forego the issue of, say, 8 percent CDs[27] in favor of borrowing in the Eurodollar market at 10 or 11 percent can help preserve solvency! On the contrary, interest ceilings "have simply subjected the commercial banking system—and the financial system more broadly—to severe structural adjustments for no social gain whatsoever."[28]

A somewhat similar situation obtains for SLA. When savings inflows slowed in 1969, the Federal Home Loan Banks floated sizeable security issues and financed SLA's new mortgage loans with expansion advances. There were times when the rate on advances was substantially below that paid by the Federal Home Loan Banks. Such a means of financing, even though temporary, is highly inefficient, as well as being inequitable to non-SLA capital users.

But there is still another, more far-reaching, equity issue involved here. As James Tobin has pointed out, rate ceilings effectively block the small saver's access to rising market rates of interest.[29] FI evolved in the economy in order to circumvent various imperfections that prevented direct access to the capital markets for small savers—e.g., lumpy investments, high transaction costs, inability to pool risk, etc. But the use of rate controls as a major means of rationing funds among the various FI results in the exploitation of those very market imperfections that the intermediaries are supposed to alleviate. Rate ceilings are binding only on those savers who are unable to enter the capital market on their own. The net effect of interest ceilings is thus to transfer interest income from the owners of savings capital into a form of rental income accruing to the intermediaries who are benefitted by the ceilings.

In spite of these inequities and inefficiencies, the fact remains that a major segment of the economy's intermediaries have emerged as a result of the shelter provided by rate regulations. In particular, the entire savings and loan industry has been consciously designed as a means of subsidizing the nation's housing production. Special tax treatment, rate regulation, Federal insurance, and the continuous use by SLA of expansion advances provided them by the Federal Home Loan Banks (whose obligations are backed by the Federal government) all

---

27. CD rates had to exceed those on Treasury bills in order to be sold in the market, and the rate on the latter in August 1969 was about 7 percent.

28. Milton Friedman, "Controls on Interest Rates Paid by Banks," *Journal of Money Credit and Banking,* II (February 1970), p. 17. In June, 1970, Regulation Q controls were suspended for negotiable CDs in excess of $100,000 and of less than 90 days maturity. While this will alleviate part of the runoff problem for the banks, there are also a number of smaller institutions whose CDs come in denominations below $100,000. The remaining ceilings on longer maturity large CDs are fairly competitive at this time, but outflows will continue to occur for small CD accounts and savings certificates. The efficiency problem has been alleviated but by no means eliminated.

29. James Tobin, "Deposit Interest Ceilings as a Monetary Control," *Journal of Money Credit and Banking,* II (February 1970), pp. 4–14.

represent real subsidies of an unknown magnitude to the mortgage market. Even if one agrees that housing subsidies are desirable for the economy, one must still object to the fact that the subsidies provided through the current savings system are inefficient and of unknown magnitude.

We have pointed out above that the NBI weathered the 1969 crisis as well as they did only because of Regulation Q's inhibitory effects on CB competition. Given the character of their mortgage portfolios, the thrift institutions are unable to adjust their deposit rates quickly to changes in market conditions. To remove summarily all interest ceilings in the economy could, *ceteris paribus*, spell disaster for the NBI. It is for this reason that the issue of ceilings must be considered in conjunction with reform of the regulations governing NBI assets and liabilities. This discussion will therefore be continued below.

5.2.3 Regional Efficiency

Optimality requires equality of returns to capital among geographic regions in the economy as well as among sectors. While the economy today exhibits significant regional interest rate differentials on similar types of loans, some of the variation can be accounted for by regional variations in risk, transactions costs, and transportation costs. It is thus also possible that regional interest rates reflect true demand and supply conditions. (This was in fact the case in the California mortgage market of the fifties.) Further discussion of the national mortgage market will provide us with a concrete example of interregional capital flows as a means by which national returns on capital can be equalized.[30]

In the fifties and early sixties, California SLA were net sellers of mortgages through the Federal National Mortgage Association (FNMA), and the associations in the New York and Boston areas were net purchasers. In addition, more than $3.7 billion flowed into California from out-of-state SLA by means of mortgage participation certificates. The California institutions also bid aggressively in the East for new deposits by advertising interest rates above those offered elsewhere in the country. Given this regionally high demand for mortgage funds, there are two ways by which capital could be induced to flow into California. (These were discussed in the Fand model presented above.) First, the western SLA could attempt to import funds from other regions by offering higher rates on savings accounts. This involves considerable advertising costs (to overcome reluctance to place funds in a distant institution), and the depositors must incur

---

30. A number of features of our current financial sector help to equalize interest rates nationally: national markets for primary securities and commercial loans, the Federal funds market, Federal Reserve discounts, and FHLB advances all help to alleviate local pressures. But there still exist significant imperfections in the market for single family mortgages and consumer loans. It will be argued here that an EMTS will tend to reduce regional variation in these markets as well.

transactions costs in the process of moving their funds. But more important, these imported funds are "hot" and will leave the region as soon as higher returns are offered elsewhere. For institutions with illiquid long-term portfolios this can precipitate severe problems when national market rates rise, or when local mortgage rates fall towards the national average. Such was, of course, the case for California SLA in 1966 and 1969.

The second means of importing capital to California is to allow out-of-state SLA to invest directly in mortgages in the state. This can be done either through direct mortgage placements by individual SLA, or through the sale of participation certificates whose proceeds are somehow made available to finance California mortgages. In fact this latter tack has been taken by three government agencies and one privately-owned corporation. FNMA and, more recently, GNMA have served as national mortgage brokers for government guaranteed mortgages, financing themselves in the market. In July, 1970 the Federal Home Loan Mortgage Corporation (FHLMC, or "Freddie Mac"), owned entirely by the twelve Federal Home Loan Banks, emerged as a buyer and seller of conventional mortgages and participations. FNMA also became authorized to hold conventional mortgage loans as of February, 1972; and in March of 1972 the private Mortgage Guaranty Insurance Corporation (MGIC) began dealing in the secondary mortgage market. GNMA has tended to specialize in HUD-subsidized housing projects; FNMA deals almost exclusively with 1500 mortgage bankers around the country; while FHLMC and MGIC provide a secondary market for the savings and loan associations.[31] Through the operation of these four institutions, a true secondary market for mortgages is *beginning* to emerge in the economy. A resilient and uniform market is, however, still in the future.

We can only conclude on the basis of our discussion in this section that the present system of financial intermediaries and their controlling agencies must be modified if an optimal national allocation of capital is to be approached in the economy.

5.3 Recommended Reforms for the Savings Industry

The potential instability inherent in the monetary system has long been recognized, and the result has been a series of national commissions to study the problems involved. The Federal Reserve System, for example, was the result of an early National Monetary Commission. More recently, in 1958, the national Commission of Money and Credit was established "in response to widespread concern as to the adequacy of the nation's monetary and financial structure and

---

31. MGIC is a subsidiary of the MGIC Investment Corporation, the largest private insurer of conventional mortgages in the country. MGIC, by specializing in loans insured by its parent, is able to avoid the expense of investigating each mortgage offered to it for sale. See "Nobody Pours It Like Fannie Mae," *Fortune,* LXXXV (June 1972), p. 86.

its regulation and control."[32] In the wake of 1966 and 1969, two further major studies were started—Irwin Friend's comprehensive *Study of the Savings and Loan Industry* for the FHLBB and the President's Commission on Financial Structure and Regulation (the Hunt Commission)—and a book was written by Leo Grebler for the Joint Savings and Loan and Mutual Savings Bank Exchange Groups. In addition, Federal legislation was introduced in 1968 that would have broadly reformed the structure of SLA and MSB.[33] Despite differences among the recommendations proposed by these various groups (and there are several significant ones), the thrust of each study indicates that many experts recognize the highly competitive relationships of the various depository financial intermediaries, and are of the opinion that institutions competing in similar markets should in most cases be governed by similar regulations. This section will describe the more important recommendations that have been made for reforms in the savings industry. Section 5.4 of this chapter will then superimpose the effects of an EMTS on these reforms in an effort to anticipate the changes in the U.S. savings industry that are required in preparation for the emergence of the EMTS.

Recommendations have been made that bear on virtually every aspect of FI operations—from charters to holding company activities. For the purposes of this discussion, however, we will confine ourselves to suggested reforms in the asset and liability structures of FI, since we have seen that it is imbalances in this area that have been central to NBI's competitive disadvantages. Moreover, in the interests of space, economic justifications provided here for the adaptation of these reforms will be brief. The reader is referred to any of the three publications cited above for further details. It should be remembered also that the discussion in this section pertains to the FI sector as it exists *currently*—sans EMTS.

5.3.1 Reforms Concerning Financial Intermediary Assets

On the asset side of the balance sheet, the emphasis in the recommendations is on freedom of choice for the individual FI in choosing its portfolio. In our discussion above we have demonstrated that both inefficiency and institutional illiquidity can result from regulatory restrictions on FI portfolios.

Several authors[34] have presented compelling arguments in favor of NBI consumer lending. Consumer loans, even if only a small (10 percent) fraction of the

---

32. *The Report of the Commission on Money and Credit,* Prentice-Hall, Inc., Englewood Cliffs, 1961, p. 1.

33. The Federal Savings Association Bill: H.R. 13718. The bill failed to pass.

34. Fand, *op. cit.*; Benston, *op. cit.*; Irwin Friend, "Changes in the Asset and Liability Structure of the Savings and Loan Industry," in the Friend *Study,* Vol. III, pp. 1355–1434, 1969; and Leo Grebler, *The Future of Thrift Institutions,* Joint Savings and Loan and Mutual Savings Bank Exchange Groups, 1969.

portfolio, can increase an institution's cash flow significantly since these loans mature in an average of only one year (versus 8 years for most mortgages). This supplemented cash flow increases the ability of the FI to cover withdrawals and/or to take advantage of changes in market interest rates. Such consumer loans also yield a return (net of costs) of up to one percentage point higher than that on mortgages, and could therefore raise the total return on a savings institution's portfolio.[35]

The principal argument of those opposed to allowing NBI to originate consumer loans is that available mortgage funds in the economy will be reduced, thus endangering the fulfillment of the national housing goals. However, Jaffee, and Fair and Jaffee,[36] have demonstrated that there is no *a priori* reason to expect a shortage of mortgage funds if savings institutions are allowed to issue consumer loans. Moreover, to the extent that a "customer relationship" or "full-service banking" is important in present inter-FI competition, consumer loans will help NBI to attract savings funds. (It is expected that NBI will continue to invest rather heavily in mortgages, so to the extent that funds are shifted from CB to NBI there will be more mortgage lending undertaken.) In their empirical study of this issue, Fair and Jaffee simulate the Hunt Commission's recommendations with the Federal Reserve-MIT-Penn econometric model, and conclude that . . .

> Allowing savings institutions extended lending powers will result in a portfolio substitution, against mortgages, and a portfolio size expansion, favoring mortgages. The net effect of the two changes on mortgages is small and may be either positive or negative depending on specific assumptions, while the effect on housing is generally positive, although small.[37]

Irwin Friend, while less definite about the net change in available mortgage funds, *does* assert that NBI consumer lending will be beneficial for the society as a whole.

> . . . The gains to the savings and loan industry in profitability, in liquidity, and in their ability to service and hence to attract customers and to meet needs for funds in periods of tight money—totally apart from the competitive improvements in consumer credit markets—are believed to compensate

---

35. Fand, *op. cit.* and Friend, *op. cit.*

36. Ray C. Fair and Dwight M. Jaffee, "An Empirical Study of the Proposals of the Hunt Commission for the Mortgage and Housing Markets," in *Policies for a More Competitive Financial System,* June 1972, Federal Reserve Bank of Boston; and Dwight M. Jaffee, "The Extended Lending, Borrowing and Service Function Proposals of the Hunt Commission Report," *Journal of Money Credit and Banking,* November 1972.

37. Fair and Jaffee, *op. cit.,* pp. 143–144.

for the *possibility* of some diversion of resources from residential mortgages over the cycle.[38]

Although these studies indicate that consumer loan powers for NBI will not seriously disturb the mortgage and housing markets, if it is found that mortgage money (or any other type of funds) is in short supply, the government's proper response will be a direct subsidy either to the homeowner or attached to the mortgage instrument itself. Subsidies may take the form of a partial payment of interest for the mortgager, blanket 100 percent Federal guarantee of the principal, an interest supplement to buyers of mortgages in a secondary market, or permission for FI to count some percentage of a mortgage's face value as legal reserves.[39] Alternatively, subsidies may be placed directly on the real asset that is to be financed. This is generally more efficient, since it avoids nonproductive shifts in the ratio of mortgage value to new housing value, and it enables the authorities to exercise greater control over the type of housing units that are subsidized. In any case, "Financing [a national goal] through control of the portfolios of financial institutions is a costly and inefficient means of allocating resources,"[40] and must be ended in the interests of economic efficiency.

Similar considerations apply to essentially all the extended asset power proposals for FI. For example, George Benston studied the adjustments of Swedish mutual savings banks after they had been given full commercial bank powers in 1967. He asserts that there was no widespread change in lending policies, but that the MSB did begin providing services that had been high profit items for the commercial banks. In other words, diversified lending powers for MSB reduced imperfections that had existed in the Swedish capital markets. We suggest that this will be precisely the result in the U.S. as well, with minimal overall impact on mortgage lending.

More generally, it must be recognized that legislated restrictions on FI portfolios concerning the fraction of assets that must be held in a given type of security (for instance, the way SLA are induced by the tax structure to hold a very high percentage of mortgages) interfere with marginal responses to market rates. It is necessary that all FI be permitted to invest in a wide range of securi-

---

38. Irwin Friend, "Changes in the Asset and Liability Structure," p. 1403, emphasis added. In a senior thesis written at Princeton University in 1972, August Moretti points out the existence of a significant difference between the Friend Study's recommendations and those of the Hunt Commission: Friend would retain the specialized mortgage function of the savings and loan industry, allowing relatively minor extensions of SLA asset powers combined with extensive new liability powers. On the other hand, the Hunt *Report* proposes the conversion of today's specialized SLA into a system of rather *diversified* lenders with wide liability powers. August J. Moretti, "The Savings and Loan Industry: Problems, Proposed Solutions and Future Housing Needs," unpublished, Senior thesis, Princeton University, 1972.

39. This last concept was put forward in the President's Commission *Report*.

40. President's Commission *Report*, p. 117.

ties. More specifically, the ability to invest prudently in corporate equities would allow FI to anticipate inflation and its effects on the real value of accumulated reserves and retained earnings; and corporate bond holdings would permit higher earnings (particularly during tight money periods) and provide an added source of liquidity reserves. Equity participations in multifamily mortgages should also be allowed in NBI portfolios. To the extent that they raise income for the lender, such participations increase the institution's solvency and channel available capital to projects with the highest productivity.

The removal of geographic restrictions on mortgage loans and the development of an active secondary market for mortgages and participations would go a long way toward protecting FI from becoming locked into an illiquid portfolio. If they were made into marketable instruments in this way, mortgages (perhaps with the aid of some form of subsidy) could compete more effectively with corporate bonds, acceptances, Treasury bills, etc., for a place in FI portfolios. As discussed above it would also be an aid to regional capital movements. Thus, efforts that are presently under way to develop a secondary mortgage market should be continued.

5.3.2 Reforms Concerning Financial Intermediary Liabilities

If the above asset reforms are indeed effected, the NBI will be in a far better position to adjust their portfolios in response to marginal variations in market rates. But the ability of NBI to compete for deposit liabilities, especially in times of rising interest rates, must also be put on a par with that of the banks. To this end, NBI should be able to segment their saver market as the banks do by offering multiple types of accounts. All intermediaries should be free to seek long-term financing through the issue of primary securities in the market, and through the issuing of longer-term, high-yielding negotiable CDs and other types of term accounts.

Moreover, the economic literature is overwhelmingly in favor of the complete elimination of interest ceilings, including the prohibition of interest on demand deposits that was legislated in 1933.[41] The inefficiencies of zero interest demand accounts were described in Chapter 3, and those of Regulation Q ceilings have been discussed previously in this chapter. While it is often conceded that emergency power to control rates should be vested in the Federal Reserve, it appears to be almost inevitable that Regulation Q and its kind will eventually disappear from everyday FI regulations.

---

41. See, for example, Tobin, *op. cit.,* Friedman, *op. cit.,* and Irwin Friend, "Summary and Recommendations."

5.3.3 Other Suggested Reforms

A more far-reaching extension of NBI liabilities concerns the making of third-party payments for private individuals and nonprofit organizations. This would severely cut into the banks' convenience advantage, placing more emphasis on price competition in the struggle for savings. Third-party payments are today said to be vital if the savings industry is to maintain its market share in the face of rising interest rates offered by CB. Defenders of the proposal also maintain that the increased competition for demand-deposit accounts would yield gains for the public in the form of better and cheaper services.

Still another recurring recommendation is that FI be allowed to manage mutual funds under the supervision of the Securities Exchange Commission. It is alleged that, in view of the rapid growth of mutual funds over the past years, still more small savers would benefit if they were to have local access to a mutual fund.

In addition, there are many recent recommendations concerning the powers that should be extended to various FI with respect to the provision of new services, chartering, branching, and regulatory supervision and auditing. These recommendations have been motivated by important considerations, but they are only peripheral to the main focus of our study and therefore they are not considered here.

5.4 Implications of the EMTS for the Suggested Reforms

The direction of the above reforms is toward the introduction of greater stability and adaptability into the structure of our current financial system. The Hunt Commission in particular viewed adaptability as a vital feature for future financial intermediaries:

> Well-functioning financial intermediaries should be able to develop and use technological opportunities without significant strain on the system. It is widely believed that the financial sector has entered a period of rapid change. Technology is expected to influence the operating methods and structure of financial institutions in important but as yet uncertain ways.[42]

We have argued, in the previous chapters of this study that these same "technological opportunities" will in fact result in the emergence of an EMTS in

---

42. President's Commission *Report*, p. 16.

the United States. As described in Chapter 4, the two most important economic features of the EMTS relating to FI behavior are:

1. The costs involved in making a financial transaction (especially nonpecuniary costs) will be decreased from what they are today. In particular, the physical location of an FI will be of no consequence for the majority of transactions.
2. There will be an increased availability of information about financial matters. Individuals will be more cognizant of, and more sensitive to, the time value of money.

In a word, the EMTS represents a sizeable step in the direction of *more competitive* savings and capital markets. These features of the EMTS will have a number of significant implications for the financial intermediaries in the economy.

5.4.1 Third Party Payments

On the basis of the historical patterns of competition for savings, we can see that feature 1 mentioned above will eliminate the relevance of the banks' claim to greater convenience. On the assumption that an individual is able to effect a transaction at any depository FI for the same cost, his choice of savings institution will be based solely on maximizing his interest income. The conclusion follows that if the total pecuniary and nonpecuniary cost of effecting savings transactions is the same at all FI, then competition will force the rates offered to be equal at all institutions. One might be tempted to infer from this situation that NBI will no longer need checking accounts in order to compete, since banking will be "no stop" under the EMTS. But it must be taken into account that commercial banks would be able to use their position as sole operator of the payments mechanism to gain significant advantage in the competition for savings. The SCOPE aspects of the EMTS will cause most wage earners to have their pay transferred directly into their demand account. The wage earner's bank would surely offer to transfer a portion of these funds into his savings account within the same institution for no charge. But we would hardly expect a free transfer to *other* FI—either banks or NBI.

Note further that this practice would not violate our assumption that all depository FI must have equal access to the EMTS. The price of a funds transfer could be the same regardless of the payee, but the fact that an interinstitutional transfer requires more resources than an intrainstitutional one would result in a higher charge for transferring funds from one's demand account into a nonbank savings account than into a bank savings account. This is exactly the situation that prevails today: there is a differential between the cost to a depositor of saving at a bank (the operator of the money system) and at other FI. Today the cost differential is largely in terms of convenience and time; under an EMTS explicit money costs will be involved.

Although transactions costs between demand deposit and time deposit accounts may by themselves imply the need for most financial intermediaries to maintain demand deposit facilities, it must be recognized that these costs under an EMTS could be very low; indeed, low enough possibly not to matter to some groups. This situation would render the above argument irrelevant. However, at least to a limited extent, one-stop banking advantages will still accrue to commercial banks if they continue to be the only intermediary offering third party payments. These advantages would include: a line of credit for easy loans (that is, the payments function will be intricately bound up with consumer lending), free and automatic transfer of funds to one's savings account when the demand balance gets over a certain level, or "one statement banking"—that is, loan, demand deposit, mortgage, and savings information all in one monthly report. Features such as these will no doubt serve to attract and hold customers. They are similar to the type of conveniences that are offered today by the CB, but in the EMTS world people are likely to be more sensitive to such considerations (particularly the first two mentioned above—the credit line and funds transfers among one's accounts). We repeat our conclusion on this matter: because of transactions cost differentials and the potential appeal of full service banking, nonbanks will be unable to compete effectively for savings without the ability to make third party payments.

Similar arguments can be repeated, although not so forcefully, regarding FI-operated mutual funds. It must be remembered that mutual funds are not fixed-dollar shares, guarantee no interest, and lack government insurance. They are therefore not appealing investments for many small, risk-averse savers. Yet assuming that a substantial number of people would utilize a mutual fund managed by their savings institution, and to the extent that FI will make transactions costs lower for their own depositors than for others, one would expect fundless FI to be at a relative disadvantage.[43] In any case, this is still another situation where institutions that compete directly should not be constrained by different regulations. All FI should be allowed the same opportunity to own mutual funds, and profitability will determine how many funds are actually created.

5.4.2 Elimination of Constraints on Assets and Liabilities

The reduced transactions costs associated with the EMTS, combined with more extensive information flows throughout the society, will together tend to make FI much more vulnerable to savings outflows than they are today. In

---

43. The question of how significant will be the number of savers who are interested in mutual funds can, of course, only be answered by empirical research sometime in the future. With proper advertising on the part of the banks, however, this number is potentially considerable.

effect every FI will be in the same situation as Teck's money-market-city MSB. The increased interest sensitivity of individuals as a result of their familiarity with merchant discounts and other manifestations of money's time value will result in wider recognition of changing market interest rates and interest rate differentials. Smaller transactions costs (again, *non*pecuniary costs are often central to any asset switch today) will make it profitable to respond to relatively small increases in rates. So the net result will be potentially more volatile deposit levels at all FI and an ever-present threat of competition from the capital markets.

This potential variability of deposit levels, which can be expected to persist in the long run, makes it imperative that FI be able to compete for funds at all times. Interest ceilings will provide but scant help for intermediaries whose rates do not keep pace with the capital markets; rather, increased interest sensitivity and small savers' increased access to the market will mean that interest ceilings *exacerbate* the inclination to disintermediate. In short, the recommendations that we have discussed concerning various maturity accounts, the elimination of interest ceilings, portfolio diversification, secondary markets for mortgages, and the right of all FI to issue long-term securities will have even more compelling economic justifications in the future with an EMTS than they do today. Individual FI, and the system of intermediaries as a whole, must be given the ability to secure funds and help maintain orderly capital markets regardless of market conditions.

5.4.3 Regional Capital Movements

In the absence of interest ceilings on deposit rates, nonprice competition for savings (for example, free gifts) will disappear and price will be the only factor by which to differentiate FI. We can therefore expect an FI which is able to offer an above-average rate of return on savings to advertise the fact thoroughly, and the more interest-sensitive savers at other FI will shift their accounts.[44] The reduced transactions costs (in this case, psychic as well as real) means that a given rate differential will attract more funds through the EMTS than it would today, so the marginal cost of funds to an institution in a capital deficient area (that is, an area where returns to capital are above the competitive average) will be lower than it is today.

Appealing again to the Fand model presented above, we see that there is a still *more* efficient solution to the problem of regional capital efficiency. If the local FI are able to sell participations in their loans, much as Federal funds are traded today, the gain to society as a whole will be greater than if individuals were to shift their deposits among FI. The presence of the EMTS and the attendant possibility of interregional competition for funds such as that described in

---

44. Today many individuals consider saving at a distant institution with distaste. We believe, however, that when all saving is effected through the EMTS such attitudes will be far less prevalent in the economy.

the preceding paragraph should tend to make FI around the country more receptive to such participation schemes—since failure to support them could lead to loss of deposits by institutions in capital-satiated areas. In sum, regional capital allocation should be more efficient with the EMTS than at the present time.

5.4.4 Summary

The discussion of this section points out the necessity for reforms in the relationship among our current financial intermediaries. Initiation of reforms such as those discussed in the Hunt Report or Friend Study will, of course, entail problems and require substantial adjustments for the industries and institutions involved. However, the problems that will be thrust upon NBI in the future, when the EMTS sharply curtails their ability to compete for savings on nonpecuniary bases, will be far more severe and widespread. If we begin to extend the powers of NBI *now*, they will then have time to acquire the expertise and competitive ability that will be required of them in the future. To delay can only increase the probability of a major crisis for the financial system at some time in the future.

The following, then, are the modifications in the regulatory structure that are most urgently needed in preparation for an EMTS.

1. All FI must be allowed to make third party payments.
2. All FI should be allowed to issue such deposit liabilities as they see fit, with no limit as to the interest rates payable on them. In addition any FI should be able to borrow in the primary securities market subject only to the regulations of the S.E.C.
3. The detailed regulation of the type and maturity of assets held by FI must be terminated. Restricting an FI's portfolio to one type of asset reduces efficiency in the capital market and will constitute an ever-present threat to the solvency of some intermediaries. All depository intermediaries must therefore be given the power to invest in the same types of market securities. In addition, current geographic restrictions on the mortgage loans of an institution, and limits on the amount of a portfolio which may be invested in participation certificates, must also be eliminated.
4. It is desirable that FI be allowed to operate mutual funds. As a result of the EMTS it is necessary that if one FI may operate a fund, then all must have at least the authority to do so.

5.5 Overview of the Future Financial System

We are now in a position to combine the discussion in Chapter 4 of the EMTS with this chapter's consideration of depository financial intermediaries.

Assuming that the above recommended reforms are in fact effected, we can proceed to sketch a profile of the intermediary system of the future. In so doing we must confine ourselves to delineating broad outlines; specific relationships in the system will be the product of particular economic costs, the actual interest sensitivity of the public, managerial drive and innovation, the exact extent of EMTS operations, and many other parameters that are simply not determinable at this time.

5.5.1 Less Specialization of Intermediaries

There will certainly be a pronounced tendency towards a single "type" of intermediary. Each of the depository FI today has strengths, weaknesses, and differentiated products that are played off against one another in the imperfect competition that prevails. But competition for savings under the EMTS will be far less imperfect. NBI will need demand accounts; CB will no longer be able to use one-stop banking as a partial substitute for competitive interest rates; and no intermediary will be effectively sheltered from the market's competition.

All FI will have the option of choosing their portfolios from the same range of assets. Each institution will make its asset choices based solely on profitability and market conditions. In view of the Federal government's persistent efforts in the past to encourage and subsidize the homebuilding industry and homeowners, we can project that mortgage loans or housing will continue to be subsidized—probably more directly than in the past. Considering the harm to the economy and to the construction industry that derives from fluctuations in the availability of mortgage funds over the cycle, a subsidy that also varies over the cycle should be considered.

All FI will be subject to similar disintermediation threats. We can therefore expect that competition will cause their portfolios to be more similar than they are today, as intermediaries substitute assets in order to achieve a desirable trade-off between risk and return. It is, however, likely (as will be argued below) that NBI will maintain some degree of specialization in mortgage lending. If this is the case, then to the extent that mortgage loans bear higher yields than CB business loans, the banks will be induced to alter their portfolios in the direction of higher yielding instruments in order to maintain competitive interest payments on their liabilities. The NBI will be reducing their committment to mortgages (as a percentage of total assets—not necessarily absolutely) in their efforts to acquire better cash flows and liquidity positions. Thus, it is not likely to be a one-sided adjustment process; rather, all intermediaries will have incentives to move away from their traditional portfolios profiles.

Finally, it will be possible for any depository FI to issue demand deposits (i.e., accounts with which transactions can be made), and nearly all of them will be compelled by forces of competition to handle transactions accounts for their customers. Once an institution begins making third party transfers it has become a part of the U.S. monetary system and therefore should be under the jurisdiction of the Federal Reserve. This is, in fact, the argument of the President's Commission *Report* and it seems to be applicable under the EMTS as well. We will discuss Federal Reserve membership further in Chapter 8 when we consider the effects of the EMTS on monetary policy.

It is to be stressed that extended powers would be used by financial intermediaries by choice and *not* by edict. With regard to augmented powers of deposit issue (third party payments and the variety of time deposits and other liabilities) it seems likely that competition will force most FI to operate in these markets. The intermediaries may, however, choose to continue specializing in their traditional areas of the asset market. This distinction arises because the various institutions have developed expertise in particular types of loans: an SLA knows well the local real estate market and has developed a good relationship with agents and builders in the area; a CB is well acquainted with the financial condition and needs of its business customers, and the customers would be reluctant to deal with a newcomer to the banking industry. This type of informal entry barrier, along with the effects of scale economies, is likely to preclude any massive shifts in institutional specialization. On the other hand, we would expect new entries into asset areas where current expertise is minimal and a high degree of imperfection (resulting in monopoly profits) exists—a prime example being consumer loans. Moreover, as more consumer lending is done through lines of credit and overdraft allowances, such loans will become intimately connected with the payment function. As we have noted above, even with the retention of some specialization in institutions' portfolios, efficient flows of funds among sectors of the economy can be obtained with sufficient competition in deposit markets. This principle is no different from the proposition that manufacturing firms, specializing in particular industries, will still achieve an optimal distribution of capital across industries, so long as there is free access to capital markets.

5.5.2 Competition Among Intermediaries

The thrust of the above discussion has clearly been that financial intermediaries in almost all respects will be more competitive. The advantages of such competition are clear and have been discussed at some length. The structural changes likely to occur as a result of the EMTS and the drawbacks of increased competition should, however, also be noted.

Discussion of intermediary competition must invariably be related to economies of scale in FI operation; but, unfortunately the existence of economies of scale in commercial bank and NBI operations is a highly controversial issue. Various studies have found alternatively no evidence for such economies, distinct

U-shaped cost curves, and economies only for the smallest banks.[45] In a related area, Benston claims to have demonstrated highly "significant" economies of scale for most aspects of SLA operation.[46] It seems that such irresolute and conflicting results are obtained for several reasons. First, two institutions of the same size in deposits can still vary extensively in terms of average account size, loan to deposit ratio, and demand deposits as a fraction of total deposits. Since a bank produces its many outputs jointly, it is difficult or impossible to assign costs properly to individual products. Second, the cost figures available are in many cases accounting data that bear little or no relation to true economic costs. For the purposes of our present study, however, there is yet a third objection to past studies of bank economies: the production function of an EMTS bank is likely to be far different from historical production functions, thereby making past studies irrelevant.

Despite the uncertainty attached to the existence of scale economies, we can make one definitive prediction: to the extent that small institutions are unable to achieve economies of scale, their ability to meet the interest rates offered by lower-cost institutions will be impaired. No longer shielded from competition by geographic isolation (that is, a local monopoly) and/or interest rate ceilings, these banks will disappear or become merged into some more efficient institution. *The EMTS can cause something approaching pure competition among banks of the future, and those with higher cost functions will inevitably suffer upon the introduction of an electronic payments system.*

From some points of view, of course, competition may not produce desirable results. The issue of the position of very small intermediaries in the EMTS has, for example, been a particular concern. It has been suggested that the demise of many small banks and nonbanks will be a necessary result of the increased competition engendered by the evolution of an EMTS. Two possible reasons have been offered in support of this allegation, but only one is actually valid. First, one could argue that the hardware requirements for automating a bank's operations to the point where it could take part in the EMTS are so great that a small bank's fixed costs per account would be prohibitively large and profitable operation would be impossible. However, this situation represents an ideal opportunity for several institutions to join together and share one computer facility. A nonprofit company could be formed by several banks (as was done in the case of bank card associations), an independent corporation could sell computer services to the banking industry, or a small institution's correspondent bank could provide it with computer services. The hardware "problem" is clearly a small obstacle.

---

45. Warren E. Moscowitz, "The Cost and Profitability of Demand Deposits: A Review of the Literature," New York State Mutual Savings Bank Association working paper, unpublished, 1971.

46. George J. Benston, "Costs of Operations and Economies of Scale in Savings and Loan Associations," in the Friend *Study,* Vol. II, pp. 677–762, 1969.

The second point—diseconomies of small scale—has already been discussed. We can only repeat our conclusion from above: if an institution's small size makes it unable to offer competitive deposit rates, competition will drive it out of the industry. This result is unavoidable.

From a static economic point of view, the elimination of such high-cost intermediaries would be a socially desirable occurrence, assuming that the process of transition can be smoothly effected.[47] However, it has long been recognized in the U.S.—both in the area of bank legislation and in economic theory—that there are substantial externalities involved in the economy's system of financial intermediaries. The failure of an FI entails considerable social costs in addition to those borne by the individuals directly involved. This type of argument is one basis for federal deposit insurance, and it is obvious that the failure of a large number of savings institutions would bring an inordinate amount of pressure to bear on the Federal government through the FDIC and FSLIC. Despite this possibility, we consider the long run advantages of increased competition in this sector of the economy to outweigh the social costs of any institutional failures that may occur as a result of EMTS innovations. Plans must, however, be developed whereby the institutions most likely to be harmed by the EMTS can be singled out for special preventive actions of some sort—be it liquidation of the intermediary, or a merger with some larger institution. It is also possible that small commercial banks will become increasingly more like today's specialized savings institutions and would have to be treated accordingly. This entire situation is one that demands extensive study and comprehensive planning on the part of today's regulatory agencies.

A second result of the EMTS will be a sharp reduction in the number of branch offices that will be maintained. This is one aspect of FI operating costs where nearly all writers agree—branch banks have higher operating costs than unit banks. The EMTS will therefore lower the cost of intermediation due to branch banks, yielding a net gain to society. However, we encounter here again the problem of how best to move resources out of the banking industry.

The nature of bank correspondent relationships will also be altered. On the one hand, there will be less need for city correspondents for routine check clearing and access to the capital markets; but, concomitantly, small institutions will find themselves in need of new and more extensive services that can only be provided by other intermediaries. The provision of certain services by correspondents will therefore need to be expanded, and will run increasingly along the lines of investment advice, easy access (for customers) to bank mutual funds, provision of computer services, and the exchange of short-term loans and participations. The relative strength of these two tendencies will be an empirical question; however, whatever the quantitative effect, correspondent relationships are

---

47. The free movement of resources among industries in the economy is usually an assumption of microeconomic theory. Unfortunately it is in a majority of cases an inapplicable one. This is an area toward which research would be well-directed.

sure to be maintained in a regime where capital markets become ever more competitive and complicated, as computerization becomes vital, and as the management of a bank's deposit accounts and credit lines becomes more complex.

It has been argued above that the EMTS will increase efficiency of capital use in the economy as a whole. Spurred on by the potential of interregional savings flows, the banks as a group should be willing to develop new instruments in the capital markets so that capital can flow quickly and easily. The result will be equalized returns to capital in all regions, without the necessity for deposit flows among regions. Goldfeld has stated that . . .

> greater allocational efficiency is served the more the differences (in regional interest rates) are related to risk, real transactions costs, and consumer preferences and the less they are related to such things as ceilings, portfolio restrictions, tax treatments, and monopolistic powers.[48]

If we follow the dictates of economic efficiency, in some cases reinforced by the existence of an EMTS, then most of the regulatory causes of inefficiency will be eliminated and any local monopoly powers which had existed will surely be destroyed by the EMTS.

5.5.3 The Customer Relationship

So far in this study the issue of the importance of customer relationships for financial intermediaries has received little mention. Direct contact between an individual and his bank will certainly decline under the EMTS, because one need never transact business at the office for routine deposits and withdrawals. In addition, one's overdraft privilege will accommodate many borrowing needs. But there will still remain the larger private loans (auto loans, mortgages, repair, and modernization) and commercial loans, and these transactions will perhaps be difficult to automate completely. In the past few years there have emerged a number of computer-programmable algorithms capable of scoring a loan applicant's credit worthiness.[49] To the extent that such algorithms are used and their results accepted by customers and banks, then an institution's location will indeed become irrelevant. However, if banks are unwilling to place complete confidence in such mechanical methods—and this might well be the case, particularly for large and/or risky loans—then the importance of the customer relationship will remain and physical location, convenience, etc., will continue to be factors of unknown magnitude in the competition for market shares.

This issue of how loans will be made by a bank represents, in other words,

---

48. Goldfeld, *op. cit.,* p. 597.

49. D.C. Ewert, "Trade Credit Management: Selection of Accounts Receivable Using a Statistical Model," unpublished Ph.D. dissertation, Stanford, 1968. Yair E. Orgler, "A Credit Scoring Model for Commercial Loans," *Journal of Money Credit and Banking* II (November 1970), pp. 435–445.

a potential bottleneck in the evolution of the EMTS. If a customer can negotiate a loan only with the institution that handles the bulk of his banking business, and if the negotiations must be carried on at the bank's offices, then an institution's physical location will remain relevant. A person who will one day request a loan from his bank is not likely to feel free to move his accounts to some remote part of the country, because of the very high cost of borrowing engendered by such action.

If the customer relationship remains an integral part of borrowing from a bank, then the economy will be unable to benefit from the full potential efficiency gains available under the EMTS; in particular, the need for customer relationships could well forestall the development of pure competition among FI. The nonpecuniary costs of issuing loans would in this case be the salvation of some smaller institutions that would otherwise be driven out of the industry by diseconomies of scale. They could become specialists in customer-relationship based lending.

5.6 Nondepository Intermediaries

The focus of this chapter has been the three most common types of depository FI in the U.S. It has been indicated how the EMTS will significantly improve the market for consumer savings, and consequently its effects will fall primarily on CB, SLA, and MSB. There are, of course, other intermediaries in the economy that cater to the savings and investment needs of the household sector; however, these institutions differ substantially from the banks and NBI in the type of products and services that they provide.

The financial environment of the future will be characterized by lowered transaction costs and greater interest sensitivity on the part of the general public—two features that are central to the market for over-the-counter savings. These features, however, are at best peripheral in relation to the demand for the liabilities of life insurance companies, mutual funds, pension funds, and credit unions. In all of these cases there is at least one particular reason for investing one's funds, none of which will be directly affected by the EMTS. For this reason we conclude quite generally that EMTS effects on nondepository intermediaries will be far less extensive than those anticipated for the depository intermediaries. We will, however, briefly consider the EMTS with respect to four types of nondepository institutions, in order to point out several particular issues in this regard.

5.6.1 Life Insurance Companies

While it is unlikely that term life insurance will be greatly affected by an EMTS, life insurance company operations could be changed in two other ways.

First, nonterm insurance, as a form of contractual individual saving, could conceivably be affected adversely by new developments in the consumer savings market. While this is possible, we expect that it will not in fact occur for two reasons. To begin with, there is apparently a significant complementarity between (term) life insurance and contractual saving programs, and thus it is likely that such a joint product will continue to be demanded. Furthermore, there is the possibility that life insurance companies may become more competitive in the return they provide on the savings portion of a nonterm policy as a reaction to higher deposit rates offered by depository intermediaries. This is a difficult proposition to evaluate, since it depends on the change in various legal restrictions, the motivation of management, and economies of scale; but it could well be the overriding factor.

The second potential effect on life insurance companies lies in the area of policy loans. Many policy loans today bear quite low interest rates, due to legal restrictions on the companies. These loans can therefore be a cheap source of funds for policy holders to invest in the capital markets during tight money periods. This form of disintermediation occurred to a significant extent in 1966 and is likely to recur in the future. The insurance companies will have to develop schemes by which to raise their loan rates in order to avoid this disintermediation.[50]

5.6.2 Credit Unions

Credit unions are a fourth kind of depository FI, and the deposits they accept are similar in most respects to those of CB and NBI. Moreover, these institutions expanded rapidly during the 1960s: deposits more than tripled to $18 billion by 1970 while membership rose from 12 million to 22.8 million. They are mutual operations that can be formed in conjunction with any previously established institution or group (often they serve the employees of a single firm), in order to provide low cost unsecured loans for members. An employer will frequently contribute office space and automatically deduct savings funds and loan repayments from employees' paychecks. Credit unions thus provide a means of automatic saving akin to that of the EMTS preauthorized savings payments.

In spite of the fact that we expect the EMTS to lower the average cost of a consumer loan by the widespread use of overdrafts, it is to be doubted that any other institution could effectively compete with the loan rates offered by credit unions to their members. This is a case where credit unions have special expertise

---

50. The Hunt Commission has recommended that life insurance companies be permitted to vary the rate of interest on their policy loans according to movements in market interest levels. This would eliminate much of the appeal that such loans currently offer individuals interested in investing in the capital market.

and a superior position. (Due to their close relationship with members, credit unions have historically had very low bad debt losses.)

Nor is it likely that many credit unions would seek to compete with other intermediaries on a sizeable scale. They are limited in purpose, nonprofit, and in the main very small. (The median level of their total deposits being $200,000, with an average of about $750,000.[51] This small size prohibits aggressive competition for deposit funds due to diseconomies of scale, and restrictions on credit union membership are likely to prevent more than a very few institutions from achieving a competitive size. For these reasons we conclude that the effects of the EMTS on credit unions will be minimal.

5.6.3 Investment Funds

In recent years there has been a great deal of growth in the area of investment funds as channels for investable capital. A management group is formed, proceeds to assemble a portfolio of assets, and sells what are essentially participations in that portfolio to the public. The funds therefore differ from depository FI in a very fundamental manner: banks and savings institutions issue deposit claims that are their own liabilities, whereas the fund management issues no direct liabilities to shareholders. Moreover, the value of an investment fund share will fluctuate in value with the market value of the fund's portfolio.

Recent growth in these funds has been the result of several types of factors. First there is a desire to specialize in the holding of a particular type of asset—real estate, corporate bonds, equities, mortgages, etc.—and specialized funds have evolved to fill these various demands. Second, many alert savers have shifted their funds out of depository intermediaries in order to escape Regulation Q restrictions of their interest earnings and to hold assets whose capital value will not be eroded by inflation. Finally, rising real incomes in the U.S. have made it possible for individuals to hold larger portfolios, which can be quite well diversified. The need for the type of risk-pooling provided by depository intermediaries has therefore been reduced; instead, individuals can assemble their own portfolios of fund shares.

The effects of the EMTS on investment funds should be mixed. To begin with, there is no reason to believe that the EMTS will alter the nature of investor preferences in the economy. There will continue to be savers who are highly risk-averse and therefore who prefer a depository institution to any sort of fund. Furthermore, the adoption of Hunt Commission-type reforms in the savings industry will make the depository FI far more attractive outlets for investable funds. There will be fewer restrictions on the assets that can be purchased by intermediaries (leading to higher portfolio yields) and, more important, interest

51. Figures given in the Hunt Commission *Report*.

rate ceilings will be absent. Disintermediation will therefore no longer be necessary in order to earn higher rates of interest on one's savings. This should tend to diminish the funds' appeal. On the other hand, the (real of perceived) liquidity of fund shares should be increased under the EMTS because both pecuniary and nonpecuniary transaction costs will fall considerably. Easier access to one's fund shares should lead to an increased flow of savings into the investment funds.

Overall we expect that the funds will continue to serve a demand in the economy for specialized investment portfolios. While there may be some tendency for depository FI to manage such funds themselves (in an attempt to internalize interinstitutional flows of capital and to reduce transaction costs through economies of scale), there is no reason why the EMTS should make such funds obsolete.

5.6.4 Consumer Loan Companies

Consumer loan and finance companies constitute the one type of nondepository intermediary that is likely to be affected significantly upon the introduction of an EMTS, primarily due to the lines of credit that will be attached to many consumers' transaction accounts. As we have noted previously, the consumer loan market is a highly imperfect one, and consumer finance companies have become an important supplier of these high profit loans. But as more NBI expand into consumer lending, and as prenegotiated lines of credit come to cover many intermediate-sized durable expenditures, the demand for consumer finance company credit is likely to decline from its present level (25.4 percent of all consumer lending in 1970, or $31 billion). We would also expect increased competition from intermediaries to reduce interest rates (and therefore the profit margin) on at least some classes of finance company loans.

5.7 Conclusion

Such a radical series of changes in the financial intermediary sector as those anticipated in this chapter are certain to have ramifications in nearly every sector of the economy. Each financial institution will find itself operating in a very new environment, as will economic units in the nonfinancial sector. The sum of all these microeconomic adaptations to the EMTS will be the changes that occur at the macro level in the economy. We therefore turn in the next two chapters to a consideration of how the various economic units of the society will be affected by the EMTS. Finally, in Chapter 8 we will be in a position to assess the overall macroeconomic implications of the EMTS.

6

Portfolio and Deposit Management by Financial Intermediaries

We are now prepared to consider specific questions concerning the behavior of financial intermediaries under an electronic monetary transfer system (EMTS). The issues to be raised are not in themselves new; they concern the availability and pricing of loans, the terms of lines of credit, the role of compensating balances, and pricing and activity charges for various types of deposits. The analysis of these topics is, however, put into a new focus by the technology and related economic changes of an EMTS.

More specifically, there are three basic properties of an EMTS that will represent new conditions and new structures within which intermediaries must operate. These properties have been discussed at length in the two previous chapters, but it is worth listing them again here, since they serve as the foundation for the analysis of this chapter. The properties are:

1. Intermediaries will face an increased competitive environment with respect to interest yields on loans and deposits and with respect to services provided.
2. Depositors, as a result of an increased availability of information and lower transactions costs, will be highly interest and cost sensitive, both in evaluating different institutions' offerings and in choosing particular types of deposits within a given institution.
3. Household borrowers, in responding to the characteristics of an instantaneous transfer system containing preauthorized payments, will require overdraft facilities on demand deposit accounts; in addition, it is anticipated that for many households more extensive lines of credit, which can be drawn on as consumer loans, will be available.

Of these three changes, the third is the most important and innovative. Kenneth J. Thygerson in a memorandum dated September 1, 1970 for the United States Savings and Loan League has stated, for example:

> The wide use of bank credit cards [today] shows quite convincingly that the ETS ["electronic transfer system"] will provide both overdraft and/or consumer credit services to the individual participant in our economy. It is becoming apparent that in any attempt to analyze the ETS from the viewpoint of the consumer, it will be almost impossible to separate the transfer function from the consumer credit function.

The special significance of preauthorized lines of credit lies in the timing of reserve outflows from the intermediary. In the case of a normal loan, the funds are removed from the lending institution as soon as the loan is granted. In contrast, there is no definite or foreseeable time lag between the issuing of a credit line and its being taken-down (i.e., used). Merely by issuing such an overdraft privilege an intermediary must give up some control over its future reserve flows and portfolio adjustments. Outstanding credit lines thus represent an added source of uncertainty in the institution's operations.

Two more general factors should also be noted at the outset. First, our analysis here will be concerned primarily with intermediary decisions and behavior with respect to household-unit borrowers and depositors. This reflects our more basic conviction that an EMTS will have relatively little effect on business and corporate borrowing and deposits (where, for example, lines of credit and high deposit-rate elasticities are currently common). Indeed, to an important degree our analysis of consumer lending decisions will consist of adapting and incorporating into intermediary-household relations certain features that now apply to intermediary-business relations. Second, we will not in this chapter distinguish between bank and nonbank financial intermediaries. It has already been noted that we expect banks to continue to specialize in business loans and deposits while it is likely that savings institutions will continue their traditional roles in mortgage lending; in the area of household-unit loans and deposits, however, both types of institutions have already developed considerable expertise, and thus we expect them to operate competitively, and hence similarly, in household loan and deposit markets.

6.1 The Management of Consumer Loans and Lines of Credit

The combination of increased competition among intermediaries and demand on the part of household-units should lead, under an EMTS, to a significant expansion in the scope of consumer lending. This lending will take the form of both short-term lending through over-draft facilities and long-term installment lending to finance major purchases. To distinguish these terms, we shall refer to the short-term loans as *over-drafts* and the long-term loans as *consumer loans.* In this section we consider the intermediaries' likely response to an expanded consumer-loan market. We begin with a consideration of the actual loan contract and then proceed to an analysis of lines of credit that can be taken-down to finance expenditures.

6.1.1 The Pricing and Availability of Consumer Loans

In many ways, the most important financial characteristics of consumer loans are closely akin to commercial loans granted to small-business enterprises.

In both cases, the ability to repay the loan depends primarily on future income streams and not on currently available net worth. It thus follows that the likelihood of default is high in both cases, and default will be a paramount factor in the lender's decision on the size and the interest rate of the loan. Consequently, we can anticipate for consumer loans what is already the case for small commercial loans; namely that the lender will place great stress on personal knowledge of the borrower and on a satisfactory past relationship between the borrower and the lending institution.

The implications of the joint factors of high default risk and a close customer relationship have been previously analyzed in detail for the commercial loan market, and thus it is possible to provide a summary of this analysis with respect to the consumer loan market.[1] Consider a lender evaluating the expected profits to be obtained on a loan of size L at an interest rate r to some customer. If we let $R = 1 + r$ be the rate factor, then the size of the loan contract, including principal and interest, will be RL. Assume the lender attaches probabilities to the likelihood of any given contract being repaid such that if x is the contract amount (RL), then $f[x]$ is the probability (density function) of full repayment. It is convenient to assume that the lender is assured of repayment for loan contracts (RL) less than some amount k and holds no hope of repayment on contracts greater than some amount K. It is also necessary to consider the lender's opportunity cost of funds used for consumer loans. In the simplest case, this cost can be set in terms of an opportunity interest rate i, or an opportunity factor $I = 1 + i$. (For the moment we shall take this factor I as given, although we shall return to the determinants of I below.)

With this basis, the lender's expected profits from a loan in the amount L at a rate factor R can then be written:

$$\pi = RL \int_{RL}^{K} f[x]\,dx + \int_{k}^{RL} xf[x]\,dx - IL. \tag{6-1}$$

The first term represents the lender's expected income for those cases in which there is no default; the second term represents the bank's expected loan repayment in the amount x when this is less than the contract amount. The third term represents the opportunity cost of the loan; that is, the opportunity rate multiplied by the amount of funds allocated to the loan.[2]

Integrating this relationship by parts, (6-1) may be written:

$$\pi = (R - I)L - \int_{k}^{RL} F[x]\,dx, \tag{6-2}$$

---

1. See Dwight M. Jaffee, *Credit Rationing and the Commercial Loan Market*, (New York: Wiley, 1971). The analysis in this section closely follows Chapter 2 of *Credit Rationing*.

2. It can be seen that the lender is assumed to maximize expected profits and that in cases of partial default the lender receives the amount x without collection costs. For more details, see Jaffee, *op. cit.*, Chapter 2.

where $F[x]$ is the cumulative distribution of $f[x]$. Differentiating (6-2) with respect to the loan size L then yields the first order condition for an expected profit maximum:

$$\frac{\partial \pi}{\partial L} = R - I - R \cdot F[RL] = R(1 - F[RL]) - I = 0 \qquad (6\text{-}3)$$

This relationship may be interpreted as expressing the optimal loan size $\hat{L}$ as a function of any given interest rate factor R.

The shape of this relationship is shown in Figure 6-1 by the curve $\hat{L} = \hat{L}[R]$. (For the moment ignore the curve $D = D[R]$.) The pertinent features are: (1) for interest rate factors R that are less than I, the lender will provide no loan at all; (2) as the interest rate factor rises to the amount R_1, the loan size will rise to the amount $\hat{L}_1$; (3) as the interest rate factor rises above R_1, the loan size actually declines and approaches zero as R approaches infinity.

The particular shape of this function is important because it raises the possibility that a borrower may only obtain a loan of some maximum size ($\hat{L}_1$ in the figure) regardless of the interest rate factor that he offers to pay. In other words, nonprice rationing of consumer loans is a distinct possibility. In order to determine whether rationing actually occurs in any given situation, it is of course necessary to know the shape of the borrower's demand function for loans and the interest rate factor that is negotiated. One example is illustrated in Figure 6-1 by a borrower's demand function $D = D[R]$. For interest rate factors less than $\bar{R}$, it can be seen that the lender will supply a loan that is smaller than the loan demanded; thus, in this range, rationing will occur.

It is still a long step from the possibility of rationing illustrated in Figure 6-1, to an empirical verification that such rationing will indeed be an important aspect of the consumer loan market under an EMTS. Based on study of the commercial loan market, however, the following appears to be a likely course for the development of the EMTS consumer loan market.[3]

1. The rate of interest r charged on consumer loans will move in response to changes in market conditions, although the variations will be less than for rates on negotiable securities traded in open markets.
2. While lenders will have incentive to discriminate between different customers in terms of rate, the existence of a variety of social and legal constraints, and usury ceilings, indicate that extensive discrimination will be hard to achieve. Thus consumer credit customers will tend to be charged the same rate. The major distinctions that might arise among customers will be on the basis of collateral.
3. With the rate of interest determined by market conditions, and with relatively little risk-differentiation among customers, the *size* of the loan will

---

3. See Jaffee, *op. cit.*, especially pp. 49–57.

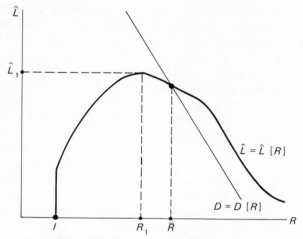

Figure 6-1. Long-Term Credit Rationing.

become the primary matter of negotiation between the lender and the borrower.

4.   In particular, borrowers will be offered a smaller loan than they desire in many cases. The size of the loan will depend on the factors determining the likelihood of loan repayment. These factors will include, among other things, the borrower's income and financial status, the type of collateral offered, and the nature of the customer's previous relationship with the lending institution.

This last point concerning the customer relationship deserves further emphasis, since it could represent a major bottleneck to the operation of an EMTS. To the extent that lending institutions weigh heavily personal contact and a customer's historic record with the institution, factors of location and convenience will still enter into intermediary competition. Alternatively, it is possible, particularly with an expanded consumer loan portfolio, that intermediaries may make greater use of objective computerized credit analyses. It is difficult to evaluate the likely outcome on this question at the present time.[4]

6.1.2 Lines of Credit for Consumer Loans

A line of credit for a consumer loan guarantees to a household unit the availability of loan funds at any time up to some specified future date. Whether

---

4. See also the discussion in Section 5.5 above.

the lender is granting a loan or approving a line of credit, he faces essentially the same problems of loan size, the rate of interest to be charged, and the maturity of the contract. Consequently, we anticipate that the lender will use the same general criteria in approving credit lines that he uses in granting standard loans.

Lines of credit do differ from standard loans, however, in that the lender must commit itself beforehand to the loan terms. By the time the line of credit is used, therefore, conditions may change and the lender may no longer wish to make the loan under the specified conditions. This suggests that lenders may be more cautious in approving lines of credit than in granting loans, and that they generally will charge the customer for the availability of the credit line.

The lending institution may adjust its behavior to the existence of lines of credit by changing the composition of its asset portfolio and by setting the terms on lines of credit so as to influence the amount of loans outstanding and the take-down rate. With respect to the portfolio composition, it would be expected that lending institutions would maintain more liquid portfolios as lines of credit are extended in order to reduce the risk of costly forced sales of hard to market securities. Specifically, shifts in portfolio holdings toward short-term assets, government securities, and, in the case of commercial banks, excess reserves should be anticipated. It may be noted, and will be discussed further in Chapter 7 below, that the shift toward more liquid portfolios by the lending institutions will be countered by a shift toward less liquid portfolios and asset holdings by household units upon the availability of lines of credits. In other words, the availability of lines of credit allows a change in the incidence of risk due to un-expected and stochastic payments toward the financial institutions and away from the household units. Owing to the economies of scale and diversification in large portfolios that may be achieved by the financial institutions, this is very likely an efficient change.

With respect to the pricing and terms of lines of credit, the rate of interest to be charged when the line is used poses the least problems. Following procedures currently used in commercial lending, it is most likely that the intermediary will charge the rate in effect on new loans at the time the line of credit is actually used. An alternative procedure would be for the lender to guarantee the rate at which the line may be used; in this case the rate could be set at some average of rates that are expected to prevail during the life of the line. But since this would entail additional risk for the intermediary, it would appear unlikely that there would be much inclination to follow this course.

With respect to the size of the line of credit, on the other hand, the lender must commit himself beforehand to some upper limit. This would be similar to the decision already discussed for new consumer loans, except that whereas the desired upper limit may change over time, the intermediary would have to commit himself to a single number for the life of the line. In particular, to the extent that the desired size of the loan contract falls, the intermediary would find himself tied to a larger than desired amount.[5] Referring to Figure 6-1 and Equation (6-3), several factors may be responsible for a reduction in the desired loan size:

1. A deterioration in the income or financial condition of the borrower will increase the likelihood of default and thus decrease the desired size of the loan.

2. A rise in the lender's opportunity rate I, owing to increases in market rates of interest, will cause the lender to seek a greater expected return on a consumer loan. This may be achieved, in general, by either raising the rate of interest on the loan, or by reducing the size of loan (thus reducing the likelihood of default.) In practice, we would expect both methods to be used, following the practice in commercial loan markets.

3. A rise in the lender's opportunity rate I, owing to internal pressures on the lender's loanable funds, will similarly make a higher expected return on consumer loans necessary. This internal pressure on loanable funds may arise, for example, because of unexpected take-downs of either commercial or consumer loans, which create problems of short-run adjustment for the intermediary. Problems of this nature are discussed further in Section (6.1.3).

Whatever means the lender uses in setting the terms of credit lines, he will still in some form have to recoup the costs and risks associated with providing the lines. Although it is difficult at this point to ascertain the specific manner in which charges for credit lines will be set, we can indicate the main possibilities, while noting that different methods may be used by different lenders and that more than one method may be adopted by the same lender. The main alternatives are:

1. Limiting the Maturity of the Line of Credit. By limiting the length of time for which the line of credit is in force, the lender can reduce the risk that changes in basic conditions may occur during the life of the credit line. Offsetting the advantage of short maturities, however, are the costs of frequent credit checks and of decision time. Also, of course, customers would naturally question the usefulness of credit lines for which the size limits were frequently changed with the state of monetary conditions. Thus, the likely result is that lines of credit will have relatively short *legal* maturities—much like bank credit cards do today—but *renewal in most cases will be automatic,* based perhaps on a computerized check for changes in the borrower's status. Only in cases indicating a significant change would the borrowing limit be redefined.

2. Including a Fee in the Loan Rate. To obtain more direct monetary compensation, the intermediary could add a special premium to the interest rate

---

5. If the desired size of the credit line rises then presumably the lender would simply increase the lending limits.

charged on the line when it is taken down. The loan rate would then include the cost of the lender's funds, a risk premium, and a "liquidity premium" to compensate the lender for the risk of providing the line. This method obviously suffers in terms of economic efficiency: holders of lines of credit who enjoy the guarantee of loan availability, but never actually make use of the available credit, would pay no charge for this service. Frequent users of the line, on the other hand, would pay more than should be rightfully assigned to their account. Even though the scheme suffers on this basis of efficiency, it does have an administrative simplicity, and would provide at least a reasonable first approach to the problem. Similar considerations also apply to the pricing of over-drafts on demand deposit accounts as noted below.

3. **Compensating Balance Requirements.**   Compensating balances are deposits maintained by borrowers or would-be borrowers as an implicit payment to the lender for a loan or line of credit. In commercial lending, compensating balances have remained something of an enigma. Both lenders and borrowers appear reluctant to discuss specific arrangements, only limited data are available on the extent and the form of the arrangements, and economists have had difficulty understanding the underlying rationale of such schemes when direct explicit pricing would seem to be both available and more efficient.[6] Given the presence of compensating balance schemes in commercial lending, however, at least the possibility of a similar scheme being adopted in consumer lending arrangements must be considered.

There appear two main routes that could be followed in adopting compensating-balance charging for credit lines. The first is an informal system in which the *quality* of the customer relationship is taken into account in determining the size of the credit line. For example, as a simple case, it is possible that lines of credit would be granted only to current customers of the lending institution. Indeed, this would be a necessary requirement if credit lines evolve as extensions of over-draft allowances available on demand deposit accounts.

The second possibility for compensating balance requirements is a more formal scheme in which an implicit cost of a line of credit is that the holder maintain some proportion of the line as a balance with the lending institution. The efficiency of such a scheme will depend on the precise manner in which it is implemented. Most analyses of the problem indicate that *minimum balance requirements*—where the customer's compensating balance is expressed in terms of the minimum balance he maintains in his account—will generally be less advantageous for the depositor than *average balance requirements*—where the customer is credited with his average balance. The explanation for this conclusion is that in the average balance case, the depositor still may use the deposit balance for transactions purposes as long as he maintains a satisfactory average account, whereas in the minimum balance case, the funds maintained as the

---

6. See also the discussion in Section 7.1.2.

compensating balance have no value to the depositor. In both cases, however, it should be noted that the intermediary must maintain reserves against the compensating balance, and this introduces a significant disadvantage from the standpoint of the institution.[7]

4. Direct Fees for Lines of Credit. Finally, the most efficient means of charging for a line of credit is an explicit and direct fee. There are many ways such fees could be constructed in terms of fixed and/or variable charges that relate to the maturity and the size of the line. The general principle, nevertheless, is clear: customers would be charged explicitly for the services provided by the line of credit. It should be noted, however, that intermediaries have in the past been reluctant to institute such direct fee systems. For example, in the current use of bank credit cards, the banks have not adopted fee schedules for either obtaining a card, or for using the credit facilities available between billing dates. This is due, presumably, to the imperfectly competitive nature of current bank credit card markets. Under the more competitive environment of an EMTS, however, it would be expected that the more efficient means of direct pricing would be used more often.

These available methods of credit line pricing may be examined further from the point of view of economic efficiency. To do this, a more formal model is useful. We shall assume that the lender has decided on the maximum loan size. (C_m) and the loan rate factor (R) in the manner described above. We assume further that the lender anticipates that on average over the life of the credit line, a loan in the amount $\bar{L}$ will actually be outstanding. The revenue that may be obtained for providing the credit line will then be determined, for each of the pricing schemes, as follows:

Direct Fee Pricing: Revenue $= w_1 C_m$. Under this scheme, the borrower pays a separate fee for the provision of the credit line regardless of whether the credit line is actually used. We assume for simplicity that the fee is proportional to the size of the line, with a proportionality factor w_1.

Including the Fee in the Loan Rate: Revenue $= w_2 \bar{L}$. Under this plan, when the credit line is used, the borrower pays not only the true loan rate (R), but also a fee that is proportional to the amount of the line used. The revenue under this plan is thus the proportionality factor (w_2) multiplied by the expected average take-down $(\bar{L})$.

Compensating Balance Fee: Revenue $= w_3 C_m \beta$. With this plan, the borrower must maintain a compensating balance with the lender in an amount equal to the balance rate times the size of the credit line (C_m). The value of this

---

7. See Douglas Hellweg, "A Note on Compensatory Balance Requirements," *Journal of Finance,* XVI (March 1961), p. 80, and William E. Gibson, "Compensating Balance Requirements," *National Banking Review,* II (March 1965), p. 390.

balance to the lender is given by β which accounts for both the opportunity rate factor I and the intermediary's reserve requirement.[8]

The total revenue that may be obtained on credit lines is thus:

$$V = w_1 C_m + w_2 \bar{L} + w_3 C_m \beta. \tag{6-4}$$

With the variables C_m, $\bar{L}$, R, and β all set for the borrower, the intermediary is then to choose the cost parameters w_1, w_2, and w_3 in such a way as to maximize profits. To determine the efficiency of the alternative pricing schemes, however, we must also consider the associated costs to the borrower. These costs will be determined as follows:

Direct Fee Pricing: Cost = $w_1 C_m$. For direct fee pricing, the borrower and lender have an equal evaluation of the cost (or revenue) associated with the fee.

Including Fee in the Loan Rate: Cost = $w_2 \bar{L}^b$. The borrower's cost under this scheme is similar to the expected revenue of the lender, except that the borrower and lender may not share the same expectations as to credit line use. Thus, $\bar{L}^b$ is the *borrower's* expected loan size, whereas $\bar{L}$ as used above is the *lender's* expected loan size.

Compensating Balance Fee: Cost = $w_3 C_m \alpha$. The amount of the compensating balance is again given by $w_3 C_m$. The factor α accounts for that proportion of the balance that would have been maintained in any case (for transactions) and the borrower's cost of funds.

The total cost to be paid by the borrower for the credit line is thus:

$$C = w_1 C_m + w_2 \bar{L}^b + w_3 C_m \alpha. \tag{6-5}$$

It is clear that in any negotiation between the lender and borrower, the lender will attempt to set the parameters w_1, w_2, and w_3 as high as possible, while the borrower will attempt to set them as low as possible. Thus, in order to analyze the actual outcome, a model of the negotiating process and of the institutional setting in which it takes place must be developed. It is possible, however, to consider directly the efficiency of alternative outcomes to the pricing problem. For an outcome to be economically efficient, the parameters should be chosen to maximize the revenue of the lender for a given value of the borrower's cost.[9]

---

8. More specifically, the higher the reserve requirement on deposits the smaller the proportion of compensating balances that may actually be used for investment, and thus the smaller the β factor. Similarly, the lower the opportunity rate I, the less the intermediary will earn on the available balances, and thus the lower will be β.

9. Equivalently, one could minimize the costs of the borrower for a given value of the lender's revenue.

Formally, using Equations (6-4), and (6-5), the problem is:

Maximize V, subject to the constraint $C = C_0$,

or using the Langrangean method,

Maximize $\psi = V - \lambda(C - C_0)$.

The first order conditions for an interior maximum are:

$$\frac{\partial \psi}{\partial w_1} = C_m(1 - \lambda) = 0 \tag{6-8a}$$

$$\frac{\partial \psi}{\partial w_2} = \bar{L} - \lambda \bar{L}^b = 0 \tag{6-8b}$$

$$\frac{\partial \psi}{\partial w_3} = C_m(\beta - \lambda \alpha) = 0. \tag{6-8c}$$

It is apparent (upon solving for λ in each equation) that for an interior solution, with C_m positive, we must have $\lambda = 1 = \bar{L}/\bar{L}^b = \beta/\alpha$. In other words, a pricing solution with all three methods used simultaneously can be efficient only if (1) the lender and borrower expect the same loan take-down rate ($\bar{L} = \bar{L}^b$) and (2) view the cost and revenue of compensating balance requirements equally ($\beta = \alpha$).[10] If these conditions are not met, then one or more of the pricing systems should not be used. More specifically, if $\bar{L} > \bar{L}^b$ (and $\alpha > B$) then only the method of including the fee in the loan charge should be used; the result follows because then the lender would anticipate a higher revenue than the cost anticipated by the borrower, making the system desirable. Similarly, if $\beta > \alpha$ (and $\bar{L} < \bar{L}^b$), then only the compensating-balance fee should be used; this would be efficient because the balance would be of more value as revenue to the lender than as a cost to the borrower, again a desirable situation. Finally, we can note that if $\bar{L} < \bar{L}^b$ and $\beta < \alpha$, then only the direct fee system should be used, and if $\bar{L} > \bar{L}^b$ and $\beta > \alpha$, then the direct fee system should not be used.

It is, of course, an empirical question which of these cases holds currently, and it is even more difficult to speculate which will hold under an EMTS. For example, as already noted, the efficiency of compensating-balance requirements depends critically on the level of reserve requirements, on the relative opportu-

---

10. This interpretation of Equation (6-8) assumes that α, β, and $\bar{L}^b$ are all determined independently of the cost parameters w_1, w_2 and w_3. If, in fact, there is a dependency, then this must be taken into account in interpreting the results.

THE ECONOMIC IMPLICATIONS OF AN EMTS

nity costs of the lender and borrower, and on the extent to which the borrower can continue to make use of compensating balances for transactions purposes. Without such data for the EMTS economy, the efficiency of the various techniques cannot be evaluated.

6.1.3 Dynamic Adjustments with Credit Lines

Regardless of how the limits and costs of lines of credit are assigned, the lender will not be able to eliminate fully the risk that large numbers of credit lines will be taken-down at the same time, thereby creating a strain on the lender's liquidity. Commercial lenders, for example, currently face an especially severe problem in this respect because business and commercial credit demands tend to be highly correlated. This high correlation of the business and commercial credit demand of individual borrowers occurs because each firm responds to essentially the same stimuli: high rates of investment or other sources of high aggregate demand, followed by reduced availability of trade credit and a large demand for funds in capital markets, accompanied by pressure on the banks' loanable reserves. Consumer lenders, on the other hand, may find the correlation of demand by individual household units to be somewhat lower. Whatever the actual case, however, the provision of lines of credit to household units will require a significant amount of adaptation on the part of the lending institutions.

More specially, we can follow through the possible adjustment paths that are available to a lending institution in periods of unexpected take-downs of consumer credit lines. To start, consider an institution with outstanding lines of credit in the amount C_m and with an average quantity of loans outstanding on these lines of $\bar{L}$. Now allow an increase in the use of credit lines (say to amount L, where $\bar{L} < L < C_m$). If this change reflects a new long-run equilibrium with respect to the proportion of credit lines that are taken-down, then in the long-run we would expect the lending institutions to adjust by changing the cost parameters and lending rates on these loans. Our concern here, however, is with a short-run situation in which the lending limits are set and the lender is responsible for meeting the demands up to the amount C_m.

The adjustment alternatives that are open to the lender can be seen most clearly from the institution's balance sheet identity, which may be written:

$$DD + TD + OS + E = L + OL + S + RR + ER \qquad (6-9)$$

where:

DD = Demand Deposits

TD = Time Deposits

OS = Other Sources of Funds

E = Net Worth

L = Consumer Loans Outstanding

OL = Other Loans Outstanding

S = Securities Held

RR = Required Reserves

ER = Excess Reserves

The left-hand side of the identity represents the alternative sources of funds and the right side of the identity represents the alternative uses of funds. In terms of Equation (6–9), the short-run disequilibrium of the lender is represented by an unexpected increase in consumer loans L. To adjust, then, the lender must either increase the available sources of funds or reduce the alternative uses of funds.

With respect to an increase in the available sources of funds, demand deposits, time deposits and equity are all currently difficult to adjust on a short-run basis. Changes in equity are difficult to effect because of the complicated procedures involved in new stock issues; changes in demand deposits are difficult to achieve because there is no interest yield that can be adjusted; and changes in time deposits are difficult both because Regulation Q ceilings may constrain the intermediary and because household units are not sufficiently interest sensitive to allow changes in the rate to be an important short-run determinant of their time-deposit holdings. Consequently, under the present regime, commercial banks have relied on other sources of funds, including various types of certificates of deposits, Eurodollar funds, and Federal Reserve discounts for their short-run adjustment. Under an EMTS, however, we would expect significant changes in these priorities. Demand deposits, for example, assuming that they yield interest, would respond to changes in the rate paid, and thus could be increased. Similarly, time-deposit holders will be significantly more interest sensitive and will have available to them transfer facilities such that the depositor may shift funds into savings accounts quickly and at relatively low cost. Consequently, we would expect that, under the EMTS, short-run adjustments by lenders would take the form more of adjusting deposit rates on both time and demand deposits, and less of acquiring funds in the (more costly) certificate and Eurodollar markets.

With respect to a reduction in alternative uses of funds in case of an unexpected take-down of consumer loans, we would expect an EMTS to have less effect on the lender's response. Currently, the lender has three main choices: he may decrease free reserves (either by decreasing excess reserves or increasing borrowed reserves), he may sell securities, or he may not renew or issue new loans to commercial or consumer borrowers. In addition, securities may be sold, although there is a question of which maturity to sell. Available empirical studies of bank behavior with respect to these alternatives have not provided a clear picture of which route intermediaries generally choose. In particular, it appears the choice depends on a complicated set of factors including the expected length of the disequilibrium, the costs of alternative transactions, expected changes in interest rates (including term structure considerations), tax considerations, and institutional and legal factors that require specific securities to be held. While this situation may not be encouraging from the standpoint of predicting bank response to short-run disequilibrium, our main concern here, and our main point, is that there are no apparent reasons why the EMTS should substantially alter bank behavior in these respects.

In summary, the addition of credit lines for household units will represent an additional source of demand for bank and other intermediary funds that may arise at unexpected or undesired moments. The intermediaries will thus have to be sensitive in setting their limits on credit lines and adopting their portfolio composition to the possibility that many of the lines may be taken-down at the same time. On the other hand, the increased interest sensitivity of depositors, and the ability to change deposit rates on all types of accounts, together with bankers' previous experience with commercial loan lines of credit, indicate that the adjustment to this aspect of an EMTS will not be especially serious. Finally, it should be added that several significant macroeconomic issues do arise in this context. First, there is the question whether the existence of readily accessible consumer credit will tend to displace in intermediary portfolios other socially important securities. One aspect of this topic was discussed in Chapter 5, where emphasis was placed on the relationship between consumer loan and mortgage loan portfolios. Second, there is the question of how the increased availability of consumer loans will affect the cyclical stability and long-run level of consumption expenditures. Third, there is the question of how intermediary borrowing will affect the velocity of money. These latter two questions are taken up in Chapter 8.

6.2 The Pricing of Time Deposits

The behavior of financial intermediaries with respect to the pricing of time deposits will be a second major area affected by the introduction of an EMTS. Currently, the interest yield set by an intermediary on its time deposits is based essentially on four factors: the yield obtained on the institution's earning assets, the costs of administering the account, the level of the reserve requirement, and the profit margin over costs. Under an EMTS, these four factors would continue to be relevant, although with some possible changes in importance. Three new factors, however, will also have to be taken into account by the intermediaries in determining their pricing policies under an EMTS.

First, the ability of depositors to transfer funds between time deposit accounts and demand deposit accounts will be significantly increased. In the present situation, such a transfer must either be done by mail, with its incumbent delays and uncertainties, or a trip must be made to the institution itself. Under the EMTS, on the other hand, such a transfer will be achieved by a telephone call. Furthermore, under an EMTS, the marginal costs of making such a transfer will be very small, and thus, given competition, we would expect the charge for this service to be also very small. Intermediaries are likely to respond to this situation under an EMTS in two ways. First, this increased flexibility for depositors should cause the intermediaries to enforce more rigorously the stated maturities of their time deposits. In the present situation, intermediaries generally allow withdrawals from passbook accounts on demand, with only minor and not always enforced rules concerning the number of such withdrawals per month. If this policy were to continue under an EMTS, however, individuals would maintain only minimal demand deposit accounts, transferring funds from time deposits to demand deposits at frequent intervals. In addition to the undesirable demand deposit-time deposit mix that would result, intermediaries would also have to undertake large fixed costs in the installation of computer power to handle the high volume of transactions between the two forms of accounts. The upshot, then, is that we expect financial intermediaries to treat time deposits as liabilities of fixed maturity, which, in general, cannot be withdrawn on demand.[11,12]

A second new factor under the EMTS will be that intermediaries will have to offer a much larger variety of maturities for their time deposits. This will arise because, as just described, if maturity dates are strictly enforced, then depositors may well require a fairly wide choice of alternatives. In fact, intermediaries may have to allow for a continuum of maturities, with the depositor selecting the maturity when he opens the account, and the rate he receives being a function of that maturity. This innovation would thus be essentially an extension of the maturity choice already offered by banks on certificates of deposit.

The third new factor under an EMTS, and one that has been discussed above, will be the increased interest rate sensitivity of depositors. This sensitivity will be reflected in the depositor's choice of secondary versus primary securities, in his choice of financial intermediaries, in the choice of his demand-deposit time-deposit mix, and in the particular maturity of his time deposits. At all these levels, financial intermediaries will face much higher interest-rate elasticities.

11. Intermediaries, at least at first, may have to allow "emergency" withdrawals on demand. It would be expected, however, that a significant charge, perhaps the loss of accrued interest, would be paid for the deposit withdrawal, and this would eliminate the possibility of any profitable shifting of funds between demand deposits and time deposits on a short-term basis.

12. The payment of interest on demand-deposit accounts is an alternative or complementary technique to meet the problem of frequent shifting between demand deposit and time deposit accounts. This possibility is discussed in Section 6.3.1.

6.2.1 A Model of Time-Deposit Pricing

The interaction of the various factors that affect time-deposit pricing can be illustrated with a simple model. We shall begin with a basic case, and then develop the effects of various extensions. To start, assume the intermediary issues only one deposit liability, purchases only one (risk-free) asset, and that the deposit and asset are of the same maturity. Furthermore, assume that the demand for deposits is an increasing function of the deposit rate, and that the yield on assets is taken as given by the intermediary. The intermediary's profit function can then be written:

$$\pi = i(kD) - r(D). \tag{6-10}$$

The first term reflects the intermediary's net income on its assets: i is the yield on assets, D is the level of deposits, and k is a factor that adjusts deposits for the costs of running the account and for reserve requirements. The second term is the cost of deposits, that is, the deposit rate r times the level of deposits D.

Differentiating this profit function with respect to the deposit rate then yields the first order condition for a profit maximum:

$$\frac{\partial \pi}{\partial r} = i(kD') - D - r(D') = 0, \tag{6-11}$$

where $D' = \partial D/\partial r$. By arranging terms we have:

$$r = ki - D/D'. \tag{6-12}$$

Equation (6-12) clearly illustrates the basic factors that determine the deposit rate. The yield on earning assets is i, and the deposit rate will be positively related to this yield. The costs of maintaining the account and the reserve requirements are implicit in k; the greater the costs or the greater the reserve ratio, the lower will be k, and thus the lower will be the deposit rate. Finally, the last term in (6-12) is a measure of the market power of the intermediary and thus is related to the intermediary's ability to obtain monopolist profits. For example, if the intermediary is a perfect competitor, then the derivative D' will be infinite, and thus the last term will be zero. Otherwise, the last term will be positive and the greater the market power of the intermediary, as measured by this term, the lower will be the deposit rate. We can thus immediately note that increased competition and interest-sensitivity in time deposit markets, which have the effect of increasing D', will lead to higher deposit rates being paid to depositors.

Table 6-1
Alternative Strategies for Deposit-Rate Setting[a]

Strategy	Asset Maturity	Liability Maturity	Net Expected Yield of Portfolio
A	1 year + 1 year	1 year + 1 year	$(i_1 + i_{1e}) - (r_1 + r_{1e})$
B	2 year	1 year + 1 year	$(2\,i_2) - (r_1 + r_{1e})$
C	1 year + 1 year	2 year	$(i_1 + i_{1e}) - (2\,r_2)$
D	2 year	2 year	$(2\,i_2) - (2\,r_2)$

[a]The calculation of the net expected yield are based, to simplify, on *simple interest* (no compounding). The cost factor k, common to all the strategies, is not shown.

6.2.2 Extension of the Model

It has been indicated that an important feature of intermediary behavior under an EMTS will be the availability of deposits of many different maturities. Thus, in order to provide a realistic model of time-deposit pricing under an EMTS, it is necessary to extend the basic model to allow for the possibility that the intermediary may issue deposits and purchase assets of various maturities. Not surprisingly, the extension of the basic model that is required is essentially an application of propositions from the theory of the term structure of interest rates. The main results are most easily illustrated with a simple example.

Assume the intermediary has a planning horizon of two years, and that it may purchase assets of maturity 1 year or 2 years, and may issue liabilities also of maturity 1 year and 2 years. Denote the yields available on the assets as i_1 and i_2 and the rates on the deposits as r_1 and r_2 respectively. Also denote the *expected* rate for 1 year assets and 1 year deposits, one year in the future, as i_{1e} and r_{1e}. With these conditions, there are four separate strategies that could be followed by an intermediary, depending on whether it takes a long or short position in the assets and deposits; these strategies are illustrated in Table 6-1. The determination of deposit rates under such conditions can be separated into two distinct parts: first, the determination of the *term structure*, that is, how r_1 and r_2 are related to one another; and, second, the determination of the *level* of the deposit rates as might be measured, for example, by the average of r_1 and r_2.

Considering the term structure problem first, the results of the *expectations hypothesis* of the term structure of interest rates are particularly useful. According to the expectations hypothesis, rates on securities of different maturities must adjust such that the expected holding yields for all available strategies are equal. For the expectations hypothesis to be valid, and for this condition to hold, there must exist a sufficiently large set of investors (depositors) and borrowers

(intermediaries) with the ability to arbitrage between deposit markets of different maturities. As we have already indicated, both the increased competition
between intermediaries and the increased interest sensitivity of depositors make
this likely to occur under an EMTS.[13]

In terms of Table 6-1, it can be seen that the expectations hypothesis
implies that the net yields shown in the last column must all be equal. Otherwise, investors would not wish to invest in one or more classes of securities, and
market forces would move the rate structure back into the proper alignment. To
illustrate, let us assume that the rate on 2 year deposits exceeds the sum of the
rate on 1 year deposits and the expected rate, for one year hence, on 1 year
deposits. From Table 6-1, it can be seen that the intermediary would follow
only strategies A and B, and would not issue any 2 year deposits. Depositors, on
the other hand, would wish to purchase only 2 year deposits. Clearly then, the
market for time deposits would not be in equilibrium, and the rates would be
forced back in line if the market were to function.

The implication of the expectations hypothesis for deposit-rate setting
therefore requires that the condition,

$$r_2 = (r_1 + r_{1e})/2, \tag{6-13}$$

hold in equilibrium. That is, deposit rates for different maturities must be such
that the holding yields for any given horizon must all be equal.[14] This result
obviously generalizes from the two year case discussed here to any fixed horizon.

While Equation (6-13) is notable for its simplicity, a somewhat more complicated, but perhaps more realistic, version of the expectations hypothesis has
been developed to incorporate *habitat* considerations.[15] A habitat may be
defined as the maturity that would be selected by an investor were everything
else, including the risk and yield on all securities, the same. Hicks, for example,
has suggested that many investors would have an inclination, everything else the
same, to invest in short maturity assets; it is also possible that certain investors,
life insurance companies for example, would be inclined toward long maturity
portfolios. Whatever the case, the existence of habitats among important groups
of depositors or among the intermediaries themselves, would lead to a bias in the

13. The main alternative to the expectations hypothesis is what may be termed the
segmentation theory. According to the segmentation theory, there exists very little interaction between markets for securities of different maturities. Thus, the deposit rates on
different maturity deposits would *each* be determined by the demand and supply for
deposits in the same manner, as described below, that the *level* of deposit rates is determined
under the expectations hypothesis.

14. This formulation assumes the payment of simple interest without compounding.
A geometric average of r_1 and r_{1e} should be used to take account of compounding.

15. See, for example, John Hicks, *Value and Capital,* second edition, (London: Oxford
University Press, 1946); and Franco Modigliani and Richard Sutch, "Innovations In Interest
Rate Policy," *American Economic Review,* (May 1966), pp. 178-197.

term structure of deposit rates such that lower deposit rates would be paid on those maturities for which there is relatively great depositor demand and/or relatively weak intermediary supply.

Assuming that the term structure of deposit rates has been determined, we can now turn to the question of the level of deposit rates. The supply of deposits by the intermediaries and the demand for deposits by the households can both be considered a function of any single deposit rate, or for convenience, a function of the average level of the deposit rate. Thus, the level of the deposit rate is determined simply such that the total market for deposits is cleared. Under conditions of perfect competition, this is the familiar equality of demand and supply. Under imperfect competition, intermediaries will set the *level of* deposit rates at some lower level, depending on the extent of their market power and the elasticity of demand. Note, however, that even under imperfect competition, as long as the expectations hypothesis holds the term structure will be determined along the lines of Equation (6–13). If the expectations hypothesis does not hold, then the term structure as well as the level of deposit rates will be a function of the market power of intermediaries and the elasticity of demand in the various markets.

6.2.3 Summary of Time-Deposit Pricing

To review the main results of this section, it would appear that the major *structural* change in the time-deposit market will be the increased availability of deposit securities for different maturities. The interest-rate pricing of these deposits would be expected to follow the principles of the term structure of interest rates and the expectations hypothesis, although with some bias toward lower rates on those maturities for which either the depositors have a preferred habitat or the intermediaries have an unpreferred habitat.

With respect to the average level of deposit rates, the most important factor is likely to be the increased competitive environment and the increased interest-rate sensitivity of depositors. Both of these factors will force intermediaries to pay higher rates on all deposit maturities. The result will be that the amount of financial intermediation in the economy will increase and that the intermediaries themselves will use interest rates as their major competitive device for attracting and maintaining time deposits.

6.3 The Pricing of Demand Deposit Accounts

The major technological and direct economic effects of the EMTS occur with respect to demand deposit accounts, and thus it may be anticipated that intermediaries will be responsive in changing their pricing policies on demand deposit accounts to the new conditions. Specifically, three conceptually distinct aspects of demand deposit accounts should be considered: the account as a short-term deposit at the intermediary; the account's use for external transfer into and out of the intermediary; and borrowing from the intermediary that occurs with the use and provision of over-draft facilities.[16]

6.3.1 The Payment of Interest on Demand Deposit Balances

We first return to an issue that was initially raised in Chapter 4—namely the payment of interest on transactions balances. It was shown in Chapter 4 that welfare maximization generally requires the payment of interest on transactions balances. But in order for this actually to occur, the intermediaries must be induced by economic forces to pay this interest, and the current legislated prohibition of interest payments on demand accounts must also be removed.

With respect to the legislated prohibition of interest on demand deposit balances, it would appear this restriction is likely to be eliminated even in the absence of the EMTS. Already, banks that wish, for competitive reasons, to pay interest on such accounts have found ways to achieve this; for example, free or low-cost services that are provided by banks are perhaps best interpreted as the payment of interest in kind.[17] Under an EMTS the prohibition against interest payments will become even more difficult to enforce. In particular, to circumvent the prohibition, banks could have customers maintain their funds in time deposit accounts (which pay interest) but agree to transfer funds into the demand deposit account whenever a third party transfer was requested. With the convenience of electronic transfers, it would be difficult for the Federal Reserve to set regulations that would effectively stop the banks from undertaking such arrangements. Consequently, we do not consider the current prohibition of interest payments on demand deposit balances a significant problem for the EMTS.

With respect to the economic forces that will induce banks and other intermediaries to pay interest on demand deposit balances, let us suppose, for the moment, that the EMTS comes into existence and that intermediaries continue to maintain traditional demand deposit accounts (from which third party payments are made but which pay no interest) and time deposit accounts (which pay interest but are of fixed maturity with no external transfer privileges). If the cost of transferring funds internally between these two types of accounts is suf-

---

16. Demand deposit accounts are being defined here as accounts from which external third party transfer may be made. This differs from the current legal definition of such accounts.

17. See Robert J. Barro and Anthony J. Santomero, "Household Money Holdings and the Demand Deposit Rate," *Journal of Money, Credit and Banking,* (May 1972).

ficiently low, then clearly funds will never be stored in the demand deposit account. Instead, depositors will take advantage of the low cost of transfer to maintain as much of their "transactions" oriented funds as possible in the shortest maturity interest-paying time deposit account.

The resulting shuffling of funds back and forth from time deposit accounts to demand deposit accounts, in addition to being socially unproductive, is likely to be unprofitable for the intermediary. In particular, the intermediary would have to maintain a sufficiently large computer to handle the large volume of internal transfers between accounts. While a fee system could be introduced to meet the costs of these internal transfers, competition between intermediaries would force a *marginal cost* pricing system which, given the high fixed costs of the computer technology, would generally still result in a loss. Consequently, intermediaries would obviously be eager to find some device that would eliminate the incentive to depositors to shift funds between demand deposits and time deposits.

The payment of a competitive interest rate on demand deposit balances would appear to be exactly the right device.[18] As a first approximation, demand deposits could be treated as very short maturity time deposits. The interest rate paid on demand deposits would then follow the same term structure relationships already developed above for time deposits. Demand deposits, of course, would still differ from time deposit accounts due to the ability to make external transfers and to use over-draft facilities from the account. Even ignoring these two issues, however, there remains the problem that demand deposits, by their very nature, can have no set maturity. Thus, even if by experience the intermediary could evaluate *ex ante* the average maturity (or turnover rate) of a demand deposit balance, there remains the possibility that *ex post* the volatility of this balance could vary widely. This uncertain volatility of demand deposit balances makes it important that the intermediary hold reserves and liquid assets to cover the stochastic cash flows. Consequently, the volatility represents a real cost to the intermediary and we must anticipate that the interest yield on demand deposit accounts will, in fact, be less than the level indicated solely by term structure considerations.

This analysis also leads to a clarification of practical issues relating to the socially optimal level of interest payment on demand deposit accounts. According to the literature on the "optimal supply of money," interest should be paid on transactions balances. But it has not always been clear at what level this rate

---

18. It may appear that the fixing of deposit maturities, the charges for transfers between time and demand deposit accounts, *and* the payment of interest on demand deposit accounts, are more tools than are necessary for the problem at hand. It should be noted, however, that the intermediaries will be attempting to meet three conditions: the competitive pricing of fees for internal transfers, limitations on the number of such transfers, and the optimal demand-deposit, time-deposit mix. Consequently, three tools are, in fact, required to meet these objectives.

should be set. Simple demonstrations of this proposition in the literature indicate only that transactions balances should yield "the" rate of interest; but while it has been understood that in practice some lower rate would have to be paid, the specific considerations have not been developed.[19] With the separation of the functions of demand deposit accounts that has been developed here, however, the issues are quite clear. First, there is the issue of maturity; we must anticipate that demand deposits would be treated as deposits of very short maturity in setting the deposit rate. Second, there are the fees for external transfers and for the use of over-draft facilities with demand deposit accounts. These fees could be interpreted as deductions from the depositor's gross yield to pay for the maintenance of his demand deposit balance. Third, there are the costs of the stochastic volatility of demand deposits; the fees charged for these costs may also be interpreted as deductions from the gross yield.

Thus we can anticipate, as a practical matter, that generally the net yield on demand deposit accounts would be significantly below the yield on time deposits. This then raises the question whether the conditions for the "optimal supply of money" are actually being met. The answer is yes; the costs that are deducted from the gross yield on demand deposits represent the real costs of managing these accounts and thus should be included in determining the socially desirable net yield. On the other hand, it does remain true, of course, that an even more desirable situation could exist if the costs of managing demand deposit accounts were reduced toward zero.[20]

6.3.2 Charges for External Transfers

The likely results under an EMTS for the pricing of external transfers from demand deposit accounts and for the use of over-draft facilities are quite clear once the payment of the gross yield for the balances is determined. With respect to the fees for transferring funds externally to and from demand deposit accounts, we have already indicated in Chapters 3 to 5 the major technological and economic factors that are relevant. In particular, it was stressed that with the appropriate marginal cost pricing for transfer services, the socially optimal volume of system use will be achieved. The details of the pricing system, however, are more difficult to anticipate. Issues such as fixed versus variable costs (depending on the size of a transaction), peak load pricing, and specific destina-

19. See, for example, Harry G. Johnson, "Is There an Optimal Supply of Money," *Journal of Finance,* (May 1970), pp. 435–442.

20. This suggests, in other words, that even when the "correct" interest yield is paid on demand deposits, a reduction in the costs of carrying out transactions is still desirable. Thus, both the payment of interest and the reduced transactions costs for demand deposits under the EMTS are steps toward the optimal supply of money.

tion changes, cannot be really settled until the precise properties of the physical system are finally developed.

One important feature of external transfer services should, however, be stressed. As a general rule, it would appear that external transfers are not likely to be a profitable service for intermediaries. This follows mainly from the technological features of transfers under an EMTS. As already indicated the real *marginal cost* of effecting a transfer under the EMTS is likely to be very low, and may be declining over a large part of the relevant range of use. The fixed costs for computer capital, on the other hand, are likely to be large. It thus follows that intermediaries would have to follow some form of *average cost* pricing if they are to avoid losses in providing this service. Unlike public utilities who face a similar problem and use their local market monopoly power to attempt to set price above marginal cost, the intermediaries will find themselves in a very competitive market in which it will be difficult to price above marginal cost. While it is not likely that the final result will find intermediaries running significant losses on transfer services, it is equally unlikely that transfer services will provide them with significant profits.

6.3.3 Charges for Over-Draft Facilities

With respect to the provision of over-draft facilities, the main terms that are to be determined are the interest rate charged when the facilities are used, the limits on the maximum credit available, the maturity of a given credit line agreement, and any charges for the availability of the credit line. For all these decisions, we expect the considerations already developed for consumer credit lines to apply with only minor changes. The most important point of negotiation will remain the size of the line of credit, and it is here that there may be one difference between an over-draft credit line and a consumer loan credit line. Whereas a consumer loan credit line will in all likelihood *not* be available to all depositors, at least some small over-draft facility will be necessary to carry out demand deposit transfers under an EMTS. Without such a facility, overdrawn accounts would be commonplace in a system with a significant number of pre-authorized transfers.

6.4 Summary

This chapter has dealt with several of the most important respects in which the operations of an intermediary will be affected under the EMTS. The basic forces causing these changes are the competitive environment of an EMTS, the interest-sensitivity of depositors, and the opportunity for the intermediaries to provide credit lines for consumer loans and demand-deposit accounts. The major implication for intermediary management will be that the institutions will have to be much more responsive to competition and market conditions if they are to continue to attract deposits. Specifically, in terms of deposits, demand deposit accounts will have to pay interest, and a variety of time deposit accounts of different maturity will have to be available. In terms of assets, the intermediaries will have to develop procedures for evaulating consumer requests for lines of credit. From a social point of view, the net result will be a significantly greater degree of financial intermediation. The effects of this intermediation on the other sectors of the economy and on macroeconomic aggregates are considered in the following two chapters.

7

Implications for the
Nonfinancial Sectors

An operational EMTS will offer a large number of new services and features
to the nonfinancial sectors of the economy, and by properly taking advantage of
these features individual economic units will be able to achieve significant savings, both pecuniary and nonpecuniary. Moreover, the increased degree of
specialization that will evolve in the management of payments and credit presents the potential for greater overall economic efficiency.

Central to the determination of the efficiency effects of the EMTS will be
the exact scheme used to price the system's services. The question of an optimal
pricing arrangement for an electronic network such as the EMTS is an interesting
one. First, there are two distinct and basic factors involved in EMTS pricing. The
first is the information switching capacity of the national computer network,
whose services will be priced by *its* owners; the second is the information processing that will be provided by banks for their customers. Almost all payments or
funds transfers will involve the use of both these segments of the EMTS.

In addition, there are three main issues affecting the optimal pricing of
EMTS services. The first issue arises from the fact that an electronic transfer
system has many similarities with the "bridge problem" of welfare economics.
After an initial large investment, marginal operating costs (in this case, the cost
of a marginal message flowing through the system) are nearly constant and
extremely low—in many instances they are effectively zero. Setting the price
equal to marginal cost therefore will lead to continuing losses. But average cost
pricing, which would produce a profit for EMTS owners, is inefficient. In addition, we must take into account the inefficiency that is inherent in operating
parallel (that is, competing) switching systems, as discussed in Chapter 4. Thus,
the first issue is equivalent to the determination of an optimal pricing scheme for
a monopolistic public utility, if we are to price EMTS services properly. There is
alaready a large literature on this topic, and we are not in a position to criticize
or expand on it here.

A second important issue is that of peak versus off-peak pricing. As was
mentioned in Chapter 4, EMTS owners should be able to exercise considerable
control over the demand for the system's services by manipulating peak prices.
There is an extensive economic literature on this topic as well. For a discussion

of peak pricing of a computer system's services in particular, the reader is referred to Sharpe's *The Economics of Computers.*[1]

The third issue to be considered in setting prices for the system is the externalities involved in the operation of a payments system. An efficient and well-functioning monetary system is a vital segment of a modern economy. Indeed, the Federal Reserve System today subsidizes the check-clearing mechanism by providing facilities to the commercial banking system, and we may well see a continuation of such national subsidies (to the EMTS operators) in the future.

Rather than attempt to deal specifically with pricing problems such as these, we will make a simplifying assumption for the purpose of our analysis in this chapter. We will suppose that there is a per-transaction charge (independent of the money value of the transaction) for any EMTS transfer of funds, which will be borne by the payor in any exchange. This charge will be considerably less than the cost of processing a check today. This assumption is probably a fair approximation to eventual EMTS pricing: the marginal costs of message switching and processing in the system will be quite low, and they should be constant up to the point where some part of the system becomes overloaded.[2] By using this price assumption, we will be able to determine the direction of change in economic activities at the micro level that will be induced by the EMTS, and it is this type of qualitative analysis that is the thrust of the current chapter. In the following sections we will examine separately the implications for corporations that deal primarily with the industrial sector, for retailers, and for consumers in the economy.

7.1 Manufacturing Firms

We stated in Chapter 4 that the EMTS will provide only limited new services for manufacturing firms, at least when compared with its effects on consumers. Corporations that require a bank line of credit can readily apply for one today, so credit lines will not be a new innovation for the firm in the future (as it will be for consumers). Similarly, cash discounts are currently a common practice in intercorporate trade and we can expect such discounts to continue when payments are made electronically. This is not, however, to imply that EMTS ramifications for the corporate sector will be small. The financial operations of manufacturing firms (particularly the smaller ones) will be affected extensively by the

---

1. William F. Sharpe, *The Economics of Computers,* (New York: Columbia University Press, New York, 1969).

2. At this point, congestion costs and waiting times will arise, thereby raising the cost of using the system. These costs could be alleviated by (1) expanding capital investment in the overloaded sector of the EMTS; or (2) arranging peak and off-peak prices so as to shift demand away from periods of peak usage.

giro aspects of the EMTS, the increased amount of financial information that flows through their banks, and the speed with which funds are transferred when payments are made in the system.

7.1.1 Financial Specialization

The fact that almost all financial transactions of the firm will pass through its bank *and be recorded there* (for any of several reasons) presents the potential for a major change in current financial practices. The crucial difference inherent in an EMTS is this: whereas under the check payment system the bank processes merely the dollar amount of a firm's checks, the giro nature of payments in the future will require that the bank's computer know the *payee* as well as the amount of each transaction. For this reason the bank will be in a prime position to replace its corporate customers' accounting departments. There is no need for exactly the same information (that is, payee, amount, date, etc.) regarding each transaction to be processed first by the bank and then by the firm. Clearly, specialization will yield economies in this area, and since the bank must process this accounting information in order to effect payments through the EMTS, *efficiency will dictate that the bank provide an accounting service for firms.*

A corporation's bank will be in a position to monitor and control virtually all financial aspects of everyday operation. Given a suitable model of corporate financial activities (cash management, inventory levels, investment policies, trade credit criteria, wage payments schedule, etc.) and an individual firm's parameters for such a model, a bank will be able to run the routine finances of a company more efficiently than the company itself. Economies of specialization will then accrue to the firm, which can reallocate its resources away from financial activities and concentrate on its primary economic function—the production of goods and services.

It has been pointed out by Mateer[3] that such a specialization of functions has already begun in the form of the lockbox system, the transfer of funds among corporate offices over the Bank Wire, the use of drafts as a means of payment, and reliance on commercial bank lines of credit as a source of secondary liquidity. As money has become ever more expensive over the past years, corporations have come to depend increasingly on their banks for succor in efficiently and cheaply running their financial operations. This more intense utilization of cash and credit has been able to emerge only as a result of an increasing supply of bank services to the nonfinancial sector. Concomitantly, the banks have seen their corporate transaction balances decline relative to expenditures, as treasurers seek to minimize their holdings of nonearning assets.

---

3. William H. Mateer, *The Checkless Society: Its Cost Implications for the Firm* (Michigan State University Business Studies, 1969).

These combined pressures of reduced balances and added costs have forced the banks to reconsider their method for receiving compensation. To cover the banks' costs in the traditional manner, compensating balances would have to be extremely high.[4] The use of direct service charges by banks is in fact becoming more common. In particular, drafts and lockboxes are regularly priced on a per item basis by many banks.

As bank-provided services continue to increase in the future we would expect this trend away from compensating balances to continue. The banks will be expanding the scope of their services to corporate customers, and bank operating costs will rise sharply as a result. In order to cover these costs, the banks would have to demand ever-higher compensating balances—balances that would significantly exceed the average transactions balances of the corporations. This phenomenon should speed general recognition of the inefficiencies that are inherent in compensating balance arrangements.[5] The fee system will therefore become more prominent, and the service income of banks will rise relative to the income from their portfolios. For similar reasons, compensatory balances for bank correspondents should also be replaced by fees. The gross level of demand deposits in the banking system will drop as compensating balance requirements become less common.

7.1.2 The Firm's Demand Deposit Balances

A large number of articles attempting to describe and predict a firm's demand for transaction balances have been developed in the corporate finance, and money and banking literatures. Perhaps typical of the sort of model that has been proposed is Miller and Orr's,[6] which describes a firm's optimal average cash level to be

$$\bar{M} = \frac{4}{3} \cdot \left(\frac{3 \cdot F \cdot s^2}{4 \cdot i} \right)^{1/3}$$

---

4. Mateer, *op. cit.*, p. 29.

5. These inefficiencies were referred to in Chapter 6 in relation to compensatory balances on credit lines. For details see William E. Gibson, "Compensating Balance Requirements," *National Banking Review* (March 1965), pp. 387–395: and Douglas Hellweg, "A Note on Compensatory Balance Requirements," *Journal of Finance* (March 1961), pp. 80–84.

6. This description is taken from Daniel Orr, *Cash Management and the Demand for Money* (New York: Praeger Publisher, 1971). The first published description of the model appeared in Merton Miller and Daniel Orr, "A Model of the Demand for Money by Firms," *Quarterly Journal of Economics,* LXXX (August 1966) pp. 413–435. Admittedly there are better assumptions to be made concerning a firm's cash flow than that it is stochastic with no trend, and Miller and Orr have been criticized on this point. However this model does reveal the reactions that we can expect from a firm under the EMTS.

where

$\bar{M}$ = Average holdings of cash balances.

F = The fixed cost per conversion of securities into cash.

s^2 = The variance of daily changes in the cash balance. (The level of daily cash flow is hypothesized by this model to be a random variable.)

i = The opportunity cost of holding money. (That is, the difference between interest paid on demand deposits and that on marketable securities.)

Potential effects of an EMTS on this type of demand for money are contained in the variables F, s^2, and i. If the EMTS lowers F for the firm directly (particularly the nonpecuniary factors in F), or if the firm takes advantage of economies of specialization by giving control of its finances to its bank and thereby lowers F, then $\bar{M}$ will tend to fall.

The effect on s^2 is more difficult to predict *a priori,* although as a first approximation it would appear that s^2 will be lowered. The EMTS could reduce short-run stochastic fluctuations in cash flows in several ways:

1. Mail float will be eliminated.
2. More orders will be paid for immediately, since the purchaser need not circulate his check through a bureaucracy. (This is similar to the argument made concerning retail convenience credit in Section 7.2.1.)
3. For credit transactions, the seller could require that a preauthorized payment for the amount of the invoice be entered against the buyer's bank account. The seller would then know exactly when payment would arrive, allowing better planned conversions between bonds (or a time account) and money.

In any case, to the extent that s^2 is reduced in these ways, so too will be the firm's demand for money drop. (And vice versa, if s^2 rises under the EMTS.)

The largest net effect on $\bar{M}$ may result, however, from the change in i for corporate transaction accounts engendered by the EMTS. Nearly half of all checks written in the U.S. are debited to business accounts; and many corporate treasurers strive to maximize their demand deposits' velocity. Such accounts entail considerable expenses for a bank, and the firms pay for their demand account activities with a compensating balance. Such balances earn no interest (and therefore the firm is incurring an opportunity cost by holding them), so a corporation's net yield on its transactions account balances is actually negative. However, the EMTS will lower bank operating costs as electronic transfers replace checks, and lead to the replacement of compensating balances by fees. The net result of these EMTS features will be a higher yield on corporate demand accounts (that is, a smaller absolute value of the negative yield, or perhaps even a positive rate of return; this will depend on actual bank costs and market yields), and thus a lower value of i in the Miller-Orr model. *Ceteris paribus,* this would lead to an increase in the optimal amount of demand deposits held by a firm.

Many writers[7] have ignored this effect on the value of i, emphasizing instead only the EMTS' ability to lower F and s^2. Consequently, they have concluded that optimal money holdings will fall sharply under the EMTS. This may well be true, but it must be recognized that the EMTS will bring three distinct types of pressure to bear on money balances, and until we can ascertain the magnitudes of the changes in F, s^2, and i, we cannot determine the effect of the EMTS on a corporation's demand for transactions balances.

A firm's demand for cash balances will also be affected by the elimination of float. The "floatless society" will have mixed effects for firms. On the benefit side for a company will be the immediate control that it gains over its accounts receivable payments. Lockbox systems will be made obsolete by instant electronic transfers, and the firm will be able to garner cost savings in the form of lower bank fees and a reduced need for working capital to finance receivables. Interest income on the amount of the former float will also accrue to the company. (Note that smaller companies will gain proportionately more than larger ones in this manner, since they were formerly unable to utilize lockboxes, etc., due to their size.) On the other hand, the corporation will no longer enjoy the benefits of float in its payments to others. Average cash balances will be driven up by virtue of the fact that the firm must maintain sufficient balances to cover all of its payments as soon as they are made. The float effects of the EMTS on corporations are thus in opposition to one another. We might expect the magnitudes of these effects to be approximately equal since cash inflows will equal outflows over a long enough period of time. As with many of the other problems posed in this study, however, verification of this expectation must await future empirical research.

7.1.3 Trade Credit

The EMTS literature has predicted that an electronic payments system will precipitate extensive changes in the means by which intercorporate trade is financed. In particular, it has been alleged that "trade credit will be largely replaced with bank credit under an electronic funds-transfer system."[8] In this

---

7. See, among others, Dennis W. Richardson, *Electric Money,* (Cambridge: The MIT Press, 1970) and Donald Hester, "Monetary Policy in the 'Checkless' Economy," *Journal of Finance,* XXVII (May 1972), pp. 279–293.

8. Dennis W. Richardson, *op. cit.*

section we will examine this and other possible modifications in trade credit that could be engendered by the introduction of the EMTS.

The close ties between a bank and a firm in the accounting of its short term cash flow raises a question of the responsibility for financing a firm's accounts receivable. In the current regime, accounts receivable are negotiated by the firm at the time of the sale to another customer. Normally, the firm then retains the accounts as assets until they are paid. In some cases, however, and especially in some industries, it is common for the receivables to be discounted at a bank or with a firm specializing in this function ("factoring"). Whenever the firm finances the receivables itself, implicitly it is allocating its working capital for this function or obtaining short run financing that can be passed on to customers in the form of new trade credit.

The efficiency and economic rationale for this arrangement depends essentially on two considerations. First, the provision of the right of deferred payment to a customer may be thought of as part of the sales cost or advertising necessary for the transaction. In this view, it is then natural for the firm to retain control over the provision of the financing, since it is best equipped to judge the profitability of the specific sale. Second, the firm may be in a better position, from its vantage point in the industry, to judge the financial status of the customer than a bank. Thus, again, the firm may continue to be the most efficient route for the provision of credit to customers in many cases.

However, we may also find that the new financial and accounting relationships between a firm and its bank will engender a larger role for the banks in financing trade credit extensions during some periods. A bank's role as accountant will provide it with first-hand knowledge of its firms' customers' payment habits. In the event that a bank's customer needs a loan, there will be no need for the bank specially to examine the quality of its accounts receivable because it will already possess the necessary information. The bank will therefore be in a prime position to factor its customer's receivables and/or to use them as collateral for short term loans. This will be a viable source of funds for a corporation under normal monetary conditions.

Such lending will not, however, constitute a universal solution for corporate liquidity problems. Smaller firms are just as likely to have difficulty procuring loans in tight money times under the EMTS as they sometimes do today. Regardless of the quality of collateral offered, there will still be times when the demand for commercial loans simply exceeds the banks' ability to grant them. Under such circumstances, interfirm trade credit will fulfill the same functions as it does today. It will continue to be a means by which firms can offer discretionary price reductions to their preferred customers, as well as a device for stimulating demand by customers who are short on cash.

While the banks will be in a stronger position to finance intercorporate trade under the EMTS, firms will still retain important advantages in the granting of such credit. We therefore conclude that the nature of intercorporate trade credit will not be radically altered by the EMTS.

7.2 Retailing Firms

A sizeable portion of a retailer's business is conducted with other firms, and as a result the EMTS will affect retail establishments in many of the same ways as manufacturing firms. In particular, retailers will have incentive to make greater use of bank financial management services, to pay fees for bank services, to take advantage of trade credit, and to adjust their average cash holdings to a new level based on the criteria described in Section 7.1. But retailers also deal directly with the consuming public; and merchants' terminals will serve as customers' input devices to the EMTS. The merchants will therefore become involved with the credit card aspects of the EMTS as well as its giro facets.

7.2.1 Credit Features of the EMTS

To the extent that bank cards and their credit lines serve as effective substitutes for merchant credit, retailers will be less in need of their own small, expensive, and inefficient credit operations. In fact, the EMTS should substantially reduce the demand for 30-day charge plans. This sort of retail credit, which comprised 16 percent of the 1970 stock of consumer credit outstanding, is largely for the convenience of consumers and the encouragement of impulse buying. Customers who use such convenience credit are free to make purchases even when they do not have a checkbook or a sufficient amount of cash with them. But the EMTS will provide instant and pervasive access to one's bank transaction account and therefore an account holder can buy conveniently (and on impulse) without short term retail credit. The economic advantage to retailers of extending such convenience credit will no longer be applicable.

But there is also retail installment credit, which is used by individuals to finance their larger purchases. While the centralization of all such consumer credit into the banking system would result in economic gains due to economies of scale, it seems doubtful that complete specialization will ever occur. To begin with, many merchants have viewed bank charge cards with distaste. In Chapter 3 we described the retailer's conception of retail credit: a merchant's willingness to grant credit is considered to be a vital concomitant of successful competition. It allows him to gain the loyalty of his clientele and also to screen out "undesirable" customers (if that is desired).[9] Monthly billings provide a useful mailing list and can double as a means of cheap advertising when flyers are stuffed into the envelope.

There will be still another force leading merchants to retain credit operations: as we showed in Chapter 6, the banks' supply of consumer credit lines is

---

9. For example, there are stores which will refuse to grant charge cards to people with less than some (rather high) annual income.

likely to fall short of demand. There will be two types of individuals who are refused bank credit—those who are bad credit risks, and those "good" risks who are rationed due to the short supply. The former group will probably be rejected in their application for retail installment credit as well; but if bank credit cannot accommodate all the good credit risks in the economy, merchants will be led by competition to offer credit plans just as they do today. In such cases installment lending would serve functions similar to those provided by interfirm trade credit: it will be a means of competing for the favor of the creditless customer by helping to finance his inventory of goods. (It is also a means of achieving price discrimination while maintaining a single advertised price.)

For these reasons it seems probable that many retailers (primarily the larger ones) will continue to maintain their credit operations. Moreover, once they are relieved of the burden of convenience credit (which is currently free to customers and therefore must operate at a loss), the more efficient retail lenders should be able to break even or earn a profit on their credit programs.[10]

7.2.2 Retail Prices in the EMTS

Because the channels through which consumer credit will be extended under the EMTS will be completely different from those of current bank card plans, merchant revenues in the future will *not* be discounted by the banks as they are today. Under current bank card schemes, the bank makes a loan to the customer each time it pays cash for a merchant's receipts. The merchant pays his bank to take over default risks and collection costs when he accepts less than par value for his sales receipts. But an EMTS transaction need not involve an extension of credit by the bank. It can be simply a giro transfer whose cost will be borne by the payor. Only when the payor's balance is insufficient to cover the purchase price does the bank extend credit, and in that case the customer bears the full cost of his credit in the form of interest that he pays on the loan. The cost to the retailer of membership in the EMTS will therefore be quite small. He must pay only for the hardware installed on his premises, plus perhaps some allocated portion of the system's overhead. There will, however, be *no discounting* of merchant receipts in the EMTS.

The merchant must be prepared to accept payments in cash and by check as well as electronically, and this can complicate the retailer's financial operations. If all payments occurred through the EMTS, then the retailer's cost of effecting transactions would be lowered from its present level. There would be no need

---

10. Even today, the larger credit programs do earn profits for the merchants. Under the EMTS the elimination (or sharp reduction) of free 30-day credit will tend to make lending more profitable. On the other hand, however, increased competition in the provision of consumer installment loans will tend to lower interest rates, and thereby to lower profits.

for cash registers, trips to the bank, or check clearing. In addition the risk of cash being stolen or lost would be nil, as would the possibility of a bad check. The merchant would not have to keep funds tied up as drawer cash for making change and he would never wait for "cash items in the process of collection" to be paid. However, as soon as the first cash or check customer arrives, the retailer must pay for the operation of two essentially separate payments mechanisms.

In order to better understand this situation we can view the various means by which a consumer is able to effect payment as so many services provided to him by the seller. Whatever the means of payment, the *end* is the same—value is exchanged. But the differences among cash, merchant credit, instant EMTS funds transfer, and bank credit lie in the costs and conveniences they provide to the parties involved. It is thus inevitable that in a perfectly competitive regime the price of a good will vary with the means of payment used to purchase it. Or, more properly, in any retail transaction the purchaser procures both a good and a "payment service," and he must pay for both. If the merchant incurs costs that vary by payments method, competition and profit-maximization will force him to pass these costs on to customers as they are incurred.

The event most likely to occur in the EMTS will be that retailers offer three "prices" on any given item, according to the customer's payment preferences.

1. Currency and checks—this price will include the value of the good, plus some surcharge for the merchant's cost of using a paper-based transactions system.
2. Transaction-time EMTS funds transfer—the price includes only the cost of the good sold. By our assumption, the payor will be separately responsible for the explicit EMTS service charges (which will be less than the surcharge imposed by the merchant in case 1 above).
3. Merchant credit—this will be composed of either case 1 or 2, plus an interest charge for the time value of money and as compensation for default risk on the loan.

This is all quite straightforward and easily derivable from a model of perfect competition. There are two noteworthy results, however, that occur in this new regime of retail prices. First, one may be liable in the future for an extra surcharge if he chooses to pay a bill with cash. If the EMTS is absolutely cheaper to operate than a paper-based system, then electronic funds will be used to effect transactions. There is an increase in equity among consumers that will result from this sort of pricing scheme. In particular, the poor, who today cannot procure credit cards, will no longer be forced to pay higher prices in support of the credit purchases of others. Since an EMTS transaction need not necessarily entail the extension of credit, the poor will be granted ID cards and transaction accounts as readily as they now procure checking accounts. It is to be expected, of course, that the poor will be extended credit lines less often and in smaller amounts than the rich; but this is no impediment to their use of the EMTS for routine transactions.

7.3 Consumers

Households in the economy will be affected by the emergence of a complete EMTS more than any other nonfinancial economic unit. The basis of EMTS ramifications throughout the economy is that the system will reduce extant imperfections and costs in the payments mechanisms and capital markets. Households, being the smallest units in the economy, tend to be greatly affected by these factors. Therefore, the EMTS will significantly modify the economic environment in which consumers operate. The result will be extensive changes in their means of payment, saving processes, and access to the capital market.

7.3.1 Transactions for Settlement

Cash and Checks. On the basis of our discussion in Section 7.2, we can describe the effects of the EMTS on the household demand for currency and checks. Most obvious in this regard is the fact that, if the cost estimates available today are valid, then EMTS transfers will dominate checks for practically all purposes. There will be no rational reason for employing a check as a means of payment when an electronic transfer can provide virtually all the economic features of a check at a lower cost. We therefore conclude that a check will be used to transfer funds only when EMTS facilities are not available.

The question of cash usage is somewhat more complex, especially since no data exist on the transactions cost of using cash. In deciding how to make a particular payment the consumer will have to weigh the cost (merchant's surcharge) and inconvenience of using cash against the cost (system transaction fees) and convenience of electronic payment. A breakeven point, above which the rational consumer will always use the EMTS to transfer funds, will be determined jointly by the cash surcharge, EMTS charges, and the consumer's attitude toward carrying cash. Further, there are many cases today where cash is employed only because one's check is not acceptable to the seller, and EMTS transfers will surely replace cash in these exchanges. There are also high crime areas (especially in cities) where the risk of carrying cash is very high. Heretofore checks have been a highly imperfect substitute for cash in such areas; but electronic transfers will be quite acceptable in lieu of cash, leading to a sizeable decrease in the demand for currency in high crime regions.

Overall we can conclude that substantially less cash will be used in the future than today; but without data on the costs involved in an optimal EMTS and the merchant transaction charges that will prevail in the future (not to mention the absence of detailed cost data for present cash usage), it is impossible to quantify this projected decrease in the demand for currency.

Demand Deposit Balances. The EMTS will affect consumers' demand for money transaction balances, just as it will for firms. Household cash flows, however, are quite different from those of a corporation. Because households tend to receive income at regular intervals, and disburse funds more or less regularly over the next payments period, the assumptions of an inventory-theoretic model of cash holdings are not too far from the true situation. That is . . .

> inventory models of the Baumol-Tobin variety when properly handled, *may be* useful instruments for the study of money demand in the household sector.[11]

We will therefore use several variants of the Baumol-Tobin model of optimal money holding in order to illustrate the EMTS' effects on household transaction balances.[12]

The individual is assumed to have two assets available to him: cash (i.e., a bank transaction account or currency) and bonds, with a fixed cost for each conversion between the two. (Instead of bonds, we might consider the earning asset for our individual to be a savings account or time deposit.) His income is received at the beginning of a period of length T and cash outflows occur at a constant rate throughout the period. In order to gain interest income from his wealth the individual will desire to hold some portion of his income in bonds, converting to cash as the need arises (see Figure 7-1). (In the course of the period all of the original income must be expended; in other words, there is no provision for saving in the model.) We assume that the individual seeks to manage his finances during the period in such a manner as to maximize his net interest income (or, correspondingly, to minimize operating costs) by properly choosing the amount of bonds converted in each transaction.

Total costs of operation for the period are

$$TC = \frac{B}{2} \cdot i \cdot T + F\left(\frac{A}{B}\right), \tag{7-1}$$

where,

---

11. Orr, *op. cit.,* p. 134 (emphasis in the original).

12. William J. Baumol, "The Transactions Demand for Cash: An Inventory Theoretic Approach," *Quarterly Journal of Economics,* LXVI (November 1952) pp. 545–556. James Tobin, "The Interest Elasticity of Transaction Demand for Cash," *Review of Economics and Statistics,* XXXVIII (August 1956), pp. 241–247.

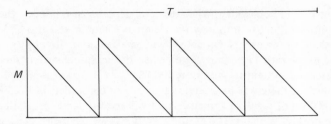

Figure 7-1. An Inventory—Theoretic Cash Model.

B =   The amount of bonds converted in each transaction.[13]

T =   The income period, in fractions of a year.

i =   The annual opportunity cost of holding money. Since demand deposits in the EMTS will earn interest, i is equal to the difference between the yield on bonds and that on demand balances.

F =   The fixed costs of a conversion between bonds and money.

A =   The total expenditures in the period.

The first term in (7-1) describes the opportunity cost of holding the average money balance ($B/2$) during the period. The second term is the total fixed costs for bond-money conversions. Differentiating TC with respect to B, we determine the optimal conversion size as:

$$B^* = \left(\frac{2 \cdot F \cdot A}{i \cdot T} \right)^{\frac{1}{2}} ,$$ (7-2)

which implies an average money balance of

$$M = \frac{B^*}{2} = \left(\frac{F \cdot A}{2 \cdot i \cdot T} \right)^{\frac{1}{2}}$$ (7-3)

Notice that (as was also the case for firms) we cannot make an *a priori* statement about the amount of cash held by an individual under the EMTS versus

---

13. Tobin, *op. cit.,* shows that the optimal scheme for conversions requires that B be constant throughout the time period.

the amount he will hold today. When demand deposits earn interest there will be a lower opportunity cost of money than there is today. F will also be lower, however, than it presently is. On net, M will be affected in direct proportion to the change in the ratio (F/i) that occurs when the economy switches over from today's payments system to the future EMTS.

In addition, there will be a service available to consumers in the EMTS—the preauthorization of regular payments—that will tend to lower M. If all of one's constant monthly payments (taxes, utilities, mortgage payment, etc.) are paid by the bank immediately upon the receipt of his income, then we should substitute $(A - P)$ for A in the above model, where P is the amount of preauthorized payments for each income period. The average cash balance maintained by the individual will thus be lower, the larger is P.

In order to determine the sum of these several pressures on M we will have to await empirical evidence concerning the changes in F, i and P that actually do occur following the introduction of the EMTS. Due to the payment of a competitive interest rate on demand account balances, households' interest income from their wealth will be higher, asset shifts between bonds and money will take place at lower transaction costs, and money will be more optimally supplied than it is today because money holdings will no longer be distorted by an artificial spread between the yields on money and earning assets.

The Payments Period.   There has been speculation in the literature that the EMTS will precipitate the more frequent payment of salaries—that the payments period will be shortened.[14] This may well be the case. Electronic transfers and automated accounting will lower the costs of making *and* receiving wage payments. At the same time wage earners will become more conscious of the fact that "wages due" constitutes an interest-free loan to their employers, and they will demand a reduction in the length of the payments period. It has been inferred that the household demand for money will *fall* as a result of the shorter payments period.[15] This is not, however, the case, as can be seen from (7-3) above. The shorter income period is reflected in a smaller value of T; but since expenditures are assumed to be made at a steady rate over time, the fraction (A/T) will remain constant. In short, the optimal level of cash balances is "independent of the frequency and regularity with which payments were received."[16]

---

14. See, for example, Hester, *op. cit.*, and George W. Mitchell, "Effects of Automation on the Structure and Functioning of Banking," *American Economic Review,* LVI (May, 1966), pp. 159–166.

15. Mitchell, *op. cit.*

16. Harry G. Johnson, *Essays in Monetary Economics,* Harvard University Press (Cambridge, 1967), p. 187. While this fact is not intuitively obvious, it is in reality an alternative statement of Tobin's result that optimality requires equal-size, equally-timed bond conversions over the payment period. Suppose we have two individuals, A who is paid annually, and B (with the same expenditure pattern and salary as A) who receives two paychecks per year. Using Equation (7-2), A decides to make 12 bond-to-money conversions in the course of the year. Therefore, on June 30, A will have exactly one-half his

The conclusion is that basic *inventory-theoretic models predict the EMTS will not tend to lower the demand for money due to a shortened payments period.*

It is possible, in fact, that this shortening of the payments period, if it goes far enough, will increase the amount of money held by households. There is always the possibility that the consumer's optimal course of action is to avoid any investment in bonds. This will occur if the transactions costs exceed the expected interest income derivable from bonds. That is, when

$$\left(\frac{A-B}{2}\right) \cdot i \cdot T - F\left(\frac{A}{B}\right) \leqslant 0 \text{ for all integer } (A/B), \text{ or}$$

$$F \geqslant \frac{T}{A}\left(\frac{A-B}{2}\right) \cdot i \cdot B.$$

Recalling that (T/A) remains a constant, we see that the right-hand side of this inequality falls as A decreases with a shortened payments period. In other words, as T falls, F is more likely to outweigh any profits gained by investing in bonds for an ever-larger segment of the population. This corner solution implies that the EMTS shorter payment period, *ceteris paribus,* may actually *increase* the average demand for money balances by households.[17]

The limiting case for the EMTS shortening of T would be the perfect synchronization of income and expenditure streams. Transactions balances would be credited instantaneously by employers at a constant rate over time. T would approach zero. In this case the model breaks down—M becomes unbounded when $T = A = 0$. Intuitively we see that if income were perfectly synchronized with outflows, the transaction demand for money will be nonexistent, as it could be today with an all-inclusive bank credit card. However, this limiting case is completely unrealistic. There will always be some fixed cost attached to making and receiving payments, and as a result the optimal payments period T will never become arbitrarily small.

7.3.2 Credit for Short-Term Financing

In Section 7.2 we demonstrated that pure convenience credit supplied by retailers will have an insignificant role under the EMTS. However, such credit

---

salary remaining (neglecting accumulated interest), which is the same amount which B plans to spend during the second half of the year. It is clear that B must find 6 conversions to be his optimal course of action, for if this were not so, A would also optimally alter his behavior beginning June 30. But that would violate Tobin's result that asset conversions be equally spaced throughout the decision period.

17. Johnson, *ibid.,* describes another situation where this result obtains. He shows that, if there is a *variable* cost for a bond-money conversion in addition to F (the fixed cost in our model), then the "optimum cash balance increases as the period decreases."

accounts for only a minor portion of total consumer credit in the U.S., and there will remain a sizeable demand for consumer loans to finance various types of expenditures. There are two distinct purposes for which a household will borrow funds. One is for the financing of its routine expenditures—as an adjunct to the management of working capital. The second cause for consumer borrowing is to allow the immediate purchase of durable goods. The motivating forces behind these two types of borrowing are quite different, and we will therefore consider them separately. We begin with short term financing.

With the growth of credit cards, consumers have been afforded an increasing amount of latitude in the management of their routine purchases. Suppose we take P (from the above exposition of Baumol's model) to be the amount of one's monthly purchases that are charged. If one receives his credit card bill on the first of each month, and is also paid on that day, then

$$M = \left(\frac{F \cdot (A - P)}{2 \cdot i \cdot T} \right)^{\frac{1}{2}} .$$
(7-4)

The larger is P, the less money one will hold.[18] In the extreme case, where $P = A$, payments and income are perfectly synchronized and $M = 0$. This tendency results from the ability to make purchases during the month without using cash. The time when income is received is thus irrelevant. As we have already emphasized, an EMTS purchase is quite different from a credit card transaction and consequently the EMTS will not precipitate perfect synchronization in this fashion. Consumer lines of credit (and/or merchant credit) will, however, be available for many individuals (at a cost), thereby making it possible to effect transactions without the immediate use of one's own funds.

A.S. Rama Sastry[19] points out that the Baumol-Tobin model implicitly assumes the cost of a cashout (that is, a negative or zero cash balance) to be infinite. This clearly is not the case for most firms; and, more important for our purposes, it is not the case for an individual with a bank card line of credit. It can be shown that when there is some finite cashout cost, the average cash balance held will be lower, and the interest elasticity of demand for money will be greater, than in the Baumol model. Sastry therefore presents a more general model which includes both the Baumol-Tobin assumption (infinite cashout cost) and the universal credit card case ($P = A$, as discussed above) as special cases. This model is depicted in Figure 7-2.

The assumptions of the model are similar to Baumol's. There are two assets, cash and bonds, with a fixed cost for each conversion between the two. Income is received at the beginning of a period of length T and cash outflows occur at a regular rate throughout the period. (Both T and A are the same as in Baumol's

18. Orr, *op. cit.*, points out this implication of credit cards for money holding.
19. A.S. Rama Sastry, "The Effect of Credit on Transactions Demand for Cash," *Journal of Finance,* XXV (September 1970), pp. 777-782.

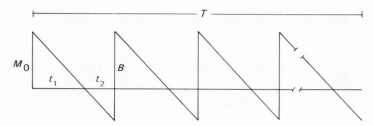

Figure 7–2. The Inventory Cash Model with Credit Lines.

analysis.) It is also assumed the individual has overdraft privileges available to him (either in the form of a credit line at his bank or as a merchant charge account) at an annual cost of r_c per dollar borrowed, prorated for the duration of the loan.[20] The individual's behavior over the period of length T consists of cycles that begin with a money balance M_0. This cash is run down at a steady rate over time t_1, after which the individual uses his overdraft allowance for time t_2. At the end of t (note that $t = t_1 + t_2$), B dollars of bonds are cashed, with which the bank is repaid (the amount $(B - M_0)$) and the money balance is again restored to M_0. The individual wishes to minimize transactions costs (maximize net interest income) over the period of length T by manipulating B and M_0.

Comparing Figures 7–1 and 7–2, we see the basic difference between the original Baumol model and this revised one to be the latter model's provision for a negative cash balance. In Sastry's framework the individual's expenditures are financed from his cash balance during the first part of each cycle and the bank finances his purchases during the last part via the credit line. There are three costs involved in managing one's cash position in this fashion:

$$\text{The opportunity cost of holding money} = \frac{M_0}{2} \cdot t_1 \cdot i$$

$$\text{the interest cost of the overdraft} = \frac{B - M_0}{2} \cdot t_2 \cdot r_c$$

and the cost of moving between bonds and money $= F$.

Total operating costs (TC) for the period are

$$TC = \left[\frac{M_0}{2} \cdot t_1 \cdot i + \left(\frac{B - M_0}{2} \right) \cdot t_2 \cdot r_c + F \right] \frac{A}{B} , \qquad (7\text{-}5)$$

where

---

20. For simplicity the ensuing analysis will refer only to bank credit lines. The same types of advantages will derive from merchant-extended credit.

B = The lot size for bond-money conversions.

M_0 = The initial holding of money.

t_1 = The time during each cycle when expenditures are financed with cash.

t_2 = The time during each cycle when expenditures are financed on the credit line.

i = The annual opportunity cost, in percent, of holding money.

r_c = The annual interest charge on overdrafts.

F = The fixed cost per bond conversion.

A = Transactions volume during period T.

Differentiating Equation (7-5) with respect to M_0 and B, and then solving simultaneously, yields the optimal values of these variables. The primary result is the optimal average money holding specified by the model, which is

$$M = \left(\frac{A \cdot F}{2 \cdot i \cdot T} \right)^{\frac{1}{2}} \left(\frac{r_c}{i + r_c} \right)^{\frac{1}{2}} \qquad (7\text{-}6)$$

Note that Baumol's average money holding is given by the first term of (7-6) alone. (In fact, Baumol's solution is a special case of Sastry's, where the cost of a cashout (r_c) is infinite.) Since the second term of (7-6) is necessarily less than unity, for any nonzero i and finite r_c the average demand deposit balance held by an individual with a bank line of credit is less than in the absence of the credit line.[21] Since the consumer always has the option of setting $B = M_0$ (that is, of not utilizing the credit available to him), the fact that the line of credit is used for financing routine expenditures indicates that the account holder is able to derive a lower net cost by employing the credit device.

Another important result of this model is its implications for individuals' responses to a change in the level of interest rates. The interest elasticity of demand for money in Baumol's model is $(-\frac{1}{2})$. As given by the Sastry model it is

$$(-\tfrac{1}{2})\left(1 + \frac{i}{i + r_c} \right).$$

---

21. In the above solution for M we ignore the possibility of a binding ceiling on the individual's line of credit. If, however, the optimal solution requires a $(B - M_0)$ larger than the credit line's limit, the consumer would substitute a corner solution where $(B - M_0)$ is equal to the ceiling. In this case he will still be better off than he was without the credit line.

This quantity is never less than Baumol's; and for nonzero i it is greater. This result gives further support to the argument in Chapter 5 that savers at financial intermediaries in the future will be more sensitive to changes in market interest rates than they are today. Overall sensitivity to interest rates will be greater under an EMTS that includes bank lines of credit.[22]

7.3.3 Credit for Long-Term Financing

Once a bank has granted its customer a line of credit it cannot control the uses to which the funds will be put. In particular, we would expect individuals with sizeable credit lines to use them as a means of financing durable goods purchases, vacations, or other medium-sized expenditures. Based on the limits of today's bank card credit lines, the maximum size purchase that is relevant here is likely to lie somewhere in the range of $300 to $1500.

The major issue—both for micro analysis and for determining the macro effects of the EMTS in Chapter 8—is,

> Do we hold currency or demand deposits to meet emergencies and to buy the "big things" we want? Or do we borrow for these purposes, and make repayment out of future income receipts.[23]

There are some households that are reluctant to borrow for their purchases of durable goods or other sizeable expenditures. Credit lines will be demanded by these households primarily as insurance against liquidity crises, and bank credit lines will rarely enter into the financing of their medium-sized purchases. The findings of Mueller and Lean[24] support this conclusion; they assert the existence of a class of consumers who frequently use their saving accounts as a place to accumulate funds with which large purchases can be made. These consumers hold liquid saving accounts against known (or unknown) future needs, and they are willing to reduce temporarily such balances in order to finance a large expenditure. They feel that their savings position provides adequate security, and they are disinclined to resort to expensive installment borrowing when there is a viable alternative. According to the results of Mueller and Lean's opinion survey,

> Families which are willing to make withdrawals from their savings accounts are for the most part those which are in a strong financial position and have

---

22. It should be noted that the implications of this model are directly related to the problem of consumer credit line pricing discussed in Chapter 6.

23. Orr, *op. cit.*, p. 145.

24. Eva Mueller and Jane Lean, "The Savings Account as a Source for Financing Large Expenditures," *Journal of Finance*, XXII (September 1967), pp. 375–393.

savings habits and motivations which have enabled them in the past to build their savings balances.[25]

But there are also the "permanent income" hypotheses of Modigliani-Brumberg-Ando and Friedman. Central to these models is the assumption that each individual has a concept of his "permanent" income (which he will tend to earn in the long run), and he plans to consume some fixed portion of this permanent income figure each year regardless of his actual earnings. For individuals whose actual income temporarily falls short of this planned level of consumption, a bank credit line will present the means for attaining a superior allocation of intertemporal consumption. We can see this from the following model.

Figure 7-3 is a basic Fisherian description of an individual's intertemporal consumption decision.[26] C_1 and C_2 are consumption in the first and second periods; W_1 and W_2 represent income in the respective periods; and r is "the" rate of interest, at which the individual can freely borrow and lend in the market. The indifference map I_i represents the consumer's attitude toward consumption in the two periods. Tangency between the market-determined budget constraint $\overline{EF}$ and the individual's indifference map yields the point at which the consumer's utility is maximized. Notice in Figure 7-3 that, with this individual's preferences, the ability to lend or borrow makes him better off unless his endowment point is Z. In the one case of point Z his income is *ex ante* distributed in the same fashion as his desired consumption, so he makes no use of the loan market.

The budget line in Figure 7-3 is a straight line due to the assumption that there is a constant r for both borrowing and lending. But this is an unrealistic assumption. Households in the U.S. are able to invest savings at a rate of about 4-6 percent in a bank account,[27] and they can borrow against future income only at significantly higher rates if such an unsecured loan is obtainable at all. This situation yields a budget line such as that of Figure 7-4, where Q is the endowment point. This new budget line has two segments whose slopes are determined by the magnitude of r_1 (the rate of interest earned on money lent (saved) by the individual) and r_b (the rate at which money can be borrowed). The old budget line is still $\overline{E_1F_1}$, and it corresponds to a single hypothetical interest rate r such that $r_1 < r < r_b$. A person with a time preference different from that indicated by Q is unambiguously worse off in our second regime.

25. *Ibid.*, p. 375.

26. Irving Fisher, *The Theory of Interest*, (New York: The Macmillan Co., 1930).

27. The "average" household may dabble in primary securities or mutual funds, but "traditionally this type of saver has emphasized liquidity and safety of principal over immediate return or growth potential." (Daniel H. Brill and Ann P. Ulrey, "The Role of Financial Intermediaries in the U.S. Capital Markets," Rederal Reserve *Bulletin* LIII (January 1967), pp. 18-31.) As a result, FI savings accounts tend to be the repository of the bulk of household financial savings. To the extent that mutual funds become more popularly used in the EMTS, this standard return on savings (r_1) may rise slightly, but it will never approach the rate at which an individual can borrow.

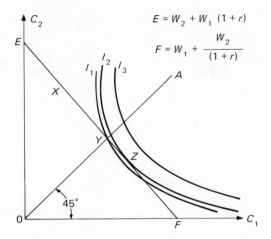

$$E = W_2 + W_1 (1 + r)$$

$$F = W_1 + \frac{W_2}{(1 + r)}$$

Figure 7-3. The Fisherian Borrowing Decision.

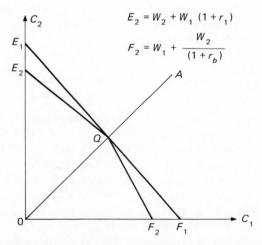

$$E_2 = W_2 + W_1 (1 + r_1)$$

$$F_2 = W_1 + \frac{W_2}{(1 + r_b)}$$

Figure 7-4. Budget Constraints in Practice.

How does the EMTS affect this situation? To begin with, the effective r_1 is raised due to lowered transaction costs in the EMTS. This rotates the left half of the budget constraint upward to E_3 in Figure 7-5. In a similar way the effective r_b is lowered when the costs of securing a loan are reduced by the presence of a precommitted line of credit. But the customer cannot borrow an unlimited amount at the effective rate r_c ($<r_b$). His budget line thus becomes $\overline{E_3 QVF_3}$, where the horizontal distance between Q and V corresponds to the maximum amount of credit available on the consumer's line. In this third regime,

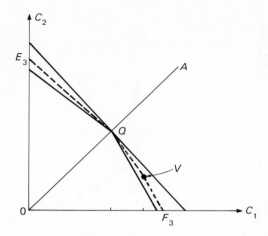

Figure 7–5. Budget Constraints with the EMTS.

made possible by the EMTS, the consumer is unambiguously better off than in the second regime, regardless of whether he saves prior to making his large expenditures (the Mueller-Lean saver) or borrows in order to smooth out his consumption path (the "permanent-income" borrower).

7.4 Summary

We have seen in this chapter that the changes induced in the nonfinancial sector of the U.S. economy by the introduction of an EMTS will be significant and pervasive. The money holdings of economic units will be affected in several ways, although we cannot predict the net result. These money balance changes will cause the velocity of money to be altered as well. Firms at all levels will become more dependent on their banks for the provision of financial and account-ing services. Individuals' access to capital markets will be enhanced, installment credit will be more perfectly supplied, and the small investor's interest sensitivity will increase in the EMTS environment. The availability of an EMTS, with its low costs of operation for merchants, will lead to a new, more competitive pricing scheme for consumer goods and services. It will also reduce the house-hold demand for currency and essentially make the check obsolete as a means of payment. In a word, the EMTS will constitute a more competitive and efficient monetary system for the economy, one which will entail significant gains for all nonfinancial units in the management of their financial affairs.

As a result of our consideration in these past two chapters of the micro-economic implications of the EMTS, we are now ready to turn to the macro-economic aspects of the system.

8 Macroeconomic Effects of the EMTS

We have shown in the preceding chapters that a United States electronic monetary transfer system (EMTS) is today both technically feasible and economically and socially desirable. But a significant impediment to the *rapid* emergence of a fully electronic payments system is to be found in the area of public acceptance. It has been stated repeatedly in the literature that a sizeable public education campaign will be necessary to popularize the techniques and new features of the EMTS.[1] It is to be expected that different economic units will react to these monetary innovations at differing speeds and with differing enthusiasm: larger corporations will be quicker to realize the potential gains than their smaller counterparts: wealthy consumers will adjust to the system more rapidly than the poor; individual financial intermediaries will vary in the extent of their involvement in the system; etc. We can, however, anticipate with confidence that the microeconomic advantages of the EMTS described in Chapters 6 and 7 will, in time, lead to the economy's complete changeover to the new payments mechanism.

Innovation in the U.S. financial sector is, of course, not a unique event. The rise of credit cards and travellers' checks, the emergence of a national market for Federal funds, the postwar secular rise in the velocity of money, the certificate of deposit and commercial paper markets, and the emergence and rapid growth of nonbank financial intermediaries, to name just a few, have all come about in reaction to some new cost or opportunity in the economy. Each of these monetary developments has had some effect on macroeconomic relationships in the society. The Gurley-Shaw debate concerning nonbank intermediaries, the study of the determinants of the velocity of money and the appropriate definition of money, and the differing views toward the efficacy of Regulation Q ceilings are just three examples of the seriousness with which economists have treated such developments in the past. The EMTS will, of course, represent a more *far-reaching* change in the nations payments system than any of those mentioned above. It will have direct effects on virtually every member of the economy. The potential effects of the EMTS on macroeconomic relationships—and hence on the government's monetary and fiscal policy—are far greater than for any recent

---

1. "Electronic Money," *Forbes,* IC (April 1, 1967), pp. 42–46. Georgia Tech Research Institute. Donald D. Hester, "Monetary Policy in the 'Checkless' Economy," *Journal of Finance,* XXVII (May 1972), pp. 279–293. E.B. Weiss, "The Marketing Implications of the Checkless Society." New York, Doyle Dane Bernbach, Inc., 1968.

U.S. monetary innovation, and consequently require serious study on the part of those responsible for controlling the economy.

There are a large number of empirical relationships that the EMTS may alter drastically: What will be the transactions and interest elasticities of the demand for (and supply of) money? Will there be changes in the consumption function and consequently in the multiplier? Will there be need for a new working definition of money, which may include credit lines and perhaps part of savings accounts? What will be the relative importance of non-Federal Reserve System member intermediaries in the channels of monetary policy? What lag structure can be expected to accompany monetary and fiscal policy operations? These and many other economic relationships will have to be reestimated and reconsidered on the basis of EMTS-generated data if fiscal and monetary policy are to maintain their efficacy. In the course of this chapter we will see that most of the macroeconomic effects of the new payments system will primarily be of a quantitative character that can be recognized and accounted for in currently available models of economic activity. (Indeed, the significant *qualitative* implications of the EMTS will be found to occur at the microeconomic level). However, these macroeconomic changes will alter many extant empirical relationships in the economy and could therefore cause difficulties if no corresponding adjustments are made by policymakers.

Since the EMTS is likely to be adopted only over a period of time, there will be an interim period during which the economy is adjusting toward the new equilibrium. In this period of adjustment, policymakers will be confronted with a double problem: first, the old econometric parameters will not be valid; second, the system will be too unstable to make any new estimates meaningful. But in the long run, after the innovations have been completed and a new equilibrium achieved, there should be no conceptual barriers to the estimation of the parameters of the new payments mechanism. Our interest in this chapter lies in the aspects by which that new equilibrium will differ from today's economic environment. The period of transition will not concern us; we can only assume that monetary and fiscal policymakers will be able to adapt properly to monetary innovations as they proceed. To be sure, there will be mistakes and difficulties during the transition period, but the experiences of that time will be unique and largely inapplicable to the conditions that will prevail in the economy in the long run.

Our discussion here will be divided into three sections. The first deals with the EMTS effects on the real sector of the economy—cyclical stability, the distribution of income, and changes in the level of consumption and production. In the second section, changes in the private monetary sector are considered; in particular, we will examine the implications for velocity, the definition of the economy's "money" supply, and the means through which credit will be extended. Finally, we will discuss the channels of monetary policy and evaluate the ways in which they will be affected by the EMTS.

8.1 Effects on the Real Sector of the Economy

8.1.1 Credit Lines and Cyclical Stability

The actual and potential effects of consumer credit on business fluctuations in the U.S. have frequently been a subject of dispute in the economic literature. It has been suggested, on one hand, that installment credit allows individuals to shift their purchases of goods (especially durables) to periods of high aggregate demand, and thus to aggravate the magnitude of the economy's fluctuations. In contrast, it is also possible that the extension of consumer credit during an economic slump could help initiate recovery and reduce fluctuations. As we have seen, the EMTS will precipitate extensive improvements in consumers' access to various capital markets and borrowing facilities. It is likely that sizeable lines of credit will be extended to many individuals in the society, and that the overall stock of available installment credit in the economy will rise. The main question then is, to what extent will the extension and use of consumer credit become more important than it is today in affecting the economy's cyclical stability. A second issue (which will be discussed in the next section of this chapter) concerns how the greater availability of consumer credit will affect the economy's overall level of consumption demand.

Cyclical Effects of Installment Credit. To begin with, we can consider the theoretical aspects of the effects of consumer credit on the cyclical variations of aggregate demand in the real sector. Of primary importance in this regard is the *timing* of credit extensions. Consumer credit provided in the midst of a recession is likely to be a significant net addition to aggregate demand for the economy. During a recession period the consumer's income is likely to be relatively low, and the availability of credit may be critical if a purchase is to be made. Furthermore, banks, for example, reduce borrowed reserves and will probably be holding excess reserves while the economic slump persists; additional loans to consumers may thus be extended without reducing loans to other sectors of the economy.

In contrast, at a peak in economic activity, lending institutions typically have low excess reserves, and thus any net addition to consumers' borrowings must displace a nearly equal amount of loans to other borrowers. This displacement may occur either through rising interest rates on loans (in which case the more interest-elastic borrowers will be displaced), or through changes in the distribution of nonprice rationing (in which case a borrower's position in the lending queue will determine the effects of the displacement). In either case, however, the extension of consumer credit contributes little to *aggregate* demand; instead, it shifts the distribution of output between investment, government, and consumption goods, causes price inflation in the consumer good sector, or both.[2]

We can thus see that consumer credit contributes most to aggregate demand when such demand is weakest, and least when aggregate demand is greatest. This becomes even more evident when one considers the timing of loan repayments. Suppose an individual takes out a loan at the beginning of an upswing. His repayment funds will be flowing back to the bank (or other lender) as it is experiencing a rising demand for funds—that is, when the bank is able to relend the funds to finance further expenditures. The consumer has thus acted in a useful contracyclical role by means of both his initial borrowing and his repayment schedule. An individual who borrows at a cyclic peak, on the other hand, has just the opposite effects: he borrows at the peak in demand and repays when demand is slack.

Shifts of consumption demand to periods of already high aggregate demand are particularly burdensome for the durable goods industries. The services of durables are consumed over a period of time following the initial consumption expenditure, so that after an initial increase in the stock of goods the consumption of durables' services can continue at the higher level with no further new production. McCracken, Mao and Fricke[3] present the following example. Suppose automobiles have a use life of ten years, and that there are 50 million autos currently operating in the country. Now let the demand for auto services rise (once and for all) by 10 percent over some short period of time. In order to satisfy this demand, the economy's stock of cars must rise to 55 million; but the *rapidity* of this increase in the durables stock is of central importance for stability in the industry. McCracken, Mao and Fricke show that if production rises by more than one-half million units per annum (that is, by more than the number of new autos demanded times their replacement rate) during the transition period, then following the initial buildup in the stock of autos, "production will first fall off and then follow the path of a regular recurring cycle."[4] A similar instability can arise in the producers' goods industry as well. A rapid fluctuation in the demand for consumer goods (durable or nondurable) can, through the accelerator, induce wide swings in the demand for capital goods.

---

2. Since future output is based on the current capital stock and current investment, the availability of consumer installment credit provides a means by which the growth rate of the economy may be altered at the margin.

3. Paul W. McCracken, James C.T. Mao, and Cedric Fricke, *Consumer Installment Credit and Public Policy*. Michigan Business Studies, Vol. VXII, No. 1, University of Michigan, Ann Arbor, Michigan, 1965.

4. *Ibid.*, p. 39.

It is thus clear that installment borrowing can be, in theory, a source of either stability or instability in the economy, depending on the factors motivating the demand for loans. What has in fact been the case? The available empirical evidence is, unfortunately, very difficult to interpret, and has lead various writers to draw conflicting conclusions on this matter. In one major study of consumer credit and its relation to public economic policy, McCracken, Mao and Fricke reported that

> The postwar turning points in consumer credit show a pattern of timing similar to that of economic activity generally . . . This broad conformity of credit cycles with those of general economic activity *warrants the presumption* that movements in consumer installment credit do result in *somewhat* wider cyclical savings in business activity.[5]

If such is indeed the case, and the same tendency persists into the future, then consumers' increased access to credit will allow them to borrow more in this cyclical fashion. Consequently, business cycle fluctuations will be aggravated.

However, this conclusion has by no means gone uncontested. Michael Evans considers the evidence on this issue and concludes:

> Far from causing distortions and recessions, increased use of consumer credit has been accompanied in recent years by a return toward full employment. The simple burden theory, which states that fluctuations in the economy are caused partially by the use of consumer credit, appears completely fallacious.[6]

If Evans' conclusion is the proper one, EMTS-generated reforms in the consumer credit sector should *diminish* the extent of cyclical variations in the economy.

It must be noted that these conclusions (and others like them) may be invalidated as a result of the changed patterns of credit availability and use that will prevail with the EMTS. It should be clear from the above discussion, however, that consumer installment credit is potentially a potent force in the U.S. economy. Whatever the eventual effects of the EMTS in this area, fiscal and monetary authorities will need to study and perhaps specifically control the consumer credit market in order to maintain stability in the economy.

Control of Cyclical Variations. The single most important feature of consumer credit lines for the purpose of studying their cyclical effect will be that the credit is actually extended on the *borrower's* initiative. Having granted a

---

5. *Ibid.,* p. 54 (emphasis added).

6. Michael K. Evans, *Macroeconomic Activity,* (New York: Harper and Row, 1969), p. 160.

line of credit, the lender has little control over when it will be taken down or in what amount. Accordingly, it must be anticipated that consumer credit take-downs will be largely insensitive to the standard monetary policies of the Federal Reserve. This raises the question of alternative monetary schemes for controlling the use of credit lines.

McCracken, Mao and Fricke argue that consumer credit extensions can be controlled today by limiting the availability of reserves to the banking and intermediary system as a whole; confronted with a shortage of loanable funds, intermediaries will curtail consumer lending in order to fulfill the loan demands of their more important customers.[7] But the extent to which available consumer credit will be rationed under the EMTS (with its precommitted credit lines) will be determined largely *prior to* the period during which the authorities wish to curtail aggregate demand. It is possible that the rate of interest applicable to consumer loans will rise, causing the more interest-sensitive borrowers to reduce their demand. In fact, such interest-sensitivity will be of greater importance under the EMTS than it is today. However, as we concluded in Chapter 6, the rate on consumer loans will probably respond only partially (and with a lag) to changes in general market conditions. Therefore, the nonprice credit rationing that has heretofore dominated the effects of interest rates in clearing the con-sumer loan market will continue to be a prominent feature of the market under the EMTS (in spite of some increase in consumers' sensitivity to interest costs). Therefore, under the EMTS the general monetary controls of the Federal Reserve System are unlikely to be sufficient to control consumer credit during an expansion.

Furthermore, it is important to note that, regardless of the nature of con-sumer credit's effects on the business cycle, such macroeconomic results are completely external to the microeconomic decisions involved in such credit extensions. Neither the lending intermediary nor the consumer has any cause to take such aggregate effects into account. If consumer overdrafts become suffi-ciently widespread, the monetary authorities may therefore find that the ability to affect credit line extensions and takedowns directly will become an important stabilization tool. This issue will be considered further in Section 8.3.

8.1.2 Other Macroeconomic Effects

The previous section has dealt with the effects of the EMTS on the econ-omy's cyclical behavior; but there are also several once-and-for-all changes that will occur as a result of the introduction of the new payments system. Each of

---

7. In addition to reducing the flow of their own consumer lending, the banks today often call their short loans to consumer finance companies, thereby further curtailing the availability of funds to the consumer sector.

these results is an aggregation of the advantages that will accrue at the micro-economic level to individual economic units as a result of the EMTS. Since the latter were discussed at length in Chapter 7, we only briefly point out here their results at the macroeconomic level.

First, we can expect a redistribution of income in favor of poorer economic units to occur for several reasons. Since fixed transaction costs (in all markets) have a greater proportionate impact at lower income levels, the EMTS, which reduces these fixed costs of effecting payments, will provide a greater percentage increase in income for those at the low end of the distribution. Likewise, the elimination of Regulation Q ceilings will result in higher interest incomes for those small investors who have heretofore been unable to enter the market directly in order to take advantage of cyclically-rising interest rates. Similarly, the payment of interest on demand deposits will be important to individuals with small incomes who are currently unable to invest a part of their transaction balances in bonds or saving accounts. Finally, a more competitive consumer credit market will result in lower interest rates in that market; since the borrowing in this market is undertaken to a great extent by the lower income groups, they will be helped disproportionately by such a development.

A second result of the EMTS will be an increase in the economy's real output. The electronic payments mechanism will be absolutely cheaper to operate than the current one, thus freeing resources to other sectors of the economy. In addition, the costs of financial intermediation should be lowered, since increased competition will drive inefficient institutions out of the industry. Finally, there will be a more efficient allocation of capital to the productive industries than obtains today, with the result that physical output should rise.

Third, the increased opportunities for borrowing under the EMTS may also have a long-run effect on the economy's average level of consumption expenditures. Abstracting from the transitional and impact effects that will occur with the shift to better borrowing opportunities, there are two basic factors that can influence the average level of consumption.[8] These can be seen most clearly in the context of a "life-cycle" theory of consumption in which the young tend to borrow and the old tend to lend. The first factor is that the interest as well as the principal of a loan must be repaid. Thus, for any given generation, while the availability of loans may allow a more optimal time-phasing of its consumption activities, the total consumption achieved over the life of the generation will be reduced by the amount of the interest payments. The second factor is that in a growing economy the removal of a binding constraint on borrowing by the

---

8. There may well be a strong initial increase in consumption as household units take advantage of their new borrowing opportunities. However, such credit must be repaid with interest in ensuing periods, and this will tend to reverse the initial jump in consumption. There should then follow an adjustment process which will terminate in a new equilibrium. Such short-run shifts and equilibrations will be part of the transition difficulties with which monetary and fiscal authorities will have to deal.

young will allow an ever-increasing level of consumption to be achieved by successive generations. Thus, the net effect on consumption depends on the relative magnitudes of these two factors. Thomas Russell, following Cass and Yaari, has demonstrated under specific conditions that consumption expenditures will rise upon the removal of a binding loan constraint if and only if the growth rate of the economy exceeds the interest rate charged on the loans.[9] In other words, the net effect on consumption will be positive whenever the positive effect of the growth factor (the growth rate) exceeds the negative effect of the interest factor (the interest rate). While this appears to be a strong theoretical proposition, in reality, unfortunately, interest rates and growth rates have tended to be of roughly the same order of magnitude, and thus no *a priori* judgment can be made.

8.2 Effects in the Monetary Sector

EMTS-generated reforms in financial intermediary operations (discussed in Chapter 5) will precipitate several major macroeconomic developments in the monetary sector of the economy. Changes in the velocity of money, the liquidity of various "near-monies," and the extent of financial intermediation undertaken in the economy will all occur, primarily as a result of changes in the market for deposit funds. These phenomena will be described in this present section, while their implications for the workings of monetary policy are considered in Section 8.3.

8.2.1 Changes in the Velocity of Money

The postwar period has seen a steady increase in the income velocity of money, from about 2.5 in 1946 to over 4 today. (This trend in velocity corresponds to the narrow definition of money: M_1 = currency in the hands of the public plus demand deposits adjusted. Throughout Section 8.2.1, "money" refers only to this M_1.) This increase in the annual turnover of the money supply relative to GNP may have occurred for several reasons. First, to the extent that money balances are economized as transactions volume increases—as predicted by inventory-theoretic models—we should observe less than proportionate increases in money balances when real income grows as it has over the postwar period. Second, to the extent that money balances are negatively related to the level of interest rates, the postwar period's secular increase in interest rates

---

9. Thomas Russell, "The Effects of Improvements in the Consumer Loan Market," unpublished paper, mimeo, 1972; and David Cass and Menahem E. Yaari, "Individual Saving, Aggregate Capital Accumulation, and Efficient Growth," in Karl Shell, Editor, *Essays on the Theory of Optimal Economic Growth*, (Cambridge: M.I.T. Press, 1967).

should have lead to a decline in money balances held relative to transactions. Third, there have been numerous developments that may have shifted the demand for money function and thereby led to higher velocity. For corporations, techniques such as lockboxes, the use of drafts and certificates of deposits, and generally better cash management have tended to lower their demand for money. Similarly, household units have increasing use of such money substitutes as credit cards and travelers' checks, and the various "near-monies" have been viewed as increasingly perfect substitutes for currency and demand deposits as a means of holding precautionary and speculative liquidity reserves.

The future impact of the EMTS on the public's demand for money has been discussed in Chapter 7, where we have seen that the EMTS is likely to produce conflicting pressures on the equilibrium level of money balances. Lower transaction costs and the availability of credit lines to many individuals will tend to lower money balances (and thus to raise velocity). In contrast, the payment of interest on transaction balances will lead to increased demand for money. There are also two further (and conflicting) factors that will affect the public's future demand for M_1. First, it was argued in Chapters 6 and 7 that there will be a strong tendency to eliminate compensating balances, replacing them with direct fees. To the extent that such required balances are in excess of firms' desired transaction balances, their elimination will reduce the demand for demand deposits and thereby raise the overall velocity of money. Furthermore, the elimination of compensating balances, which are insensitive to changes in market interest rate fluctuations, will work to increase the *variability* of the income velocity of money.

The second factor influencing money holdings and velocity will be a shift in the ownership of demand deposit balances. Today only about 75 percent of American households own a bank checking account; but the increased convenience and lower transaction costs of an EMTS should cause nearly all Americans to enter the system. This occurrence will precipitate two results. First, the household sector will shift between currency and demand balances, and to the extent that the transaction velocities of these two differ, the velocity of M_1 will be affected as well. Second, since demand deposits of the household sector are generally less interest-sensitive and have a lower velocity than those of the corporate sector, we would expect this development to counteract (at least partially) the increased velocity and greater variability of corporate money holdings that were discussed above.

We have noted here the various conflicting pressures that will be brought to bear on the demand for money balances under an EMTS. However, since we are unable to determine the magnitude of these forces *a priori,* the aggregate effect of the EMTS on money's velocity must remain an empirical issue. *Velocity and its variability may either rise or fall upon the emergence of the EMTS.*

It is important to recognize that the measure of money's velocity is crucially related to another economic issue, the proper definition of "money" itself.

Velocity is important in monetary theory largely because it provides a means of relating total output to some known (and controllable) factor, the money supply. For example, from the traditional equation of exchange, $MV = PQ$, if velocity (V) is known in advance, then changes in the money supply (M) will have a predictable effect on total transactions (PQ). From the standpoint of monetary policy, then, we can either attempt to predict velocity with accuracy given a *theoretically* desirable definition of money;[10] or we can attempt to define *empirically* a monetary variable such that the velocity of this variable remains nearly constant.[11] In either case, control of the relevant monetary aggregate would allow the Federal Reserve to control the volume of transactions undertaken in the economy.

In the course of the past twenty years, the Federal Reserve has utilized a variety of "indicators" to measure the effectiveness of its policies. Interest rate levels, general credit conditions, and various monetary aggregates have all been used at one time or another, but the monetary authorities have yet to discover a single "best" indicator.[12] For the purposes of our study, it is necessary to realize that the EMTS is likely to alter the significance of any monetary indicator that has heretofore been used. In particular, the relationship between M_1 and other liquid assets may be changed drastically in the future. We will therefore turn to a consideration of EMTS implications for a definition of money that will be more relevant for Federal Reserve policymakers.

8.2.2 The Definition of Money

Keynes differentiated three separate needs that money fulfills for its holders: First, and most obviously, money serves to effect *transactions*; second, money serves as a *precaution* against the possibility that nonmoney assets may be temporarily illiquid or transferable to money only at a capital loss; and, third, there is a *speculative* demand for money that causes it to be held when an expected rise in interest rates would cause capital losses on bonds. In short, money can serve as a means of storing wealth without the risk of capital value change and as a source of precautionary liquidity, as well as being the means of exchange. Moreover, these three functions of money were seen by Keynes to be closely interrelated.

The ideal definition of money for the purposes of monetary policy will

---

10. George Garvy and Martin Blyn, *The Velocity of Money*. Federal Reserve Bank of New York, 1969.

11. This latter approach is, of course, the one favored by Milton Friedman and the so-called new quantity theorists.

12. In fact, Federal Reserve "mistakes" have often been attributed to the use of the wrong indicator—see Phillip Cagan, *Recent Monetary Policy and the Inflation,* Washington, D.C., The American Enterprise Institute, 1971.

reflect changes in all three aspects of the public's money holdings. This is, in fact, the opinion of George W. Mitchell, whose "preference for monetary aggregates either as a guide or gauge is generally for those that measure liquidity changes in the economy."[13] (That is, changes in the total stock of liquid assets in the hands of the public.) The EMTS will add some important considerations to the construction of such a liquidity aggregate.

Means of Exchange. In Chapters 2 and 3 we enumerated and discussed the features of various entities that can presently be used in the course of trade for effecting payments. Currency and demand deposits must certainly be included in any monetary aggregate because of their central role in settling debts. But industrial trade credit and consumer credit are also commonly employed in the exchange of resources. How are they to be included in an empirical definition of money? Similarly, how should consumer EMTS lines of credit best be treated?

Keynes was among the first to argue for the inclusion of over-draft allowances as a segment of the money supply; and others have pursued the issue.[14] In particular, it is the *unused* portion of over-draft allowances (or trade credit allowances) that should be added to the narrowly defined money supply, and *not* the the amount of credit already extended. This may be illustrated with a single example. Assume a narrowly defined money supply of 100 and unused bank over-draft allowances of 10. Let the over-drafts of 6 be drawn on—that is, used in order to make payment. The narrowly defined money supply is then 106, and unused over-drafts have fallen to 4. It would be double counting to include *used* over-drafts in the monetary aggregate variable, because they are already included in the demand deposit portion of the money supply. Clearly, funds in the economy available to finance transactions are unchanged by the taking down of a credit line, and this fact is reflected by including only unused over-drafts in the definition of the money stock.

The situation is similar but more complicated in the case of trade or consumer credit. The proceeds of the extension of such credit are not demand deposit funds, but rather a nonnegotiable, short-term instrument—accounts receivable. This instrument may be a near-money, and therefore a liquid means of storing wealth; however, expended trade credit can never be used by its holder to finance further expenditures directly. Accounts receivable are not a means of exchange, and therefore should only be counted in the money supply if they can be "monetized" by the firm's bank (as is the case with any other

---

13. George W. Mitchell, "A New Look at Monetary Policy Instruments," *Journal of Money, Credit and Banking,* III (May 1971), pp. 381–390.

14. John M. Keynes, *Treatise on Money,* Vol. I. (New York: Harcourt Brace and Company, 1930); R.W. Clower, "Theoretical Foundations of Monetary Policy," and H.G. Johnson, "Discussion," both in G. Clayton, J.C. Gilbert and R. Sedgwick, editors, *Monetary Theory and Monetary Policy in the 1970s,* London: Oxford University Press, 1971; Arthur B. Laffer, "Trade Credit and the Money Market," *Journal of Political Economy,* (March/April 1970), pp. 239–267.

asset). If such monetization does indeed occur then they will already be included in the narrowly defined money supply. It is thus the *unused* portion of available trade credit that must be added to the narrow definition of money.

The importance of including unexpended trade credit and consumer credit in the Federal Reserve monetary aggregate will be substantially greater with an EMTS than it is today. Utilization of overdraft facilities in the U.S. is likely to increase sharply under the EMTS, as a large number of households negotiate for credit lines that will frequently be employed. Presently a large volume of bank credit lines to firms does exist; but these are frequently demanded only as security for commercial paper issued by the corporations. In most of these cases it is never intended that the lines will be taken down, and they are therefore not really relevant to the money supply. This situation could well change when consumers are given sizeable amounts of overdraft facilities; the Federal Reserve will then be faced with the task of estimating the extent to which outstanding credit lines are expected (by their holders) to be used during a given period of time. It is this portion of aggregate credit lines that will be integral to the money supply.

Store of Value. The fact that money is a riskless means of storing value accounts for its precautionary and speculative uses. But there are available today several other assets which, in addition to being virtually riskless, return a positive yield. Indeed, many writers contend that the nontransactions demand for money is totally dominated by a demand for savings and time accounts and other short-term securities.[15] This situation will certainly persist under the EMTS. In particular, the liquidity of savings and time deposits should become greater as a result of the lower transaction costs attached to dealing in such securities, and the public's increased interest sensitivity will lead individuals to concentrate their idle (that is, nontransactions) cash balances in interest-bearing accounts to a greater extent than they do today. In this fashion we expect that the EMTS will increase the overall importance of nonmoney liquid assets in the portfolios of households and corporations. In addition, households may at least partially substitute their newly-procured credit lines for precautionary reserves that had previously been held in demand accounts or near-money assets, thereby inducing still further shifts away from traditional liquid portfolio positions.

The attempt to amalgamate cash, demand deposits, credit lines, savings accounts, etc., into an aggregate liquidity indicator will of necessity be an empirical problem. It has been found in past studies that various near-money assets differ in the liquidity they provide to their owners.[16] This will continue to

---

15. Garvy and Blyn, *op. cit.*, David Laidler, "The Definition of Money: Theoretical and Empirical Problems," *Journal of Money Credit and Banking*, I (August 1969), pp. 508–525. George W. Mitchell, "A New Look at Monetary Policy Instruments," Journal of Money Credit and Banking, III (May 1971), pp. 381–390.

16. See, for example, Tong Hun Lee, "Substitutability of Non-bank Intermediary Liabilities for Money: The Empirical Evidence," *Journal of Finance*, XXX (September 1966), pp. 441–458.

prevail in the future, although the EMTS may perhaps alter the relative liquidity of various instruments. Furthermore, use of near monies and credit lines as substitutes for M_1 varies over the business cycle in response to interest rates, changes in the availability of credit, etc. Such shifts will also have to be accounted for in constructing a new monetary aggregate variable.

8.2.3 The Channels of Credit Extension

The future system of financial intermediaries will be characterized by more nearly perfect competition than exists today. Correspondingly, there should emerge a better allocation of capital and an increased ability for all intermediaries to compete for funds either by gaining deposits or issuing subordinated debentures. The proportion of society's capital that is channelled through intermediaries should therefore rise from its present level. In addition, intermediaries will be free to raise their deposit rates when market yields threaten to cause disintermediation. As a result, there will be less cyclical shifting of credit funds between intermediaries and the open market as has occurred during recent tight money periods.

This increase in the relative importance of intermediary lending raises the question of the place of credit rationing in the EMTS economy. Intermediary lending has always been characterized by nonprice rationing of credit, as well as the more standard price (interest rate) rationing mechanism. Nonprice rationing of intermediary credit can occur both in the long run equilibrium and, *a fortiori*, during cyclical tight money periods.[17] The EMTS is unlikely to have any significant effects on the existence of equilibrium nonprice credit rationing. Such behavior on the part of lenders is rational due to usury ceilings, the financial characteristics of potential borrowers, and other situations for which the EMTS will have no direct implications.

Cyclical nonprice credit rationing, in contrast, should be considerably less prevalent under the EMTS than it is today. Such rationing arises as a result of a difference between the intermediary's *desired* interest rate on its loans (which is equal to its marginal cost of loanable funds) and the actual loan rate (which is constrained at least partially by institutional factors). Under the current regime, during the periods of monetary tightness the desired loan rate rises as the marginal cost of loanable funds rises, but actual intermediary loan rates tend to follow only with a lag. In the interim, short-term credit rationing occurs. Under an EMTS, however, the differential between the desired loan rate and the quoted rate is less likely to move in so marked a cyclical fashion. First, the marginal cost of bank funds during expansionary periods will vary less when Regulation Q ceilings have been eliminated. Currently, when Regulation Q ceilings constrain

---

17. For a further discussion of the theory of nonprice credit rationing, see Dwight M. Jaffee, *Credit Rationing and the Commercial Loan Market,* (New York: John Wiley and Sons, 1971.)

banks, the *marginal* cost of funds rises abruptly above the *average* cost as the institutions attempt to obtain funds from unconventional sources, while the quoted loan rates tend to move quite sluggishly. Without Regulation Q ceilings, intermediaries' marginal cost of funds will rise less sharply, and consequently the loan rate differential will be smaller. Second, the elimination of Regulation Q and the effects of a more competitive loan market, combined with an increased awareness of interest rate charges on the part of the public, should allow the banks to change quoted loan rates more freely. Both of these effects will thus reduce the role of nonprice factors in rationing credit during tight money times. This, in turn, will affect the lags involved with contractionary monetary policy, as will be discussed in the next section.

8.3 Monetary Policy Under the EMTS

The efficacy and usefulness of contracyclical monetary policy in the U.S. has long been an issue of debate in the economic and banking literatures. This same debate obviously applies to our discussion of the EMTS. In this section we will therefore examine the theory and practice of Federal Reserve monetary control, and extrapolate these operations into the future. First, however, it is important to consider (and dismiss) the possibility that the EMTS may precipitate far-reaching changes in the theoretical aspects of monetary control.

8.3.1 The Theory of Monetary Control
Under an EMTS

In its essential features, monetary control is based on the monetary authority's ability to determine the "high-powered" monetary base. While this base may be used as currency for the nonbank sectors of the economy, and may rise and fall with variations in float outstanding, the predominant part of the base is held by the banking system as reserves. By varying this reserve base, the monetary authority affects interest rates and controls the ability of the banking system to expand its assets. The linkage between control of the monetary base and the real sector is, however, by no means a perfect one, for so-called "leakages" and "slippages" are quite common. First, the Federal Reserve must accurately determine in advance the proper policy operations required to produce a desired change in the monetary base. The base, in turn, is not rigidly related to the money supply because of float, currency holdings, and bank holdings of excess reserves. Finally, changes in the level of interest rates and the availability of bank credit will have varying effects on production and investment in the real sector, due to varying interest elasticities of demand for loans, the differential effects of credit rationing, etc.

The EMTS will embody several features that bear directly on the processes of monetary control. One immediate result will be a significant reduction in the extent of leakages of high-powered money: we have already pointed out that nonbank holdings of currency will be substantially reduced; and float will essentially vanish. This would, then, appear to bode well for the accuracy of monetary policy.

We can attempt to quantify the effects of these developments in the following standard model of the money supply process. Let:

D =   Demand deposits.

$\bar{C}$ =   Currency held by nonbank sectors (exogenously determined).

M =   The narrowly defined money supply.

H =   The high-powered money base.

R =   Reserves required by the regulatory authorities.

E =   Excess reserves held by the banks.

$\bar{T}$ =   Time deposits at commercial banks (exogenously determined).

r_d =   Reserve requirement against demand deposits (that is, required reserves as a fraction of deposit balances).

r_t =   Reserve requirement against time deposits.

The following identities then follow:

$$M = \bar{C} + D \qquad\qquad\qquad\qquad\qquad\qquad\qquad\qquad (8\text{-}1)$$

$$H = R + E + \bar{C} \qquad\qquad\qquad\qquad\qquad\qquad\qquad (8\text{-}2)$$

$$R = r_d D + r_t \bar{T} \qquad\qquad\qquad\qquad\qquad\qquad\qquad (8\text{-}3)$$

Equation (8-1) defines the money supply; Equation (8-2) specifies that the monetary base must be held either as bank reserves (required or excess) or by the public; and Equation (8-3) defines the level of the banking system's required reserves. Solving (8-3) for D and substituting into (8-1) then yields:

$$M = \bar{C} + (R - r_t \bar{T})/r_d \qquad\qquad\qquad\qquad\qquad\qquad (8\text{-}4)$$

Solving (8-2) for R, substituting into (8-4) and arranging terms, we obtain

$$M = [H - E - r_t \bar{T} - (1 - r_d)\,\bar{C}]\,/r_d. \qquad\qquad\qquad (8\text{-}5)$$

Equation (8-5) represents a money stock formula consisting of the high-powered money base less leakages to excess reserves, time-deposit reserves, and the currency held by the nonbank public, all multiplied by $1/r_d$. The EMTS will directly affect only two variables in (8-5)—$\overline{C}$ and H. Float is a net addition to the high-powered money base H, and from (8-5) we can see that as float decreases, so too will M. Therefore, in order to maintain a constant supply of money the authorities will have to inject new reserves into the banking system to replace those lost as float disappears.[18] Second, Equation (8-5) shows that the money supply will expand with any drop in $\overline{C}$, *ceteris paribus.* Since $\overline{C}$ will be a great deal lower with the EMTS than it is today, the Federal Reserve will have to contract H in order to offset the expansionary influence of the change in $\overline{C}$.

There are also at least two indirect effects of the EMTS on M that are illustrated in Equation (8-5). First, it can be seen that any increase in excess reserves (E) will reduce M. It was noted in Chapter 6 that the banks are likely to maintain greater excess reserves under the EMTS, in response to the existence of stochastic consumer credit line takedowns. The attendant decrease in M will offset the changes induced by float and $\overline{C}$. Second, we can see that the level of time deposits directly affects M. Time deposit balances in the banking system will almost certainly change under the EMTS, but the direction of that change is uncertain. There should be a net inflow of funds to time accounts as a result of better intermediation; and there will also be funds shifted between time and demand accounts due to reduced transaction costs, some shortening of the payment period, and the payment of interest on demand deposits. We cannot, however, predict the direction of this shift *a priori,* and consequently the net effect on time deposit balances is also unknown at this time.

The monetary authority should be able to adjust to all of these (direct and indirect) effects with relatively little trouble. There is, however, one further issue to be considered. Under the current regime, banks hold vault cash and Federal Reserve deposits for three reasons: first, to meet over-the-counter cash flows; second, to meet adverse interbank clearings; and third, to satisfy reserve requirements. It has been pointed out by James Tobin and William Brainard, however, that the efficacy of today's open market operations could be retained even without formal reserve requirements, since the banking system would still continue to hold high-powered money reserves to meet the over-the-counter and the adverse clearing flows.[19] Under an EMTS, over-the-counter flows are likely

---

18. The Board of Governors of the Federal Reserve has already taken action similar to this: In September, 1972 reserve requirements were lowered at the same time that Regulation D was altered to require the overnight payment of all checks. See Chapter 5 for a futher discussion of these regulation changes.

19. See James Tobin and William Brainard, "Financial Intermediaries and the Effectiveness of Monetary Controls," *American Economic Review* (May 1963), pp. 383–400; and William Brainard, "Financial Intermediaries and a Theory of Monetary Control," *Yale Economic Essays* (Fall 1964), pp. 431–482.

to be trivial, and it is possible that the variability of interbank clearings will be significantly reduced. The incentives for banks to hold reserves will thus be reduced if not eliminated. Consequently, with an EMTS, much more than with the present system, it is critical that the Federal Reserve continue to impose reserve requirements on the banking system. However, *so long as the banks are required to hold some fixed level of reserves, monetary policy will continue to operate in its traditional manner.*

8.3.2. Existing Federal Reserve Control Tools

We can thus expect that the *modus operandi* of the Federal Reserve's current "weapons" will not be seriously impaired by the EMTS. Reserve requirements, open market operations, and the discount window should all have the same types of effects as they do today (as can be seen in Equation (8-5)). We have already pointed out that specific functional relationships in the economy will be different under the EMTS; but once these new functions are estimated (by no means a small or easy task, but one which presents no *theoretical* obstacles), the Federal Reserve should be able to manipulate reserves and interest rates with no more difficulty than it does today. Changes in the scale of policy operations (for example, the size of a change in reserve requirements, or the dollar amount of open market security sales) will be necessary, but the responses of the banking system should be similar to what they have been in the past.

In fact, we would expect future monetary policy to be more efficient and easier to effect for three reasons. First and most important, better information flows will be available with an EMTS. Policymakers will have the capacity to accumulate virtually any conceivable type of financial data on a real-time basis. In such an environment, the recognition lag attached to policy operations will be shortened drastically. We feel that this particular aspect of the EMTS presents a great potential for the future importance of monetary policy operations as a means of maintaining economic stability in the United States.[20]

Second, it seems likely that regulations concerning Federal Reserve authority will be altered in some fashion. Today about 45 percent of all commercial banks, holding some 80 percent of total deposits, are Federal Reserve members. The Federal Reserve's control over such a large majority of the banking system's resources is generally said to be sufficient for the purposes of monetary policy. However, many of the largest banks in the country maintain their membership in the System only because of the check clearing services provided to members. These large banks rarely borrow at the discount window, and often find Federal Reserve regulations and reserve requirements to be bothersome or confining.

---

20. This potential gain to the society that would be incorporated into the EMTS ability to provide aggregate financial data represents still another argument for Federal Reserve supervision of the design stage of the EMTS. See Section 4.2.4.

Under a privately-owned EMTS which provides services to all intermediaries on equal terms, there will be little to prevent these institutions from seeking a charter in some state with relatively low reserve requirements and dropping out of the Federal Reserve System altogether. Such action by even a few "mega-banks" could seriously impair the Federal Reserve's influence in the economy. It would therefore seem desirable to change federal regulations such that all institutions offering third party payments either join the Federal Reserve System or at least meet federally imposed reserve requirements. (This is in fact the recommendation of the Hunt Commission.) Such action would be equitable for the intermediaries involved and would provide the Federal Reserve with better control over the economy, in addition to removing the threat of a dangerous drop in System membership.

Finally, the reduction of float to zero will considerably simplify the day-to-day operations of the FOMC trading desk, allowing it to concentrate more on "offensive" System policies.

There is also one significant area in which the introduction of an EMTS may complicate or impair monetary policy: Monetary policy's contractionary effects will be transmitted to the real sector with a slower speed in the EMTS regime where credit rationing is less prevalent than today. Donald Tucker demonstrates that one effect of nonprice credit rationing on an economy is likely to be that tight money conditions spread through the economy faster than in an environment where rationing is absent.[21] Under the EMTS, nominal interest rates may fluctuate more over a cycle than they do today, but the *true* cost of borrowed funds (which includes a shadow price reflecting the complete unavailability of funds to some borrowers) will vary less. Consequently, in the absence of rationing, the economy will adjust to contractionary Federal Reserve policies only with a longer lag.

On net, however, we expect that the potential advantages contained in the EMTS for monetary policy are likely to outweigh any additional problems that may be created. The Federal Reserve will encounter difficulties primarily during the period of transition to the EMTS; but once the new stable environment occurs, and its parameters are known, monetary policy should be able to reclaim its role as an effective policy tool.

8.3.3. A Special Case: The Regulation of Consumer Credit Lines

In Section 8.1.1 we showed that traditional monetary policy by itself may be inadequate to control installment credit that is extended via consumer over-

21. Donald Tucker, "Credit Rationing, Interest Rate Lags, and Monetary Policy Speed," *Quarterly Journal of Economics,* LXXII, (February 1968), pp. 54–84.

draft facilities under the EMTS. However, it is possible that such credit will become a major stabilizing or destabilizing force in the future economy, and as such should be under the control of the monetary authorities. In this section we will consider several ways in which such control might be effected in a regime where installment credit is extended largely through consumers' bank credit lines.

To begin with, we must point out that selective credit controls (that is, Federal Reserve control of specific assets of the banking system, interest rates, down payments, maturity, etc.) are ineffectual by themselves in a system where borrowers have access to several alternative sources of credit. Donald Hodgman[22] has argued that selective credit controls are effective only to the extent that borrowers are unable to alter the channels through which they obtain credit. In the particular case of consumers, the main sources of credit besides the banking system are consumer finance companies and trade credit from merchants. In the absence of general monetary tightness, therefore, selective controls on banks' consumer loans would have only minimal effects on the amount of installment credit extended in the economy.

We can see, then, that neither general monetary controls nor selective credit controls alone will be able to deal adequately with cyclical variations in consumer credit line takedowns. This will be a problem to the extent that installment credit becomes a major destabilizing (or stabilizing) force in the economy. Selective credit controls can, however, be used to alter "the profitability of specific credit instruments and categories."[23] In a regime of general monetary restraint, this result is equivalent to altering the *incidence* of monetary policy. Therefore, if the Federal Reserve determines that consumer credit lines must be specifically controlled during tight money periods, selective policy instruments could be effective. Such selective controls may take several forms, among which are the following:

1. If the *ceteris paribus* level of credit lines extended is deemed too large, the Federal Reserve could impose a reserve requirement against such lines, and vary the level of the required reserves as policy dictates. This would cause banks to contract their outstanding lines by refusing to renew credit arrangements as they expire. Furthermore, the banks may be induced in this manner to raise the interest rate applicable to lines already outstanding that are drawn on, thereby lowering the demand for installment credit somewhat.
2. A special subsidy (or tax) could be attached to consumer overdrafts outstanding, thus altering the effective rate of interest derivable from such loans. This subsidy (tax) could be varied over the cycle.

---

22. Donald Hodgman, "Selective Credit Controls," *Journal of Money, Credit and Banking*, IV, (May 1972), pp. 342–359.

23. *Ibid.*, p. 357.

3.   FDIC insurance payments could be varied according to the level of out-
     standing consumer credit, either its absolute amount, or as a percentage of
     total assets. More generally, it would be efficient for FDIC insurance rates
     to vary with the overall riskiness of a bank's lending and portfolio policies.
4.   An absolute limit could be set on consumer credit lines—either as a dollar
     amount or as a percentage of total assets. This type of quota would entail
     all the well-known inefficiencies of quota rationing schemes, but nonethe-
     less it is quite possible that the simplicity and ease of enforcement of this
     sort of scheme may cause it to be chosen by authorities as the primary
     means of controlling aggregate credit line extensions.
5.   Finally, the maturity of consumer loans could be limited by the Federal
     Reserve, as has on occasion been done in the past.

It seems very likely that some scheme along these lines will be needed by
the Federal Reserve as a new "weapon" of monetary control if consumer credit
becomes a significant force in the economy under the EMTS. There is also a
related issue to be considered: if consumer credit is indeed a destabilizing influence in the economy, what should be the role of the discount window in helping banks to cover their credit line takedowns? Regulation A of the Federal
Reserve System states that:

> Federal Reserve credit is generally extended on a short-term basis to a
> member bank in order to enable it to adjust its asset position when neces-
> sary because of developments such as a sudden withdrawal of deposits or
> seasonal requirements for credit beyond those which can reasonably be met
> by the use of the bank's own resources.[24]

In view of the wording of this Regulation it is clear that the Federal Reserve
Banks could view a sharp and sudden increase in the takedown rate of a bank's
credit lines as a legitimate reason for advances. A precedent for (and *caveat*
regarding) these actions, indeed, can be found in the policy of the FHLBB with
respect to SLA mortgage lending commitments. In 1966 it was made system
policy for the Home Loan Banks to extend expansion advances to "meet season-
al needs or to meet commitments that would have been at realistic levels except
for adverse cash flow developments."[25] However, during the 1966 crisis, advances
were denied to SLA which were still extending new commitments; the FHLBB
showed itself unwilling to finance indiscriminate SLA mortgage commitments.
      The implication for Federal Reserve advances to banks in the future seems
to be clear: An increase in line take-downs will be legitimate grounds for an

---

24. *The Federal Reserve System: Purposes and Functions,* Federal Reserve Board of
Governors. Washington D.C., 1963, p. 43.

25. Federal Home Loan Bank Board *Annual Report,* 1966, as quoted in Robert M.
Fisher, "The Availability of Mortgage Lending Commitments," Federal Reserve Board of
Governors, 1969, p. 8.

advance provided that a bank's commitments are at a "realistic" level. The Federal Reserve cannot stand ready to cover any and all bank credit lines without sacrificing a good deal of the potency of contractionary monetary policies.

If credit line takedowns do vary procyclically and if the Federal Reserve *were* automatically to grant advances in such situations, then it would simultaneously have to engage in large government security sales in order to counteract these reserves extended to certain banks at a time of peak credit demand. There would thus be a shifting of pressure from the borrowing bank's portfolio to the portfolios of other banks in the system. Indeed, the recognition of consumer credit demands as a valid reason for Federal Reserve advances would result in a socially inefficient overissuing of such credit lines by individual banks. In such an environment a bank would not have to bear the full costs of portfolio adjustments made necessary by its credit lines, but could instead shift these costs to other institutions by means of its access to the discount window. Contractionary monetary policies will be more effective if banks plan their portfolios under the assumption that any excessive credit lines issued must be covered from internal sources only.

8.4 Summary

Innovation in a society's payments system on the scale represented by the EMTS is bound to precipitate widespread changes in the parameters of the economy's functional relationships; but these will be largely quantitative. The liquidity of various assets will be changed, and money's velocity will be altered; credit in the economy will be extended through somewhat different channels; output will rise in the economy, accompanied by shifts in the distribution of income, changes in the relative importance of private and public expenditures, and a possible shift in the society's investment schedule. Monetary policy however, should continue to operate as it has in the past, with the possible exception that widespread credit lines may complicate the monetary authority's stabilization tasks. On the other hand, however, better information flows in the economy should be important in helping the Federal Reserve to determine the proper course of action to be followed at any given time.

Overall, it is apparent that the macroeconomic implications of the EMTS will be far less revolutionary and of less importance than the microeconomic changes which were discussed in the preceding two chapters.

9   Summary and Conclusions

In the course of this study, four major themes concerning the effects of an electronic monetary transfer system (EMTS) on the economy have been developed. These themes relate to the *feasibility of an EMTS*, the general *efficiency benefits* that will be derived from its use, *the benefits to individual sectors* of the economy that will be derived from its use, and the *macroeconomic implications* of the EMTS. In concluding the study in this chapter, we shall attempt to summarize our main conclusions in these four areas.

9.1 Feasibility of the EMTS

We have argued that the impetus for the EMTS originates in the increasing costs that will be necessary for the maintenance of a paper-oriented transfer system. In Chapter 3, it was indicated specifically how high the costs of check transfer are today and how, without significant opportunities for further automation, these costs are likely to rise further in the future. Similarly, it was noted that credit cards, whatever their popularity in current use, do not solve this problem; indeed, in terms of creating expensive paper flows, credit cards are distinctly a step in the wrong direction. In contrast, in Chapter 4 we documented as well as possible the likely costs of an EMTS. Every indication is that the EMTS will be absolutely less expensive than the current system of check and credit card paper transfer. It is here that we find the principal economic motivation for the adoption of the new system.

On this basis we expect that the EMTS will be desired, and indeed sought after, by both the commercial banking industry and by the Federal Reserve System. It is in fact already clear from issued statements that progress toward an EMTS will be welcomed by these groups. In a similar way, we can foresee no serious difficulties in the acceptance of the EMTS either by other participants in the financial markets or by corporations (both manufacturing and retailing). These groups, with perhaps the exception of nonbank depository intermediaries, will receive a variety of direct benefits from the EMTS with very few offsetting disadvantages. The nonbank depository intermediaries will also receive important direct benefits, but there will be more offsets especially in terms of the risks of operating in a new and more competitive environment; as we have developed in Chapter 5, however, (and summarize below), the net advantages to these institutions are clearly positive and large, and we cannot see a case for any serious problem for the acceptance of the EMTS by these institutions.

In contrast to financial institutions and corporations, it has been argued strongly by some that consumers (household units) may be reluctant to accept the EMTS. For example, experience with automated tellers and with pilot EMTS programs has in some cases indicated a strong reluctance on the part of consumers to deal with a fully automated and electronic system. In addition, there are important social concerns that arise with a system in which a mass of data on individuals is stored and easily accessible. We do not have evidence with which we can directly confront this forecast of consumer reluctance to use the EMTS. Indeed, it is understandable and no doubt will occur. We remain convinced, however, that the cost and efficiency advantages that will be available under the EMTS must in the end win out. To put it briefly, reluctance has its price, and we believe that the consumer sector, when confronted with the distinctly lower costs and the convenience factors of the EMTS, will realize that *it* is the sector that, in fact, has the most to gain under the EMTS.

We find that the actual form the EMTS will take is more in doubt than the ultimate acceptance of the system. We have been able to develop what are the likely broad outlines of the system. First, the system will include two major computer-related systems: the national switching network, and the banks' computerized data processing units. The national switching network will thus exist as a national communication link similar to the telephone system and it will accept inputs from computers (of individual units), retail store terminals, and individual telephones. The data processing units will then receive data from the network and reply to it with information on the status of accounts, as well as, of course, updating all accounts. In addition to this basic structure, it is apparent that a large number of other features of the system must be developed; for example, problems of security and means for providing back-up facilities in case of computer or system failure must be developed. These issues have been discussed in Chapter 4 and we have indicated the reasons why none of them should present serious hurdles for the EMTS. It is equally clear, however, that a great deal of work and planning remains to be done.

9.2 Efficiency Benefits of the EMTS

We have stressed in our study that the EMTS will provide benefits, direct cost savings aside, in terms of more efficiency in the financial markets. Efficiency is defined here in the sense that services are priced at their (socially optimal) marginal cost. We have shown a large number of cases in which either the EMTS will directly lead to gains in efficiency or in which it will lead to changes that themselves will bring forth more efficient pricing.

With respect to efficiency gains provided directly by the EMTS, three main points should be mentioned:

1. It is expected under the EMTS (with government prodding if necessary) that the price for making fund transfers will be set at the appropriate marginal cost. For the present check clearing and credit card system, the price for most check transfers and credit card purchases is well below the true cost to the economy. This has lead to an overuse of the payments system. With an EMTS, in contrast, the costs of transfer will be lower so that a larger volume of transactions can be handled efficiently, and it is expected that the efficient volume of transactions will in fact be achieved.

2. The complete separation of transactions for settlement and the provision of credit facilities and loans should be achieved under the EMTS. As we have developed in Chapters 2 and 4, such a separation is necessary for the proper pricing of transactions fees and loan interest charges. Under the present system, and particularly with credit cards, the settlement transactions and credit provision are inefficiently integrated.

3. A large part of the relevant data on financial and goods transactions will be stored and available for immediate access with the EMTS. While the availability of this data may be disturbing if it is allowed to be misused— and safeguards will have to be developed to prevent this—it is apparent that such information, particularly when available on an instantaneous basis, will be of great value for achieving proper monetary and fiscal stabilization policies.

Gains in efficiency will also be attributable to the EMTS to the extent that it provides the basis for a more competitive financial system. Numerous examples of this type have been cited in the text, so that here we shall simply list four of the most important cases:

1. A more optimal and efficient flow of funds, both among industries and among regions of the economy, should be achieved.
2. Consumer loan markets should be significantly expanded, including the provision of overdraft facilities for short-term consumer loans and lines of credit for larger and long-term consumer loans.
3. The payment of interest on demand deposit balances should occur, resulting in a more optimal supply of money.
4. Financial institutions will be motivated to move toward more direct and explicit systems for setting fees on the services they provide.

There is one important factor, however, that may be responsible for limiting some of the gains in efficiency that could be achieved under the EMTS: the need for direct customer relationships between the borrower and the lending institution in the provision of loans. Under the present system, both in commercial loans and in household loans (consumer loans and mortgages), direct and personal contact between the borrower and the lender is considered an important part of most loan negotiations. This leads to, or is at least symptomatic of, a degree of imperfect competition in the loan markets, and it may be responsible for imperfect competition in related markets (such as deposits). Imperfect competition occurs when there is need for direct contact because convenience factors such as the location of the institution, the number of branches, and the history of the borrower's relationship to the lending institution become relevant to the loan negotiation. It can be hoped, and surely will occur to an important extent, that loan negotiations of this sort will become less personal under the EMTS as lenders rely more on computer-generated analyses (and the newly available data) for loan decisions. To the extent that personal customer relationships remain important, however, the gains in efficiency under the EMTS will be limited.

9.3 Sectoral Benefits and Effects of the EMTS

Our study has distinguished among the financial sector, the nonfinancial, corporate (and governmental) sector, and the household sector as parts of the economy that will be effected in significantly different ways by the EMTS. Thus, for the purposes of summary, each of them should be considered separately.

9.3.1 The Financial Sector

With respect to the financial sector, the most important effect is that the competitive environment of the EMTS will require a large number of changes in the structure and regulation of the institutions that operate in this sector. It is interesting, in particular, that many of the changes that we expect to occur under the EMTS have already been suggested in recent proposals for the restructuring of the financial markets (see the Hunt Commission Report and Chapter 5). These structural and regulatory changes include third party payments, extended asset powers, and more flexible liability issue powers for all financial intermediaries (particularly the savings institutions), as well as the elimination of deposit rate ceilings on both demand deposits and time deposits.

Important questions that arise in this context concern whether there will be significant changes in the degree of specialization of financial intermediaries and in the number of, and competitive relationship among, the remaining institutions. Our answers to these questions are quite definite, and they indicate that the changes are not likely to be as great as some have suggested. For example, we anticipate the extended lending and borrowering powers of the depository intermediaries will have the effect of making them more alike and hence less specialized. But while we expect the current distinctions between these institutions to become blurred, by no means do we expect the distinctions to be eliminated. In particular, due to established expertise and historical relationships we anticipate that commercial banks will continue to specialize in the provision of loans to business enterprise. Similarly, we anticipate that savings institutions will continue to specialize in the provision of mortgage funds. It is, thus, primarily in the area of consumer loans that the institutions will have their greatest overlap and in which innovations can be most expected. While the EMTS in some ways will bring conflicting pressures to bear on the specialized financial institutions (for example life insurance companies, investment funds, and credit unions), we expect their position to remain essentially unaffected. In contrast, we anticipate that the condition of a more competitive consumer loan market will reduce the significance of consumer finance companies.

9.3.2 Nonfinancial Corporations

We expect that the effects of the EMTS on nonfinancial corporations will be quite varied depending on the specific sector and size of the corporation. On the general level, however, we anticipate that all corporations will be effected, more or less, by three considerations:

1. Corporations will allow banks and other financial institutions to handle an increasing share of their financial matters. This will arise because the financial institutions under the EMTS will process a great part of the data relating to the corporations' trade credit collections and debits and will be able to monitor the firm's cash flow position. It thus will be efficient, and hence less costly, for the banks to take over these functions.

2. Relatively small changes in the manner in which trade credit is financed will occur with the EMTS. It has been suggested by some writers that, under an EMTS, banks will directly finance a large share of the trade credit that is currently financed by corporations themselves. We recognize that there would be important advantages in this change, and that some movement in this direction should be expected. We still find, however, that corporations will wish to maintain primary control over the granting of receivable loans, both for competitive reasons and to achieve price discrimination.

3. The effects of the EMTS on demand deposit balances of corporations will be ambiguous. Following inventory-theoretic models, lowered transactions costs and the reduced volatility of corporate cash flow should reduce corporate demand deposit balances. But the payment of interest on demand deposits should stimulate the holding of such balances, and thus the net effect is not known *a priori*.

We also anticipate that two subsets of nonfinancial corporations—small firms and retailing firms—will receive special benefits under an EMTS. For small firms, diseconomies of small scale in billing and credit operations are important and thus the advantages of bank management of their short-run financing and cash flow will be great. Also, we can expect that the amount of cyclical credit rationing, which presently is directed primarily at these smaller firms, will be reduced; thus small firms will have to rely less on trade credit from large firms in tight money periods than they have heretofore. We do not anticipate, however, that this factor will be fully eliminated, and the rationing of small firms by banks and the capital markets will exist even under the EMTS.

With respect to retail firms, the major effect of the EMTS will concern their credit operations. Under the present system these firms grant a large amount of "free" credit to household units with credit card and in-house convenience credit purchases. There is, of course, a cost to such credit and it is presumably met by a higher average price on the goods sold. With the EMTS, however, we have seen that a much sharper line should be drawn between the payment for goods and the provision of credit. In particular, we expect that "discounts" will be allowed on purchases made with instantaneous transfer for an EMTS account; or equivalently, that a "premium" in terms of explicit interest charges will be set on purchases made with the use of credit. Furthermore, an increasing proportion of such credit should be provided by financial institutions directly, although retailers will maintain installment credit facilities (which should generally be profitable for them) and may retain some limited forms of convenience credit.

9.3.3 Household Units

In many ways household units (consumers) will be the prime beneficiaries of the EMTS. On a general level the EMTS will create a more competitive set of financial markets and will make available to the household units a variety of services and economies of scale that have until now been available only to large corporations. Furthermore, it can be expected that the lowest income household units will gain the most under the EMTS. Three examples can illustrate these points.

1. We have indicated that the costs for all types of transactions—both goods purchases and financial asset transfers—will be lower under the EMTS. A large part of the *number* of total transactions in the economy are made by the smallest household units and thus the fixed cost per transaction looms large. With the reduction in such costs a direct gain will accrue to these household units.

2. We anticipate several changes in the treatment of demand deposit balances, all of which should benefit small household units: interest will be paid on the balances, preauthorized transfers will be available, and over-draft facilities, at least in small amounts, will be provided to many units.

3. We expect significant modifications in the provision of large and long-term consumer loans. We have already noted that we expect this market to become more competitive with direct benefits to the consuming units. In addition, we have argued that lines of credits will become available to household units under the EMTS, much as such lines are already available to large corporations.

9.4 Macroeconomic and Policy-Related
Effects of the EMTS

We have noted in Chapter 8, and it is a point worth stressing, that we expect the major impacts of the EMTS will be experienced on the microeconomic level. In this microeconomic category, for example, the various efficiency and sectoral benefits discussed in the previous two sections of this chapter should be classified. Of course, new behavior on the part of individual economic units, when aggregated over all such units, amount to shifts and changes in the elasticities of macroeconomic relationships. These shifts and changes will necessitate adjustments on the part of policy-makers, particularly the monetary authority, in planning the strength and timing of policy measures. Furthermore, many of the *quantitative* results now available concerning the impacts of policy on macroeconomic variables will have to be reestimated under the regime of the EMTS, and this may prove difficult during the transition period when a sufficient set of data for efficient estimates of the new parameters will not be available. In particular, we have suggested that the appropriate definition of money and the velocity of the monetary variable may be changed under the EMTS in ways that are not fully predicatable *a priori*; consequently new empirical results will have to be obtained under the EMTS. In the long-run, however, the EMTS presents no new conceptual problems in this regard, and we expect that the measurement of macroeconomic relationships will be achieved as readily and at least as well under the EMTS as it is today.

There are, however, four summary points that can be made concerning the macroeconomic impacts of the EMTS:

1. The level of financial intermediation, both by depository institutions and by brokers and dealers developing "funds" of particular assets, will be increased under the EMTS. This will create a larger and no doubt more interest-sensitive flow of funds in the economy. We also anticipate that the system will be more self-regulating than it is presently, since institutions will have greater freedom in the choice of assets and in the issue of liabilities.

2. There is no *a priori* expectation for the direction of change in the general price level under an EMTS, although two factors that will affect the empirical outcome may be noted. First, as just indicated, the EMTS will create changes in the relevant monetary variable and in its velocity of circulation. Second, the EMTS will force a separation of transactions for settlement and the provision of credit such that instantaneous settlement will receive a discount relative to credit transactions (or equivalently credit transactions will pay a relative premium). We stress, however, that there is no *a priori* expectation of the direction of these changes, and we anticipate in fact, that the net effects will be small and probably negligible.

3. We anticipate that monetary policy will be carried out under the EMTS in much the same way it is today. The traditional tools of monetary policy— open market operations, discount loans from the Federal Reserve, and reserve requirements—will continue to operate in much the same manner. Indeed, the increased availability of data under the EMTS should significantly reduce the problems associated with policy decision-making. The channels for the *modus operandi* of monetary policy may be changed, with a smaller amount of cyclical credit rationing occurring, and thus interest rates may become more important indicators of monetary tightness. Also, preauthorized lines of credit to consumers will expand, with some adjustment necessary on the part of the Federal Reserve. This adjustment could involve the possible use of selective credit controls (although we remain in doubt as to their effectiveness), and the provision of discount loans, when financial institutions experience unexpected take-downs on credit lines during periods in which the monetary authority is attempting to enforce a tight money policy. Overall, however, we expect the main problem for the monetary authority will be its adjustment to the new set of parameters that govern the empirical relationships.

Finally, one should anticipate that a major issue of policy as the EMTS is introduced will concern the ownership of the payments system. Ownership is mixed under the present system, with the private banking system carrying out the majority of transfers, other private enterprises owning and leasing computer hardware and some transmission lines, and the Federal Reserve maintaining an overall regulatory framework and providing significant subsidies to the check-clearing system. We expect, under the EMTS, that the ownership of "in-house" computer facilities for the processing of data and maintenance of accounts will continue to take a variety of forms, and that, in general, these systems will be privately run. With respect to the central switching network, however, we foresee more difficult policy questions. Specifically, the central network will have many properties of a public utility in that parallel lines may be inefficient, standardization of interfacing between components of the system will be critical, and economies of scale typical of "natural monopolies" are likely to prevail. This, then, is an area of public policy that should receive special attention.

References

A Study of the Savings and Loan Industry, Organized and edited by Irwin Friend, to be submitted to the Federal Home Loan Bank Board, Washington, D.C.: Government Printing Office, July 1969.

Allen, Jimmy B., "Factors Determining the Volume of Certificates of Deposits Outstanding: A Case Study of the Drain Off in 1969," *The American Economist,* XV (Fall 1971), pp. 32–37.

Arrow, K.J. and Hahn, F.H., *General Competitive Analysis,* San Francisco: Holden-Day, Inc., 1971.

Barro, Robert J. and Anthony J. Santomero, "Household Money Holdings and the Demand Deposit Rate," *Journal of Money Credit and Banking* (May 1972).

Baumol, William J., *Economic Theory and Operations Analysis,* Englewood Cliffs: Prentice-Hall Inc., 1965.

Benston, George J., "Costs of Operation and Economies of Scale in Savings and Loan Associations," In the Friend *Study*, Vol. II, pp. 677–762.

——, "Economies of Scale of Financial Institutions," *Journal of Money, Credit and Banking,* IV (May 1972), pp. 312–341.

——, "Savings Banking and the Public Interest," *Journal of Money Credit and Banking,* IV (February 1972, Part 2), pp. 133–226.

Board of Governors of the Federal Reserve System, *The Federal Reserve System, Purposes and Functions,* Washington: D.C., 1963.

Bond, Richard E., "Deposit Composition and Commercial Bank Earnings," *Journal of Finance,* XXVI (March 1971), pp. 39–50.

Brainard, William, "Financial Intermediaries and a Theory of Monetary Control, *Yale Economic Essays* (Fall 1964).

Brechling, F.P.R. and R.G. Lipsey, "Trade Credit and Monetary Policy," *The Economic Journal,* LXXII (December 1963) pp. 618–641.

Brill, Daniel H. and Ann P. Ulrey, "The Role of Financial Intermediaries in the U.S. Capital Markets," Federal Reserve *Bulletin,* LIII (January 1967), pp. 18–31.

Cagan, Phillip, *Determinants and Effects of Changes in the Stock of Money 1875-1960,* New York: Columbia University Press, 1965.

——, *Recent Monetary Policy and the Inflation, From 1965 to August 1971,* Washington, D.C.: American Enterprise Institute, 1971.

Cass, David and Menahem E. Yaari, "Individual Saving, Aggregate Capital Accumulation, and Efficient Growth," in Karl Shell, editor, *Essays on the Theory of Optimal Economic Growth,* Cambridge: M.I.T. Press, 1967.

Chandavarkar, Anand G., "Unused Bank Overdrafts: Their Implications for Monetary Analysis and Policy," *IMF Staff Papers,* XV (November 1968), pp. 491–519.

Chase, Samuel B. Jr., "Financial Structure and Regulation: Some Knotty Problems," *Journal of Finance,* XXVI (May 1971), pp. 585–598.

Clower, Robert, "A Reconsideration of the Microfoundations of Monetary Theory," *Western Economic Journal*, 6.

Clower, Robert, *Monetary Theory: Selected Readings,* Baltimore: Penguin Books, 1970.

Clower, Robert, "Is There an Optimal Supply of Money," *Journal of Finance* (May 1970).

Clower, Robert, "Theoretical Foundations of Monetary Policy," in G. Clayton, J.C. Gilbert, and R. Sedgwick, editors, *Monetary Theory and Policy in the 1970s,* London: Oxford University Press, 1971.

Cox, B.; Dana, A.W.; and Zeidler, H.M., *A Techno-Economic Study of Methods of Improving the Payments Mechanism,* Menlo Park, California: Stanford Research Institute, December 1966.

Davis, Richard G., "An Analysis of Quantitative Credit Controls and Related Devices," *Brookings Papers on Economic Activities, #1,* 1971.

Edwards, George D., "A Quick Fix for the Bank Card," *The Bankers Magazine,* CLV (Spring 1972), pp. 81–85.

Einzig, Paul, *Primitive Money* London: Eyre Spottiswoode, 1949.
  "Electronic Funds Transfers: Is PaCHEK a Foot in the Door?" *Savings and Loan News* (September 1971).

"Electronic Money," *Forbes*, IC (April 1, 1967), pp. 42–46.

"Electronic Money: The Atlanta Project," *Savings and Loan News* (August 1972), pp. 36–43.

Evans, Michael K. *Macroeconomic Activity,* New York: Harper and Row, 1969.

Fair, Ray C. and Dwight M. Jaffee, "An Empirical Study of the Proposals of the Hunt Commission for the Mortgage and Housing Markets," in *Policies for a More Competitive Financial System,* June 1972, Federal Reserve Bank of Boston.

Fand, David I. "Financial Regulation and the Allocative Efficiency of our Capital Markets," *National Banking Review*, III (September 1965), pp. 55–65.

——, "Savings Intermediaries and Consumer Credit Markets," In the Friend *Study*, Vol. IV, pp. 1437–78.

Federal Home Loan Bank Board, *Annual Report,* 1966, 1968, 1969, 1970.

Federal Home Loan Bank Board. "Cycles in Mortgage Credit Availability and the 1966 Experience," In *A Study of Mortgage Credit*, Subcommittee on Housing and Urban Affairs, Committee on Banking and Currency, United States Senate, May 22, 1967 (Washington D.C.: Government Printing Office), pp. 19–40.

Federal Reserve Bank of Boston, "Electronic Money . . . and the Payments Mechanism," 1967 *Annual Report.*

——, "The Payments Mechanism . . . Another Look," *Proceedings of the 47th Annual Stockholders Meeting,* 1971.

Feige, Edgar L. and Michael Parkin, "The Optimal Quantity of Money, Bonds, Commodity Inventories, and Capital," *American Economic Review*, LXI (June 1971), pp. 335–349.

Fenstermarket, Jay Van, "Bank Charge Cards- A Step Toward the 'Checkless' Society," in Fenstermaker, ed. *Readings in Financial Markets and Institutions*, New York: Meredith Corp., 1969.

Fisher, Irving, *The Theory of Interest,* New York: The MacMillan Co., 1930.

Fisher, Robert Moore, "The Availability of Mortgage Lending Commitments," Federal Reserve Board of Governors, 1969.

Forbes, Ronald W., "An Analysis of the Supply of Consumer Instalment Credit," Unpublished Ph.D. dissertation, State University of New York at Buffalo, 1968.

Friedman, Milton, "Controls on Interest Rates Paid by Banks," *Journal of Money Credit and Banking,* II (February 1970), pp. 15–32.

Friend, Irwin. "Changes in the Asset and Liability Structure of the Savings and Loan Industry." In the Friend *Study,* Vol. III, pp. 1353–1433.

Frost, Robert A., "Banking Services, Minimum Cash Balances, and the Firm's Demand for Money," *Journal of Finance* XXV (December 1970), pp. 1029–40.

Galbraith, John A., *The Economics of Banking Operations,* Montreal: McGill University Press, 1963.

Gambs, Carl M., "The Economics of An Automated Payments Mechanism," Unpublished Ph.D. dissertation, Yale University, 1972.

Garvy, George, "Structural Aspects of Money Velocity," *Quarterly Journal of Economics,* LXXIII (August 1959) pp. 429–447.

——, and Martin Blyn, *The Velocity of Money,* Federal Reserve Bank of New York, 1969.

Georgia Tech Research Institute, *Research on Improvements of the Payments Mechanism,* Federal Reserve Bank of Atlanta, July 1971.

Gibson, Donald M.T., *The Strategic and Operational Significance of the Credit Card for Commercial Banks*, Research Report #42 to the Federal Reserve Bank of Boston, August 1968.

Gibson, William E., "Compensating Balance Requirements," *National Banking Review*, II (March 1965), pp. 387–95.

"The Giro, the Computer, and Checkless Banking," *Monthly Review* of the Federal Reserve Bank of Richmond (April 1966), pp. 2–5.

Goldfeld, Stephen M., *Commercial Bank Behavior and Economic Activity,* Amsterdam: North-Holland Publishing Company, 1966.

——, "Savings and Loan Associations and the Market for Savings: Allocative Efficiency," In the Friend *Study,* Vol. II, pp. 569–658.

Grebler, Leo, *The Future of Thrift Institutions*, Joint Savings and Loan and Mutual Savings Bank Exchange Groups, June 1969.

Gregory, Robert H. and Herbert Jacobs, "A Study of the Transfer of Credit in Relation to the Banking System," MIT Dynamic Analysis and Control Laboratory Report #87 (Cambridge, 1954).

Hahn, Frank, "Equilibrium with Transactions Costs," *Econometrica* (May 1970).

Hellweg, Douglas, "A Note on Compensatory Balance Requirements," *Journal of Finance* XVI (March 1961), pp. 80–84.

Hester, Donald D., "Monetary Policy in 'Checkless' Economy," *Journal of Finance,* XXVII (May 1972), pp. 279–293.

Hicks, John, "A Suggestion for Simplifying the Theory of Money," *Economica,* (February 1935).

Hicks, John, *Value and Capital,* second edition, London: Oxford University Press, 1946.

Hodgman, Donald R., "Selective Credit Controls," *Journal of Money Credit and Banking,* IV (May 1972), pp. 342–359.

Hume, David, "Of Money," in *Essays* London: Oxford University Press, 1963.

Jaffee, Dwight M., "Barter Economies, Monetary Economics, and the Walrasian System," Unpublished, August 1971.

——, *Credit Rationing and the Commercial Loan Market,* New York: John Wiley and Sons, 1971.

——, "The Entry of Savings Institutions into the Consumer Loan Market," Unpublished, 1971.

——, "The Extended Lending, Borrowing, and Service Function Proposals of the Hunt Commission Report," *Journal of Money Credit and Banking* November 1972.

——, "Transactions Costs and the Optimal Supply of Money," Unpublished, 1971.

——, and Thomas Russell, "Are Credit Cards Inflationary?" Unpublished, August 1971.

Jevons, W. Stanley, *Money and the Mechanism of Exchange,* London: Kegan Paul, Trench, Trubner and Co., Ltd., 1902.

Johnson, Harry G., "Inside Money, Outside Money, Income, Wealth, and Welfare in Monetary Theory," *Journal of Money Credit and Banking,* I (February 1969), pp. 30–45.

Junk, Paul E., "Monetary Policy and the Extension of Trade Credit," *Southern Economic Journal,* XXX (January 1964), pp. 274–77.

Kane, Edward J. and Burton G. Malkiel, "Bank Portfolio Allocation, Deposit Variability, and the Availability Doctrine," *Quarterly Journal of Economics,* LXXIX (February 1965), pp. 113–134.

Kessel, Reuben A., "The Allocation of Mortgage Funds," In the Friend *Study,* Vol. II, pp. 659–676.

Keynes, John M., *A Treatise on Money,* New York: Harcourt, Brace and Company, 1930.

Krooss, Herman E. and Martin R. Blyn, *A History of Financial Intermediaries,* New York: Random House, Inc., 1971.

Laffer, Arthur B., "Trade Credit and the Money Market," *Journal of Political Economy,* LXXVII (March/April 1970), pp. 239–267.

Laidler, David, "The Definition of Money: Theoretical and Empirical Problems," *Journal of Money Credit and Banking,* I (August 1969), pp. 508–525.

Lawrence, Robert J. and Duane Lougee, "Determinants of Correspondent Banking Relationships," *Journal of Money Credit and Banking,* II (August 1970), pp. 358–69.

Lee, Tong Hun, "Substitutability of Non-bank Intermediary Liabilities for Money: The Empirical Evidence," *Journal of Finance,* XXX (September 1966), pp. 441–458.

Long, Robert H. and Linda M. Fenner, *An Electronic Network for Interbank Payment Communications,* Park Ridge, Ill.,: Bank Administration Institute 1969.

Malkiel, Burton G., *The Term Structure of Interest Rates: Theory, Empirical Evidence, and Applications,* New York: McCalb Seiler Publishing Company, 1970.

Marvell, Thomas B., *The Federal Home Loan Bank Board,* New York: Frederick A. Praeger, 1969.

Mateer, William H., *The Checkless Society: Its Cost Implications for the Firm,* Michigan Business Studies, 1969, Michigan State University.

Mayer, Thomas, *Monetary Policy in the United States,* New York: Random House, Inc., 1968.

McCracken, Paul W.; Mao, James C.T.; and Fricke, Cedric, *Consumer Installment Credit and Public Policy,* Michigan Business Studies, Vol. XVII No. 1, University of Michigan, Ann Arbor, Michigan, 1965.

Meltzer, Allan H., "Mercantile Credit, Monetary Policy, and Size of Firms, *Review of Economics and Statistics* XLII (November 1960), pp. 429–437.

Mill, John Stuart, *Principles of Political Economy,* New York: Augustus M. Kelly Reprint, 1969.

Minsky, Hyman P., "Financial Instability Revisited: The Economics of Disaster," Steering Committee for the Fundamental Reappraisal of the Discount Mechanism, Board of Governors of the Federal Reserve, January 1970.

Mitchell, George W., "Effects of Automation on the Structure and Functioning of Banking," *American Economic Review* LVI (May 1966), pp. 159–166.

——, "A New Look at Monetary Policy Instruments," *Journal of Money Credit and Banking,* III (May 1971), pp. 381–390.

——, "Paying and Being Paid- The Convenience and Economics of Electronic Transfer of Funds," In "The Payments Mechanism . . . Another Look," Federal Reserve Bank of Boston, 1971.

Modigliani, Franco and Richard Sutch, "Innovations in Interest Rate Policy," *American Economic Review,* (May 1966).

Moretti, August J., "The Savings and Loan Industry: Problems, Proposed Solutions, and Future Housing Needs," Unpublished senior thesis, Princeton University, 1972.

Moscowitz, Warren Earnest, "The Cost and Profitability of Demand Deposits: A Review of the Literature." Unpublished, Prepared for the Savings Bank Association of New York State, December 1971.

——, "The Theory of Compensating Balances," Unpublished Ph.D. Dissertation, Massachusetts Institute of Technology, 1971.

Mueller, Eva and Jane Lean, "The Savings Account as a Source for Financing Large Expenditures," *Journal of Finance,* XXII (September 1967), pp. 375–393.

Nadiri, M.I., "The Determinants of Trade Credit in the U.S. Total Manufacturing Sector," *Econometrica,* XXXVII (July 1969), pp. 408–422.

Niehans, Jurg, "Money and Barter in General Equilibrium with Transactions Costs," *American Economic Review* (December 1971).

Niehans, Jurg, "Money in a Static Theory of Optimal Payments Arrangements," *Journal of Money, Credit and Banking,* I (November 1969), pp. 706–736.

Orgler, Yair E., "A Credit Scoring Model for Commercial Loans." *Journal of Money, Credit and Banking,* II (November 1970), pp. 435–445.

Orr, Daniel, *Cash Management and the Demand for Money,* New York: Praeger Publishers, 1971.

——, and W.G. Mellon, "Stochastic Reserve Losses and the Expansion of Bank Credit," *American Economic Review* LI (September 1961), pp. 614–623.

Proceedings, National Automation Conference 1967, New York: American Bankers Association, 1967.

Report of the Commission on Money and Credit, Frazar B. Wilde, chairman, Englewood Cliffs: Prentice-Hall, Inc., 1961.

Report of the President's Commission on Financial Structure and Regulation, Reed O. Hunt, chairman, Washington, D.C.: Government Printing Office, December 1971.

Reistad, Dale L., "Beyond the Credit Card," *The Bankers Magazine,* CLIV (Spring 1971), pp. 96–100.

Richardson, Dennis W., "The Potential Impact of Technical Innovations on the Transactions Demand for Money Balances," *Marquette Business Review,* CI (Winter 1967), pp. 138–144.

Richardson, Dennis W., *Electric Money: Evolution of an Electronic Funds Transfer System,* Cambridge, Mass.: The MIT Press, 1970.

Ritter, Lawrence S., "Income Velocity and Anti-Inflationary Monetary Policy," American Economic Review, IL (March 1959), pp. 120–129.

——, and Thomas R. Atkinson, "Monetary Theory and Policy in the Payments System of the Future," *Journal of Money, Credit and Banking,* II (November 1970), pp. 493–503.

Russell, Thomas, "The Effects of Improvements in the Consumer Loan Market," Unpublished paper, mimeo, 1972.

——, *Economics of Bank Credit Cards,* Ph.D dissertation submitted to Cambridge University, 1972.

Sametz, Arnold W., "Cyclical and Growth Problems Facing the Savings and Loan Industry– Policy Implications and Suggested Reforms," *The Bulletin* of the Institute of Finance of the Graduate School of Business Administration of New York University, March 1968.

Samuelson, Paul A., "An Analytic Evaluation of Interest Rate Ceilings for Savings and Loan Associations and Competitive Institutions," In the Friend *Study,* Vol. IV, pp. 1561–1590.

——, "Samuelson on the Neoclassical Dichotomy: A Reply," *Canadian Journal of Economics* (May 1972).

Sastry, A.S. Rama, "The Effect of Credit on Transactions Demand for Cash," *Journal of Finance,* XXV (September 1970), pp. 777–782.

Saving, Thomas R., "Transactions Costs and the Demand for Money," *American Economic Review,* LXI (June 1971), pp. 407–420.

Sharpe, William F., *The Economics of Computers,* New York: Columbia University Press, 1969.

Shay, Robert P., "Major Developments in the Market for Consumer Credit Since the End of World War II," In Fenstermaker (ed.), 1969.

Starr, Ross M., "Exchange in Barter and Monetary Economies," *Quarterly Journal of Economics* (May 1972).

Strunk, Norman, "Electronic Funds Transfers: The Game Plan," *Savings and Loan News,* August1971.

Teck, Alan, *Mutual Savings Banks and Savings and Loan Associations: Aspects of Growth,* New York: Columbia University Press, 1968.

Teigen, R.L. and W. L. Smith, ed., *Readings in Money National Income and Stabilization Policy,* Homewood: Richard D. Irwin, 1970.

Thomson, F.P., *Money in the Computer Age,* London: Pergamon Press, 1968.

Tobin, James, "Commercial Banks as Creators of 'Money'," in Deane Carson, editor, *Banking and Monetary Studies,* Homewood, Richard D. Irwin, Inc., 1963.

———, "Deposit Interest Ceilings as a Monetary Control," *Journal of Money, Credit and Banking,* II (February 1970), pp. 4–14.

———, "The Interest-Elasticity of Transactions Demand for Cash," *Review of Economics and Statistics,* XLII (August 1960), pp. 276–279.

———, and William Brainard, "Financial Intermediaries and the Effectiveness of Monetary Controls," *American Economic Review* (May 1963).

"Tomorrow is Coming! But Don't Worry, The Payments System for Tomorrow May be Here Already," *Savings and Loan News,* October 1971.

Tsiang, S. C., "A Critical Note on the Optimum Supply of Money," *Journal of Money, Credit and Banking,* I (May 1969), pp. 266–280.

Tucker, Donald P., "Credit Rationing, Interest Rate Lags, and Monetary Policy Speed," *Quarterly Journal of Economics,* LXXII (February 1968), pp. 54–84.

U.S. Savings and Loan League, *Savings and Loan Fact Book,* 1969, 1970, 1971.

Veendorp, E.C.H. "General Equilibrium Theory for a Barter Economy," *Western Economic Journal* (March 1970).

Vernon, Jack R., "Competition for Savings Deposits: The Recent Experience," *National Banking Review,* IV (December 1966), pp. 183–192.

Walras, Leon, *Elements of Pure Economics,* William Jaffe Translator, London: George Allen and Unwin Ltd., 1954.

Weiss, E.B., "The Marketing Implications of the Checkless Society," New York: Doyle Dane Bernbach, Inc., 1968.

White, William H., "Trade Credit and Monetary Policy: A Reconciliation," *The Economic Journal,* LXXIV (December 1964), pp. 935–945.

Willis, Parker B., "A Study of the Market for Federal Funds," Prepared for the Steering Committee for the Fundamental Reappraisal of the Discount Mechanism Appointed by the Board of Governors of the Federal Reserve System. March 1967.

———, "The Secondary Market for Negotiable Certificates of Deposit," Prepared for the Steering Committee etc." 1967.

Index

207

About the Authors

Mark J. Flannery was born in Jersey City in 1950. He attended Princeton University, where he studied economics and was graduated with highest honors in 1972. Currently he is pursuing a Ph.D. in economics at Yale University. His research interests lie in the areas of macroeconomic theory and money and banking. In addition to this book, he is coauthor of articles that have appeared in computer journals.

Dwight M. Jaffee was born in 1943 in Chicago. He studied economics at Oberlin College and Northwestern University and was graduated from North-Western in 1964 with highest honors. He received his Ph.D. from the Massachusetts Institute of Technology in 1968. His research interests are primarily in monetary theory and policy and the structure of financial markets. He is author of *Credit Rationing and the Commercial Loan Market,* co-editor of *Savings Deposits, Mortgages, and Housing: Studies for the Federal Reserve-MIT-Penn Economic Model,* and author of articles in various professional journals. He has been a consultant to the U.S. Treasury, the Department of Housing and Urban Development, and the Federal Home Loan Bank Board. He has been in the economics department of Princeton University since 1968, where he is currently an associate professor.